N°4 PLATFORM N°5

GOLDEN AGE
OF THE
GREAT WESTERN
RAILWAY

Patrick Stephens Limited, a member of the Haynes Publishing Group, has published authoritative, quality books for enthusiasts for more than twenty years. During that time the company has established a reputation as one of the world's leading publishers of books on aviation, maritime, military, model-making, motor cycling, motoring, motor racing, railway and railway modelling subjects. Readers or authors with suggestions for books they would like to see published are invited to write to: The Editorial Director, Patrick Stephens Limited, Sparkford, Nr Yeovil, Somerset BA22 7JJ.

THE
GOLDEN AGE
OF THE
GREAT WESTERN
RAILWAY
1895 — 1914

TIM BRYAN

Patrick Stephens Limited

For my parents, with gratitude, and in memory of my father
John Bryan 1928–1990

First published in 1991

British Library Cataloguing in Publication Data

Bryan, Tim
    The golden age of the Great Western Railway : 1895–1914.
    1. England. Railway services: Great Western Railway, history
    I. Title
    385.0942

    ISBN 1-85260-150-7

Patrick Stephens Limited is a member of the Haynes Publishing Group,
Sparkford, Nr Yeovil, Somerset BA22 7JJ.

Printed in Great Britain

10   9   8   7   6   5   4   3   2   1

CONTENTS

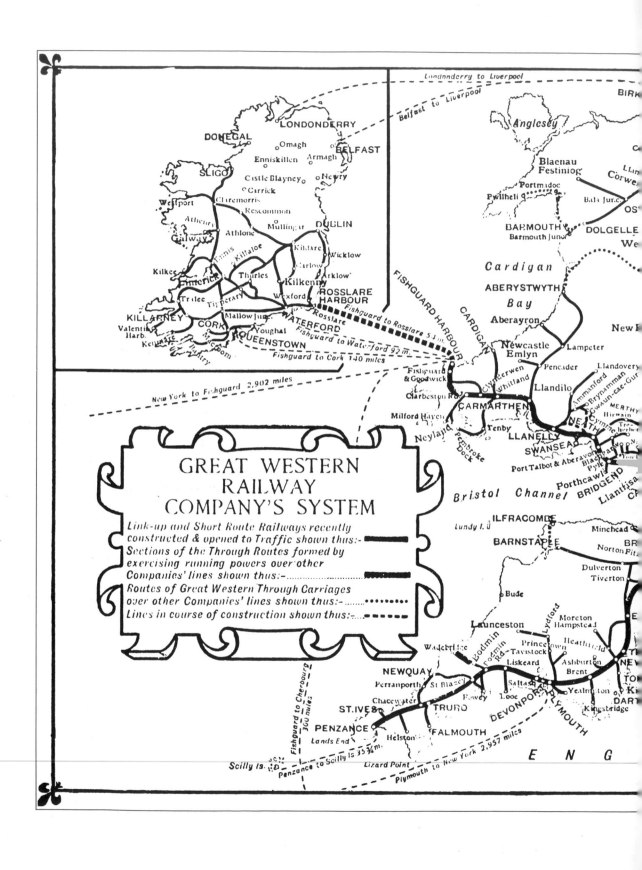

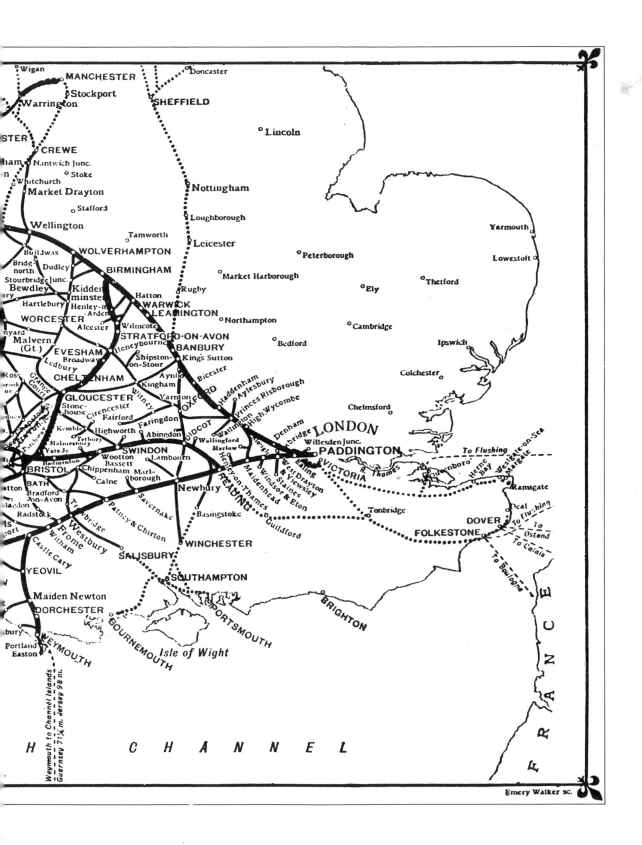

GREAT WESTERN RAILWAY
Picturesque Cornwall
COMFORTABLE HOTELS
EXPRESS CORRIDOR TRAINS
TOURIST TICKETS
SLEEPING CARS
CHEAP EXCURSIONS DURING SUMMER MONTHS FROM LONDON & PRINCIPAL STATIONS.
J. L. WILKINSON General Manager.

ACKNOWLEDGEMENTS

NO project of this kind can be possible without the assistance of a large number of individuals and institutions. Considerable help has been forthcoming from the Public Record Office, Kew, and the Reference Libraries at Birmingham, Bristol and Swindon. Thanks are also due to BR Public Affairs, Swindon, the Great Western Society, Didcot, the National Union of Railwaymen, the Science Museum, the Severn Valley Railway, the National Railway Museum, York, and the *Western Mail*, Cardiff.

I am also grateful to all those who have made photographs available for reproduction; unless credited otherwise, all remaining pictures are by the author, or are from his collection. In some cases these are the work of unknown postcard photographers of the period, whose source is no longer readily identifiable; it is hoped that this sincere acknowledgement will be accepted.

Much material has been drawn from the GWR Museum collection at Swindon, and I am grateful to the Borough of Thamesdown Museum Service for permission to reproduce various items.

The staff of Thamesdown Museum Service, the GWR Museum in particular, have also been supportive of the project, and I would also like to thank all my friends and colleagues at Swindon, including John Woodward, Lesley Crennell, Clive Berry, Elizabeth Day, Robert Dickinson, Marion Flanagan, Marion Robins, Neil Swatton and Derek Stacey.

As well as the large establishments who have been most helpful, I am also grateful to a large number of individual friends and colleagues for their assistance. Apologies are tendered in advance to anyone I have missed! Thanks are due to: Brian Arman, C. Blade, Elizabeth Bryan, Trevor Cockbill, Ian Coulson, John Flanagan, John Gibbons, Ken Gibbs, Peter Good, Fred Gray, Denis Griffiths, Derek Harrison, Ivor Huddy, David Hyde, Colin Jenkins, Clare and Martin Joyce, Roy Nash, Bill Parker, Alan Parrett, Peter Rance, D. Scott-Warren, Chris Tagholm, Duncan and Jackie Thom, Nigel and Janene Thomas, Roger Trayhurn and Michael Wyatt.

My family have also been very supportive throughout the writing

An early GWR advertising poster issued in the late 1890s. (National Railway Museum Collection)

of this book, and I owe a particular debt to my wife Ann, who patiently put up with me whilst I researched and typed; she also read through the manuscript, and made many useful corrections and suggestions.

PREFACE

THE era from just before the death of Queen Victoria to the outbreak of the Great War in 1914 has been characterized by many historians as an 'Indian Summer' or a 'Golden Age' between the seemingly endless reign of Victoria and the slaughter of a whole generation on the fields of France. It was, as one commentator put it, 'an age of ceaseless unrest and agitation'. On their country estates, the old order watched with increasing trepidation, as the nature of the British nation changed dramatically. The rise of industry, and the exodus from rural parts to the ever-growing cities, was also matched by a growth in the middle class suburbs, spreading their tentacles from the centres of towns. Despite all this growth, there was also a less palpable aspect to this progress; away from the luxury, the working classes struggled to survive, and never was the gap between rich and poor more apparent than in this era.

It has also been agreed by many that this period was also a 'Golden Age' for railways in this country; after the rapid expansion of the Victorian era, the British railway network was virtually complete, with some exceptions, and most railway companies were striving to bring other aspects of their services up to scratch. Rail travellers during this period had the benefit of more modern and efficient locomotives, comfortable, well-constructed carriages, and train services whose speed and punctuality was unequalled for some considerable period.

The number of railway staff employed was a high point, too, reaching around 650,000 in 1913. This enabled high standards of maintenance and cleanliness to be achieved, not seen since; the high polish on even the lowliest goods engine was a feature on many British lines of the period.

In the years before the First World War, the railways had not begun to feel seriously the chill wind of competition from road transport. The motor car began to grow rapidly in popularity during the era, but owning a car was still largely the province of the rich, and the majority of the population still used the train as their main mode of transport. It was the advent of the tram which was the main source of competition for the railways, and the Great Western, like other companies of the period, took its own steps to tackle this threat.

Goods were still carried predominantly by rail, and improvements in motive power and rolling-stock meant that larger quantities of goods, especially coal, could be moved even faster.

All these improvements and benefits were, of course, achieved at some cost, not only in financial but also in human terms; this human cost was borne in general by the railway workforce. The companies argued that employment on the railway was secure and, indeed, this could not be denied; but hours were long, and the rewards meagre. Victorian management styles still persisted, and to compound matters, wages actually fell in real terms during the Edwardian period. Trade Unions became more influential, but the railway companies refused to even recognize their existence for some considerable period.

As for so many of the railway companies, the years between 1895 and 1914 were a 'Golden Age' for the Great Western Railway, although it was much more than that. It was also the period when the company regained its pre-eminence amongst the railway companies of Britain, after a long period of gloom, depression and torpor. By 1914 it was the foremost railway in the country, and its rolling-stock, services and passenger facilities were second to none. This book tells the story of that 'Golden Age', and the enormous outpouring of innovation and growth in the years before the Great War.

The book does not attempt, however, to give a detailed year by year history of the era, but takes a broader approach, looking at the main themes of the period and hopefully giving the reader a flavour of the heady atmosphere of that long-gone era of 80 years ago. It is perhaps becoming something of a cliché to argue that above of all railway companies, the Great Western has attracted the most attention from railway historians; the author, like many others, owes a great debt to those distinguished writers who have admirably chronicled the history of this great company.

Apart from these published sources, this volume also draws heavily on the literature issued by the Great Western itself, for it was in this period that the company first became a major producer of books and pamphlets. Its own house periodical, the *Great Western Railway Magazine*, was also put on a firmer footing in the early years of the twentieth century, and provides us with invaluable information on how the railway operated. This publication, and some of the more workday items, such as rule-books and memoranda, gives us a vivid insight into the running of the great railway empire. After looking at the two great centres of the GWR in the period, Paddington and Swindon, the reader will be taken out on a journey round the railway network, to discover some of the characters and events of the era.

INTRODUCTION

ON 1 October 1895, crowds gathered at a variety of locations along Brunel's old main line between Swindon and Bristol to witness an event of tremendous significance in the development of the Great Western Railway; and at the very heart of the GWR network, Swindon, large crowds of workmen emerged from the great engineering works in order to witness the passing of the 'Cornishman' express. To the casual observer, this may not have been anything out of the ordinary, but to those with even the slightest interest in 'God's Wonderful Railway', it was clear that this was no ordinary day. It could be argued with some justification that the events of the day formed the beginnings of the company's growth into what the *Statist* magazine called 'the most vigorous railway company in the country'[1].

What made the passing of the 'Cornishman' on that October morning so significant was that, for the first time, a non-stop train ran from Paddington to Bristol without making the obligatory stop at Swindon for refreshment. Until that date, the Great Western had been tied by a lease agreed by the company in its earliest days. When the time had come to build the station at Swindon in the early 1840s, the company had found itself short of capital, drained perhaps by the expense of some of Brunel's more elaborate schemes; as a result, it had entered into an arrangement with a London firm, J. & C. Rigby, who agreed to build the station with refreshment rooms, part of the embryonic railway works, and cottages to house the new workforce of the company's operation at Swindon. In return for this, Rigby's were to receive the rents from the cottages and the refreshment rooms; the agreement entered into also stated that all passengers trains were to stop at the station for 10 minutes, to enable travellers to take refreshments.

To many railway historians and enthusiasts, the rest of the story is a familiar one; the 10-minute stop, which may well have semed a convenience in the 1840s, soon became an albatross round the neck of the company when it attempted to speed up its express services. Despite various attempts by the Great Western to rid itself of the agreement in the law courts, the lease remained watertight. What made matters worse for the company's pride was that the lease was sold on various occasions, from one firm to another, for increasingly higher sums. In 1881 the lease was sold to one H.G. Lake for no less than £70,000, the vendor, J.W. Chater, having doubled his investment in less than a year.

It was not until 1895, however, that the company felt able to end this relic of the Broad Gauge era once and for all; in that year it bought out the remaining years of the lease for the princely sum of £100,000, a not inconsiderable amount, which was paid for by an annual charge against revenue which lasted until 1920. The first train, already mentioned, left Paddington at 10.30 am, hauled by the Dean 'Single' *Lord of the Isles* which was, the *Great Western Railway Magazine* reported, 'one of the company's finest and most powerful locomotives'.[2] At Paddington, like Swindon, hundreds of staff crowded on to the platforms in order to get a view of the train. The 'novel' experience of running through Swindon non-stop over, the 'Cornishman' reached Bristol in 2 hours 10 minutes, ending once and for all what had been called an 'intolerable inconvenience'.

The conclusion of the 'Swindon Question'[3], as the company

The interior of Swindon's infamous refreshment rooms around 1901. (GWR Museum, Swindon)

Chairman Earl Cawdor later called it, marked the beginning of a vibrant period of rebirth for the company, which one commentator called the 'Great Awakening'. As already indicated, this book is a chronicle of some of the significant events of those years after 1895, before the First World War put an end to the hopes, dreams and lives of many involved in the running of this great railway company.

It is of course an oversimplification to argue that all the development in the years before the Great War began after the ending of the Swindon refreshment room lease. As the reader progresses through the various chapters of this book, it will become apparent that moves to end the torpor and depression suffered by the Great Western in the latter part of the nineteenth century had begun in the early 1890s; indeed, the company's own historian, E.T. McDermot, argued that the beginnings of a recovery by the GWR could be traced back as far as 1888, when N.J. Burlinson was appointed as Superintendent of the Line. But the abolition of the 10-minute stop, and the commencement of non-stop running on the Great Western main line between Bristol and London, is perhaps a most appropriate place to commence our story.

By 1910, the company was able to boast in one of its own publications that for 'every year for nearly a decade, the GWR has added for its patrons' benefit some new facility of a notable nature'. It could further add that those ten years had been 'a period of enterprise, of inauguration and progress in many directions'[4]. Much attention was paid both at the time and in more recent years to this spirit of 'enterprise', and in this book it is hoped that the reader will get some impression of the developments ocurring on the Great Western at this time, and hopefully some hint of the atmosphere of the period.

But what did this enterprise entail, and why was it necessary at all? The GWR had always had the reputation of being one of the most respected and powerful railways in Great Britain. Its foundations were laid by the great engineer Isambard Kingdom Brunel, who designed an ambitious Broad Gauge railway system with a distinctive character of its own. By the latter part of the nineteenth century, however, it had become apparent that the company had lost its pre-eminence amongst the other railway companies of the era, and although having been such an important innovator in the days of Brunel and Gooch, had fallen well behind other lines in terms of its train speeds, journey times and locomotive and rolling-stock design. Many of its stations dated back to the earliest days of the railway, and were totally unsuited to the demands of increasing traffic.

The company had the greatest track mileage of any railway in Britain, yet it had hardly a single really direct route to any town of importance on its network, apart from Bristol. As one contemporary writer noted, if there were two competing routes, the Great Western one was usually the longest. Its rambling network of lines, with its generously timed train services, led it to be ridiculed as the 'Great

A photograph typical of the GWR before the 'Great Awakening' — an unidentified 'Duke' Class 4-4-0 on a Bristol express near Bath. (Swindon Reference Library)

Way Round'. The railway was, as another writer called it, a 'slumbering giant'.

At this stage, the reader might find a brief summary of company progress in the years before the First World War useful before moving into the narrative proper. In essence, the 'Golden Age' was dominated by the Great Western's efforts to shorten its route network, and thus speed its journey times. This involved the building of entirely new lines of some considerable substance, consisting of the Bristol & South Wales Direct Railway and the Great Western & Great Central Joint line. It also entailed the building of what became known as 'cut-offs', these being smaller lines which bypassed slower sections of established routes, the Stert and Castle Cary railways were good examples of this.

Other smaller improvements were also made to the Great Western's main lines. Bottlenecks were eliminated by the remodelling of trackwork, as in the case of the building of a new junction for the Berks & Hants line at Reading in 1913. Lines were widened, doubled or even quadrupled in some places. Many of the features of the old Broad Gauge system were removed — old bridges, tunnels and viaducts were replaced, and track was realigned for faster running. Many stations and goods depots were rebuilt, and facilities for the travelling public were drastically improved. In some cases, as in that of the remodelling of Birmingham Snow Hill, considerable sums of money were expended to improve matters.

The Great Western also spent over a million pounds in its efforts to create a deep-water port of its own at Fishguard. Although initially intended as the terminal for Irish cross-Channel traffic, it soon became apparent that the company had rather more ambitious hopes for the port. The calling of Atlantic liners such as the *Mauretania* in 1908 brought prestige and revenue to the railway, although the port was never to develop on the scale the company originally envisaged.

During the period, Swindon Works turned out a series of modern, powerful and reliable locomotives with which the new services planned by the company could be efficiently run. With increased passenger comfort in mind, carriage design was also the subject of much improvement. A whole series of more minor developments were made, as the company came to terms with competition from other sources like trams — new steam 'railmotors', the forerunners of today's diesel railcars, were introduced to serve newly created 'halts', small low-cost stations built in suburban or less populated rural locations. The company also responded to the advent of the internal combustion engine by introducing motor transport, not only for the carriage of goods, but also as feeders to its railway passenger service.

A postcard view of the new era; a two-hour Bristol express hauled by Churchward 'Star' Class No 4016 Knight of the Golden Fleece *near Slough.*

This brief description has only given the slightest hint of the kind of work done by the company in the period, and the ensuing narrative will hopefully acquaint the reader more closely with the

themes and characters of the period. We are perhaps fortunate that the company was well aware of the value of publicity at that time, and as a result, was not slow in alerting the public to the great strides it was itself taking. The Great Western's new publicity department played two important roles: it promoted itself vigorously, disseminating information about its triumphs and progress to not only the world at large but also, importantly, to its own workforce. It also played a critical role in promoting the holiday area it served, especially the 'Cornish Riviera,' which to a large extent it was responsible for developing on a substantial scale. This it did by issuing numerous well-written books, leaflets and other publications, and producing a series of eye-catching posters which exhorted passengers to 'See Your Own Country First'!

Before taking the reader on a journey on the Great Western network of the era, it would be useful to spend some time analysing

why this 'Great Awakening' took place in the first place. To a large extent, the Broad Gauge foundations laid by Brunel, which we have already mentioned, were themselves a cause of the company's decline in the latter years of the nineteenth century. When the Great Engineer had formulated his Broad Gauge system in the early days of the railway, although spending a great deal of effort in justifying the theoretical advantages of the wider track gauge, it could be argued that rather less time was spent in working out the practical problems which would ensue in later years. Interchange between Broad and 'narrow' (as the Great Western disparagingly called it) was an expensive and time-consuming process, and it became clear that the existence of two major railway networks, each with its own different track gauge, was not a situation which could continue indefinitely.

The events of the 'Gauge War' and the Royal Commission of 1845 are another story, but it is nevertheless true to say that the adoption and retention of the Broad Gauge was a significant factor in allowing the Great Western to fall behind many of its competitors. When conversion was completed in 1892, the company had to count the considerable cost of not only relaying track, but also rebuilding locomotives and rolling-stock. It was said that the final conversion of the remaining 177 miles of Broad Gauge line on one weekend in May of 1892 itself cost nearly a million pounds.

At a half-yearly company meeting some years later, in February 1895, an increase of £37,776 in maintenance of trackwork was reported which was almost entirely due to the relaying of permanent way related to the conversion of gauge. Although the track gauge itself had been adjusted, there was still a great deal of the old 'baulk' road track to be replaced. The Chairman, Viscount Emlyn, told shareholders, 'You must bear in mind that our first duty is to see that your permanent way is in first class condition, and that you have a safe road for the public to travel over'[5].

One further factor in the slow progress of the Great Western in the latter part of the nineteenth century was the effects of a general financial depression which took effect in the 1870s. Indeed, until around 1895 there was widespread gloom in the business world

The sad sight of broad gauge locomotives at Swindon in 1892, prior to their scrapping; many of the engines are still in a finely polished condition. (GWR Museum, Swindon)

generally, and a consequent lack of investment, especially compared with the enormous period of growth which had preceded it in the early Victorian era. The rise of the United States and Germany as serious competitors in the industrial field, and the fall in demand for shipping after the opening of the Suez Canal, led to a general crisis of confidence. Railways in general, and the Great Western in particular, felt the effects of this depression, and the company experienced a slowing in the growth of passenger receipts, especially after 1876. Investment by the company dropped, and in the 20 years after 1877 only 400 route miles were added. Under the careful Chairmanship of Sir Daniel Gooch, economy was the watchword; fewer new engines were built, but instead old locomotives were refurbished to prolong their working lives.

The caution and economy practised during those lean years had a debilitating long-term effect on the company, and it would take some years for it to fully recover. Speaking in 1906, W.J. Scott declared that he was 'proud of the work which this company has done. It has been spoken of as the "Sleeping Giant", but I do not think the Great Western has been sleeping; he has only been waiting development and biding his time'[6].

By the latter years of the 1890s, not only had the GWR escaped the worst effects of the financial depression, but had also acquired the calibre of staff which would provide the impetus of the company's rapid expansion in the next ten years or so; to a large extent, poor management had also been significant in holding back progress. The old Great Western was typified by G.N. Tyrell, Superintendent of the Line until 1888, who was 'cautious, anxious, scared of speeds over 40 mph'[7] and had controlled the timings of GWR trains for 24 years until they were some of the slowest in England. With the death of the company Chairman Sir Daniel Gooch in 1889, one of the last links with the earliest days of the company was finally severed; new ideas started to flow in, removing much of the arrogance and complacency which had characterized the Great Western for so long. Even as late as 1889, the *Great Western Railway Magazine* was able to smugly report that 'engines that work the broad gauge today are practically unaltered from those of as long ago as 1846'[8].

Even before the real onset of expansion of the Great Western, it is clear that the new management was aware of the potential the company had. Speaking in 1899, J.L. Wilkinson, who had taken over as General Manager in 1896, noted that 'we are trying to make ours the biggest railway in every respect in the kingdom...we want to make our big undertaking *the* undertaking of the country'[9]. Wilkinson was ably assisted by his Chairman, Earl Cawdor, who in the space of ten years persuaded what had been a very cautious and conservative company Board to accept many of the changes necessary to rid itself of the 'Great Way Round' image. At the time he was appointed, June 1895, he was the youngest Chairman of a British railway. It was clear that he did not consider the post to be a sinecure, and spent a great deal of time on company affairs. The new lines to South Wales and Birmingham, and the smaller 'cut-offs', were all started during his period of office, and his influence gave a secure foundation to the growth of the company.

Earl Cawdor left the Great Western with some regret, when appointed as First Lord of the Admiralty in 1905, and his successor was the very able Alfred Baldwin MP, who had been a Board member since 1901. Two years earlier, the company had suffered another loss when James Wilkinson, the General Manager, had died. The Great Western was, however, extremely fortunate in the choice of his successor. The man appointed in July 1903 was James Inglis, who was to be the driving force behind much of the company's most important work in the period before the First World War.

Inglis had been born in Aberdeen in 1851, and had experienced a varied career on numerous railway concerns before joining the Great Western in 1892. Prior to his appointment as General Manager, he had been Chief Civil Engineer, a post which had given him a wide knowledge of the great expansion being carried out by the Great Western in this 'Golden Age'. Indeed, he had come to prominence as

This view of No 3384 Omdurman embodies much of the spirit of the 'Golden Age'. Just look at the highly polished finish on the engine — on its frame, the patterned finish known as 'guivering' can be seen, achieved by the clever use of tallow. (GWR Museum, Swindon)

Parliamentary witness for the Great Western in many of the most important schemes which underpinned the abolition of the 'Great Way Round' tag; these included the Acton & Wycombe line, the Bristol & South Wales Direct Railway, the new route to the West of England, and other miscellaneous schemes such as Fishguard Harbour.

James Inglis thus had an ideal background for a railway which was undergoing such momentous change, and proved to be an able administrator as well as manager. There was much consternation at Paddington when his death was announced on 19 December 1912, but it is likely that the tremendous stress of running such an enormous operation had taken its toll. Inglis' successor, Frank Potter, was in every way as able a candidate. A company man through and through, he had started on the GWR in the Goods Department at Paddington in 1869, and had risen up through the ranks before serving as Chief Assistant to Inglis for nearly eight years, a formidable apprenticeship for the testing post which he then accepted. Potter, too, died in office in 1919, worn out by the strain of such a demanding job, particularly during the dark years of the First World War.

The influx of 'new blood' into the company was not merely confined to the upper strata of management; the 'Golden Age' was also characterized by the retirement of many older railway employees, a considerable number of whom had started their

*Great Western progress:
Churchward 4-4-2* Bride of
Lammermoor, *built in
1905 and seen at an unknown
location, possibly Yeovil,
sometime before 1912, in
which year it was rebuilt as a
4-6-0.* (Alan Parrett
Collection)

working lives in the earliest days of the Great Western. The *Great
Western Railway Magazine* reported that 1897 would be a significant
year, since it marked the first great departure of these 'old servants'
who, it added, had 'followed the fortunes of the company throughout
the whole Victorian era'[10]. One such example of this kind of worker
had been singled out some 12 months before, in June 1896, when the
magazine reported the retirement of Guard Benjamin Jeans, who
had completed his service with the company after 54 years.[11]

It is therefore worth emphasizing that with the wind of change
blowing through the Great Western, it was not merely the old guard
of the management who were being replaced — the same applied to
the workforce at large. Without this process, the company would
have continued to be haunted by the ghosts of the Broad Gauge era,
but as the pages of the *Great Western Railway Magazine*, the
proceedings of the Swindon Engineering Society and the Lecture and
Debating Society show, a new wave of company employees did exist,
keen to participate in the renaissance of the Great Western, and its
ongoing spirit of 'enterprise'.

Having set the scene, and looked at why the Great Western began
this process of change and growth, it is now time for the reader to
embark on a journey of discovery on the Great Western Railway in
its 'Golden Age'.

PART ONE

PADDINGTON, GATEWAY TO THE EMPIRE

This postcard view of the station, although lacking somewhat in clarity, does echo GWR claims that the terminus was thronged with 'picturesque types of modern humanity'.

IT is appropriate that we commence our survey of the Great Western Railway during its 'Golden Age' in the environs of Brunel's great terminus at Paddington. It was the largest, busiest and most important station on the railway, an embarkation point as well as a destination for all the new and improved services developed during this period. Its busy platforms were a gateway to both the great city of London, heart of the British Empire, and to all points west.

The *Great Western Railway Magazine* of the time described its platforms as being thronged with 'picturesque types of modern humanity'[1]. These included 'rosy-cheeked schoolgirls...clear-eyed midshipmanites...parties of medieval looking Russian emigrants... and always the rapidly-moving businessman'[2]. Homely as this description may have been, the station must have been a tremendously bustling place to be in the years before the First World War. Busy it certainly was; in 1913 alone some 2,150,358 tickets were issued at the station's booking offices, with receipts totalling £1,261,611[3].

More importantly, however, Paddington had another prominent role in this period, as the administrative powerhouse of the railway. It was from the company's Paddington headquarters that many of the important decisions concerning the expansion and development of the GWR system emanated. With the major exceptions of the Locomotive, Carriage and Wagon Department, based at Swindon, and the Signal and Telegraph Department, based at Reading, almost all the major departments of the company were situated in the large complex of offices located in and around the great station.

This chapter will hopefully show the reader both facets of this great station—its day-to-day workings and special events, as well as its administrative headquarters role. Before dealing with the latter aspect of operations though, we shall return to describe the everyday running of the station and its expansion during the period.

THE STATION
AT WORK

PASSENGERS and visitors to Brunel's Paddington station cannot help but admire the graceful arches of the station train shed even today, but as we will see in a moment, the station came close to being completely redeveloped in the era 1895–1914. In the late 1890s the station was largely as it had been when first opened. Although the structure had been added to and improved in the years since its construction and opening in 1854, it was not until the period before the First World War that any major developments took place. Indeed, the company was moved to state in 1896 that despite rumours to the contrary, the station was 'far short of having

The end of an era: in Broad Gauge days, a Dean 2-2-2 'Convertible' and a 4-2-2 'single' prepare to take an express westwards. (Brian Arman Collection)

reached its maximum'[4]. In retrospect, one can imagine that the GWR was not perhaps telling the whole truth, and in a short space of time the layout of the station and the lines running towards Westbourne Park were strangling the efficient movement of trains in and out of Paddington.

It is difficult to envisage the transformation which must have taken place between the establishment of the original Paddington station in 1838, and the period we are describing. To put this into context, it is worth recalling that by the time the Great Western was contemplating replacing its original wooden terminus with Brunel's new structure, the population of the village of Paddington was around 46,000. Contemporary descriptions noted that the original station was surrounded by trees and shrubs. By the turn of the century though, the whole area had been swallowed up into the ever-growing sprawl of London. It is recorded that the population of Paddington rose by around 10,000 per decade, reaching a peak in the period after 1910 of some 144,000. Indeed, by this time the population of London itself had reached over $4\frac{1}{2}$ millions, a not inconsiderable total.

The original Paddington station was, then, replaced in 1854 by Brunel's great train shed, consisting of three roof spans, two smaller ones of 69 ft 6 ins and 68 feet respectively, and one larger span of 102 ft 6 ins. These great arches were supported by cast iron columns

resting on enormous foundations of concrete and brick. What almost certainly made Brunel's structure much more attractive was that over one-third of its area was glazed. Having worked on the committee of design for the Crystal Palace of 1851, the large expanses of glass used in this building inspired Brunel to use Joseph Paxton's patent glass and glazing bars in his station design. Matthew Digby-Wyatt, an architect who had worked with Brunel on the Crystal Palace scheme, was brought in to provide wrought iron decoration to Brunel's basic design.[5]

Before alteration, Paddington covered an area of eight acres covered, and two acres uncovered. Nine platforms were provided, five for departing trains, four for arrivals. These varied in length from 730 feet to 810 feet (platforms 3, 4 and 5). Milk traffic was also catered for, with a special 330-foot platform.

It was obvious, however, that as the railway's fortunes improved, and the company's spirit of enterprise manifested itself in new lines and new train services, Brunel's original layout for the station, based largely on the needs of the Broad Gauge era, would become less than satisfactory; with over 300 trains passing in and out of the terminus every 24 hours, some modernization was not merely advisable, but necessary.

Work on the major improvements needed did not commence until 1913, when the GWR Directors approved a scheme for the extension of the arrival side of the station, with the provision of three additional

platform sidings; these would eventually be numbered 10, 11 and 12. This involved considerable work, with the removal of the old 'High Level' goods yard, and excavation of the site to rail level. Whilst this was being done, the opportunity was taken to level and remodel the permanent way, and add new drainage.

A new milk platform was constructed, some 600 feet in length, a useful innovation being that the level of the platform corresponded to that of the flooring of the milk carts, so that churns could be rolled directly from railway van to cart. Anyone who has tried to manhandle a full milk churn will agree that this must have been a boon to the station staff!

Much attention was paid to milk traffic by the company, and for good reason. As early as 1896 it was estimated that the Great Western, Great Eastern, London & South Western, and London & North Western railways brought some 20 million gallons of milk into London each year.[6] With the expansion of London's population, the Great Western was faced with a thirsty market, but one which could earn the company a considerable amount of revenue. By 1914, even with the improved facilities which had been installed, it was clear that milk traffic was still causing the Great Western management a few problems; it was reported that in a 12-hour period, 33 full truck loads and nearly 400 churns delivered from guards vans on the ordinary passenger services arrived at the station. Further problems arose from the sheer number of empty churns — in the 24 hours of 3 November 1913, some 4,890 empty milk churns were unloaded at Paddington.[7]

The most significant aspect of the development and enlargement was the construction of a new roof span to cover the three additional

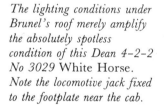

The lighting conditions under Brunel's roof merely amplify the absolutely spotless condition of this Dean 4-2-2 No 3029 White Horse. *Note the locomotive jack fixed to the footplate near the cab.*

One of the newly replaced bridges on the route between Paddington and Old Oak can be seen in the background of this 1913 view of Churchward 'Star' No 4007 Rising Star *leaving the terminus.* (Swindon Reference Library)

platforms. It was of much the same design as the three Brunel originals, except that it was made from steel rather than wrought iron. It was also, at 109 feet, larger than the Brunel arches. When preparatory work on the station extensions began it was found that the original untied roof spans had moved horizontally to the north, so much so that the columns holding up the roof of the northernmost span were $5\frac{1}{2}$ inches out of true! The strain this imbalance had put on the foundations also meant that the bolts holding the columns were in very poor condition. Combining this with the tendency of wrought iron to become rather brittle over the years, it was recommended that all the roof columns be replaced.[8]

This job was not fully completed until the mid 1920s, but was undertaken in the very real fear that if a locomotive had been derailed in the terminus and had hit a roof column, serious consequences could have befallen Paddington! The addition of a completely new roof span did, however, give the whole station roof structure much more stability. It ought to be pointed out though, that the Directors resisted a request from the Civil Engineer to replace the entire roof at the time and, as a result, despite the efforts of German bombers in the Second World War, much of Brunel's original station still survives today.

The construction of the new platforms and the additional roof span was supplemented by a great deal of other preparatory work in the years before the Great War. The increased traffic using the station was slowed considerably by the various brick arch bridges between the terminus and Old Oak Common. Both empty coaching stock and locomotives had to be moved between the station and the latter location, where the engine shed and carriage sidings were situated. The large number of train movements involved meant that often traffic was obstructed.

The outbreak of war prevented the replacement of all of the ten bridges between Paddington and Old Oak Common, but a start was made in freeing more space for additional trackwork. It was reported in 1910 that the girders used in the replacement of the Westbourne Terrace Bridge were the largest put up on the GWR since the erection of Brunel's Royal Albert Bridge at Saltash in 1859. The new bridge, with two spans of steelwork measuring 200 feet each, replaced a brick structure of 11 spans.[9]

A further innovation was the building of what was known as an 'Engine Line Bridge' in 1911. This was basically a flyover crossing the main running lines; the demand for room and better facilities for the handling of stock between Old Oak and Paddington led to the construction of this substantial bridge and two inclines of some three-quarters of a mile in length.[10]

Returning to the station precincts, a further improvement which benefited passengers and staff alike was the provision of high-quality lighting in the lofty arches of the great terminus. As early as 1880 electricity had been used to illuminate the premises, making it one of the first major public buildings in the capital to be lit by the 'new-fangled' electricity; the 34 lamps were installed by the Anglo-American Brush Electric Company. The system used by this rather grandly named company only lasted some four years in service, the contract being taken over by a company run by no less a personage than Sir Daniel Gooch himself. The 64 lamps used in this system continued in use until 1907, when a new electricity generating station at Park Royal was opened by the GWR. This supplied not only Paddington station but also the electrified Waterloo & City commuter lines as well as many other depots in the West London areas. Sub-stations were provided at Royal Oak, Old Oak Common and Shepherds Bush.[11] With the modernization of the generating plant, an opportunity was also taken to renew the light fittings which dated largely from Gooch's time. The 136 replacement lamps were substantially more powerful, and must have been a distinct improvement. One can imagine that on a dark overcast winter's day, with the station full of locomotive steam, smoke and the ever-present London smog, the traveller would need all the assistance he could get.

Before describing the actual working of the station, let us leave this chronicle of heavy engineering improvement at Paddington on a lighter note. The year 1910 saw further significant advances in passenger comfort with the opening of new lavatories, baths and a hairdressing salon under platform 1, the principal departure platform. Excavations under the station allowed the construction of a steel and concrete frame in which these facilities were situated.

Passengers then had access to what the company called a 'handsome' hairdressing salon[12], hot and cold baths and toilet facilites of the highest standard. It was noted that the public 'had not been slow to realize the advantage of the fact that they may now be shaven, shorn and shampooed while waiting for their train'[13]. Contemporary sources do not make it clear as to whether these improvements extended as far as the Ladies Waiting Rooms, although a new confectionery and tobacco kiosk erected on platform 1 at around the same time must certainly have been of benefit to passengers of either sex.

Not all the improvements appear to have been met with unaninmous public approval; writing in 1913, Lord Monkswell, after praising Paddington and many of the developments that had taken place, noted that the 'apparent endlessness of the new addition to No 1 departure platform suggests rather long and tiring walks may have to be taken'[14]. Indeed, at 1,150 feet, platform 1 was rather longer than platforms at other London termini, the longest at Euston being 900 feet and at Marylebone 843 feet; both platforms 2 and 3 at Paddington were also well over 1,000 feet long.[15]

The less energetic reader may be pleased to know that in recent

The Bookstall at Paddington in August 1913. As well as newspapers and magazines, the company's own publications are well in evidence. The large poster casually pinned up on the right-hand end of the stall would be much prized by enthusiasts today, the author included! (National Railway Museum Collection)

years British Rail, in their extensions to the 'Lawn' circulating area at Paddington, have actually shortened the station's platforms again! The comparatively long platforms may well of course have reflected the heaviness of the traffic dealt with at the station, particularly on summer Saturdays. Although it may seem obvious to the GWR enthusiast, it is worth reiterating that Paddington was the premier departure point for all the important express trains run by the company in this period, and many less glamorous besides. All the routes described later in this book had services originating from Paddington, as we shall see.

Several examples may emphasize how busy Paddington was. Easter 1907 saw a large number of trains leaving the capital for both the West Country and Ireland (via the newly opened Fishguard route). On both 27 and 28 March of that year, the 'Cornish Riviera Limited' was divided into two portions. The first portion for Cornwall consisted of nine eight-wheeled carriages and one twelve-wheeler, with 428 passengers on board. The second portion for Exeter left with ten eight-wheeled carriages, including 'slip' carriages for intermediate stations. This train carried 305 passengers. The 3.30 pm to Falmouth consisted of a staggering 16 eight-wheelers and one solitary six-wheeled carriage; the Churchward 'Saint' Class locomotive No 2903 *Lady of Lyons* was said to have kept good time to Westbury, reaching there in 99 minutes, although one can imagine that it found the going rather harder on the steeply inclined lines in South Devon and Cornwall.[16]

Heavy traffic was not always confined to the summer months, however; on 21 December 1912 a Churchward 'Star' No 4020 *Knight Commander* was observed hauling a similar load of 16 eight-wheelers on the 11.50 Paddington-Kingswear service.[17]

It goes without saying that the smooth running of a station handling this sort of traffic depended largely on the substantial staff employed. Just prior to the outbreak of the First World War this

The postcard photographer has easily captured the enormous proportions of the Great Western's only 'Pacific', No 111 The Great Bear. *Its massive boiler capacity was a match for any task allotted to it, although its unwieldy size limited its use on many routes.*

Three 'likely lads', probably porters at Paddington. This photograph is also valuable for the detail of the GWR posters in the background. (GWR Museum, Swindon)

totalled 549, not including around 150 extra porters brought in to cope with the additional seasonal traffic just described. This enormous figure included some 20 different occupations; apart from the obvious Guards, Porters and Ticket Collectors, there were 24 Policemen, 27 Booking Clerks, 10 Lavatory Attendants (five male, five female), two 'Bill Posters' and two 'Horse Loaders'.

This number also did not include a large and separate Parcels staff, or the Goods Department, of which more later. The Stationmaster and his considerable workforce presided over around 153 departures and 154 arrivals in any 24-hour period, with this number rising to around 180 arrivals and departures during the summer months.[18]

It is also worth noting the nature of the traffic going to and from Paddington; it was essentially different from that of many other London termini in that it consisted mainly of long-distance trains. Even those services which could be called 'suburban' had longer mileages than was usual, and were quite different from the services running into Liverpool Street or Charing Cross, for example. In a later part of this book, the company's suburban business will be touched on further.

Since there were no run-round facilities at the station, a good deal of shunting and empty stock movement was necessary. When a train arrived from the West Country, for example, after the train engine

A superb period photograph of special traffic at Paddington. A 'County' tank has just brought in the stock for a special train to Windsor for one of the Royal Garden Parties. The distinguished party-goers are respectfully watched by crowds on other platforms. (National Railway Museum Collection)

had been uncoupled it was standard practice for a pilot locomotive to pull the empty stock away to Old Oak before the train engine could then depart to the shed to be serviced. In the case of trains departing from Paddington, the procedure was reversed, with a pilot bringing the empty carriages into the station, uncoupling and remaining at the buffer stops at the end of the platform line until the timetabled train had departed, hauled by its main-line locomotive. With these arrangements in mind, it was calculated that a truer figure for train movements in and out of the station in a 24-hour period was around 1,272.

As contemporary sources noted, the public merely glancing at timetable posters would have had little idea of the magnitude of operations at the enormous station. The increase and improvement in train services during the 'Golden Age' can only have exacerbated work at Paddington. As well as the purely statistical increase in the numbers of passengers carried, it is also evident from contemporary records that as time went on the customer became much harder to please. Certainly, in this respect the GWR may have become a victim of its own success. As standards on the railway improved in general, so the travelling public expected more. It became clear that there could be no going back on the great strides made, and it was only the exceptional conditions created by the Great War which caused some substantial deterioration in the quality of service offered by the company.

Before leaving our description of operations in the passenger station, it is worth highlighting one further aspect of work at Paddington which was carried out mainly at night; this was the large newspaper traffic. During the late Victorian and Edwardian period, the foundations of what we would now call the 'popular press' were laid; the introduction of Alfred Harmsworth's *Daily Mail* in 1896 marked the beginning of the popularizing of newspapers. Before this time, papers like *The Times* had been produced primarily for the

G. W. R.

LONDON EVENING AMUSEMENTS.

On SATURDAY, Dec. 7th,

A FAST HALF-DAY EXCURSION TRAIN will run to

LONDON

PADDINGTON STATION,

With through bookings to the following CITY and SUBURBAN STATIONS, viz.:—

EDGWARE ROAD,	*MOORGATE STREET,	HAMMERSMITH,
BAKER STREET,	*BISHOPSGATE,	UXBRIDGE ROAD,
PORTLAND ROAD,	*ALDGATE,	KENSINGTON
GOWER STREET,	WESTBOURNE PARK,	(ADDISON ROAD),
KING'S CROSS,	NOTTING HILL &	WEST BROMPTON,
*FARRINGDON ST.,	LADBROKE GROVE	CHELSEA & FULHAM,
*ALDERSGATE ST.,	LATIMER ROAD,	BATTERSEA and
	SHEPHERD'S BUSH,	CLAPHAM JUNCTION

A Passengers booking to these stations travel via Paddington or via Westbourne Park, if the train stops at Westbourne Park, proceeding from Bishop's Road or Westbourne Park by ordinary trains, and returning by trains shewn on the other side to Bishop's Road to join the return excursion train from Paddington Station. Paddington terminus is connected with Bishop's Road Station by a covered way.

Passengers to and from West Brompton, Chelsea and Fulham, Battersea, and Clapham Junction also change at Kensington (Addison Road).

N.B.—Unless otherwise stated passengers on the return journey change at Bishop's Road.

RETURN FARES, THIRD CLASS.

LEAVING	AT	To all Stations shewn above except those marked *				To Farringdon Street and other Stations marked *			
		To return same day.	To return Monday, Dec. 9th.	To return Wednesday, Dec. 11th.	To return Saturday, Dec. 14th.	To return same day.	To return Monday, Dec. 9th.	To return Wednesday, Dec. 11th.	To return Saturday, Dec. 14th.
		s. d.	s. d.	s. d.	s. d.	s. d.	s. d.	s. d.	s. d.
	P.M.								
Clifton Down ...	1 53								
Redland ...	1 55								
Montpelier ...	1 58								
Ashley Hill ...	1a19	4 3	9 0	10 0	12 0	4 6	9 3	10 3	12 3
Stapleton Road ..	2 3								
Lawrence Hill ...	2 12								
Bedminster ...	1 47								
St. Anne's Park ...	1b45								
BATH	2 35	—	8 6	9 6	11 0	5 6	8 9	9 9	11 3
SWINDON ...	3 25	3 9	7 0	7 6	8 6	4 0	7 3	7 9	8 9

a Change at Stapleton Road.   *b* Change at Bath.

Arriving at Paddington at 5.5 p.m.

This train will stop 5 minutes at Swindon, where passengers can obtain refreshments.

FREQUENT TRAINS run from and to PADDINGTON and WESTBOURNE PARK and Shepherd's Bush, HAMMERSMITH, KENSINGTON, (Addison Road), and also to and from all Stations on the DISTRICT and METROPOLITAN Railways, including HOUNSLOW, Osterley, MILL HILL PARK, TURNHAM GREEN, WIMBLEDON, PUTNEY, WALHAM GREEN, EARL'S COURT, South Kensington, VICTORIA, Westminster, CHARING CROSS, Temple, Blackfriars, MANSION HOUSE, NEW CROSS, Deptford Road, WHITECHAPEL, Mile End, Bow Road, Upton Park, EAST HAM, Cannon Street, Monument, Mark Lane, ALDGATE, BISHOPSGATE, MOORGATE STREET, Aldersgate Street, Farringdon Street, KING'S CROSS, Gower Street, Portland Road, Swiss Cottage, St. John's Wood Road, BAKER STREET, etc.

Although many excursions ran out of Paddington, a considerable number ran the other way. This example dates from 1907.

better off and better educated 'man of leisure'. To be sure, its dense, detailed printed text was not an easy read!

The *Daily Mail* and Arthur Pearson's *Daily Express*, first published in 1900, were the complete antithesis of this; they were much more concise, better designed, and appealed to a mass market, containing photographs and feature articles for all members of the family. Most significantly for the Great Western, newspapers like these had a wide national circulation (the *Mail* having a daily circulation of around one million copies at this time). The success of such papers depended on rapid distribution, and the GWR was not slow in anticipating the significance of this traffic.

Special trains were put on including, for example, the 2.50 am Newspaper train for the West of England. This had vans for Swansea (via Gloucester), Bristol, Exeter, Gloucester and Plymouth, as well as a special vehicle for Wymans Ltd, who had taken over the newspaper kiosk franchise from W.H. Smith in the early 1900s. It was estimated that around 1,400 bundles of newspapers weighing around 23 tons were dispatched from Paddington each day, the newspaper firms delivering to the station in the early hours of the morning in a variety of motor and horse-drawn vehicles. As railways had done earlier in the century, popular newspapers probably helped to knit together the British population in a way that had not been possible in the past, and as the carriers of this form of communication, the GWR played no small role in this business.

'Star' Class No 4015 Knight of St John *does not seem as clean as some of the other locomotives pictured at Paddington in this section of the book.*

THE GOODS
DEPARTMENT

JUST on the outer limits of the Paddington terminus was the goods station. Like its passenger counterpart, it was an extremely large undertaking, dealing with a substantial volume of goods both in and out. The 13-acre premises covered the site of the original 1838 Broad Gauge station, tradition contending that what was known as the 'down stores' was originally the old station booking office.[19] By 1914 almost all trace of this had gone, the ever-increasing business done by the depot necessitating the modernization of both the buildings and the yard. As has been hinted at earlier in this section, the growth of London and its population had caused the Great Western (and other railway companies) to expand and develop its services to cope with the increased demand. The Metropolis was particularly dependent on railways for the shipping in of fresh food and other consumer items.

By the outbreak of the First World War, the GWR had added other large goods depots to that at Paddington; these included a 'City' station at Smithfield, situated under the Central Meat Market scheme and connected to the market halls by hydraulic lifts, so that meat, poultry and other perishable goods could be delivered straight from the company's trucks to the market without cartage. A larger operation was the opening of a substantial goods depot at South Lambeth, deep in the heart of South London. This shed accommodated some 70 wagons, with a three-floor warehouse above. Equipped with the latest electric cranes and traversers, the *Great Western Railway Magazine*, chronicling its opening in January 1913, reported that the depot was conveniently situated to accommodating traffic in the districts of Battersea, Kennington, Brixton, Peckham, Clapham, Camberwell, Wandsworth, Bermondsey and Southwark.[20] It is clear from this list that the Great Western was certainly not afraid to take its battle for custom deep into the heart of its rivals' territory!

Another GWR correspondent writing in the same period saw the company's goods arrangements in the capital as 'a great hand held out either to grasp the traffic of the Metropolis and Port of London,

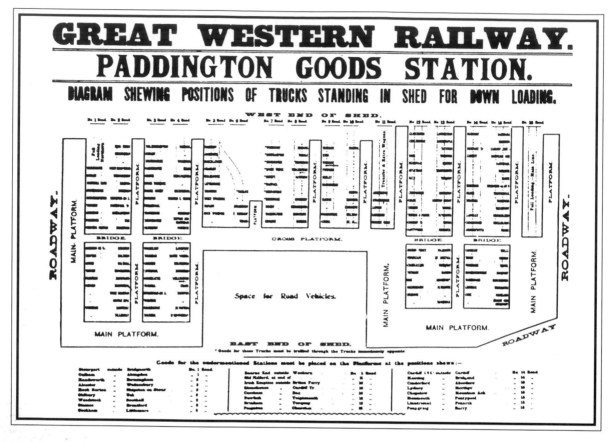

A diagram showing arrangements in the Paddington Goods Depot before the First World War. (GWR (London) Lecture & Debating Society)

or shower blessings on its inhabitants in the shape of foodstuffs of all descriptions brought in from the provinces'[21]. These generalities will hopefully help the reader to remember why the facilities provided by the company did exist, and to make the following description of the Goods Department at Paddington seem more relevant.

The improvements mentioned briefly above were in an unfortunate sense assisted by a disastrous fire which occurred at the station on 22 June 1896. What had been known as the 'Northern Warehouse' was reduced to a ruin in something less then three hours, and at one stage there had been a distinct danger that the fire could have spread much further. Despite the effects of this calamity, the department still managed to function, albeit in a reduced manner, until new premises became available.

New office facilties were built, since the old premises had been of a very primitive order. One can imagine the enormous amounts of paperwork which needed to be processed each week; and it is calculated that a million items were processed every year. Further improvements were made in the goods station itself in April 1898, with the replacement of a series of small wagon turntables, originally placed across the entrance to the shed and which had given access to different platforms. The new arrangements consisted of a 40-foot extension to the platforms, increasing the capacity of the depot by 60 wagons. At the same time, the 32 horses used for shunting were replaced by a series of hydraulic capstans. The men looking after the horses did not, however, lose their jobs — they were re-employed as 'capstan men'! All in all, these improvements, together with other general modernization, helped to bring the goods station out of the 'Broad Gauge' era.

A distinct pattern could be discerned in the way that the depot functioned. Between noon and midnight, the majority of the traffic bound for other parts of the Great Western Railway network was sorted, checked and loaded onto the correct wagon. The period between midnight and noon saw the reverse of this process, with the unloading and sorting of incoming goods for the London market itself.

A rather more detailed account of operations may enlighten the reader still further. During the afternoon, various loads of goods collected by the GWR's own vehicles were brought to the goods depot. After being sorted, weighed and having the consignment note recorded, the goods were then loaded on to the correct vehicle; this could be a complicated process if, for example, a van load of butter

One of the more far-flung locations to which the company's 'station truck' would have eventually reached; this small station was at Redbrook, in the Forest of Dean. (National Railway Museum Collection)

had to be distributed to perhaps 100 different towns on the Great Western system. This of course meant that the platform clerks at Paddington goods station had probably the best geographical knowledge of the Great Western system of anyone who worked for that great organization.

'London is the great storehouse of the world,'[22] declared Mr H.C. Law, the Goods Manager at Paddington in 1908, and he went on to list the produce arriving in London from the colonies. He further commented that in the course of a year 'there is not a town or village…that does not draw supplies of some kind or other from London'[23]. Some 32 goods trains were dispatched from Paddington each day, with smaller stations being served by the GWR system of 'station trucks'. These were wagons serving a particular stretch of line; for example, in 1908 truck number 69 served the line between

GOODS WORKERS.

LONDON.

Grade.	1st year.	2nd year.	3rd year.	4th year.	5th year.	6th year.	7th year.	8th year.	9th year.	10th year.	11th year.	Maxi-mum.
Foremen	30/-	31/-	32/-	33/-	34/-	35/-	36/-	37/-	38/-	39/-	40/-	40/-
Assistant Foremen	26/-	27/-	28/-	29/-	30/-	31/-	32/-	33/-	34/-	35/-	–	35/-
Checkers	26/-	27/-	28/-	29/-	30/-	31/-	–	–	–	–	–	31/-
Warehousemen	26/-	27/-	28/-	29/-	30/-	31/-	–	–	–	–	–	31/-
Stowers	23/-	24/-	25/-	26/-	–	–	–	–	–	–	–	26/-
Callers-off	23/-	24/-	25/-	26/-	–	–	–	–	–	–	–	26/-
Loaders	23/-	24/-	25/-	26/-	–	–	–	–	–	–	–	26/-
Porters, including Lampmen and Cranemen	20/-	21/-	22/-	23/-	24/-	–	–	–	–	–	–	24/-
Porters (Mileage and Yard), including Adult Number Takers	21/-	22/-	23/-	24/-	–	–	–	–	–	–	–	24/-
Weighbridgemen	23/-	24/-	25/-	26/-	27/-	–	–	–	–	–	–	27/-
Policemen	23/-	24/-	25/-	26/-	27/-	28/-	–	–	–	–	–	28/-
Police Sergeants	26/-	27/-	28/-	29/-	30/-	31/-	32/-	33/-	34/-	35/-	–	35/-
Timekeepers	23/-	24/-	25/-	26/-	27/-	28/-	–	–	–	–	–	28/*
Lad Porters	10/-	12/-	14/-	16/-	–	–	–	–	–	–	–	16/-

* Paddington Station, 30/-

A page from a booklet listing wage rates issued by Frank Potter, the General Manager, in August 1912.

A four-horse team is needed to haul this prodigious load from Paddington. The author feels that in this case, there might just be the hint of overloading! (National Railway Museum Collection)

Par and Newquay in Cornwall, including the stations at Par itself, St Blazey, Bridges, Bugle, Roche, St Columb Road and Newquay. The idea was probably cost-effective, although it did not always guarantee the rapid delivery of goods to some of the more far-flung outposts of the Great Western empire!

The busiest period by far at Paddington goods depot was after midnight, when the unloading and sorting of incoming goods began in earnest. Much of the traffic was of course seasonal, but all-the-year round traffic included such items as hardware, including buckets, baths, screws and nails, from the Staffordshire district, Wiltshire bacon, West of England serge and confectionery and Bristol cocoa and tobacco; and other products dealt with included chairs, blankets and carpets.

Seasonal and perishable traffic included Cornish herrings and mackerel, asparagus from the Vale of Evesham, Cornish broccoli, and new potatoes and early flowers from the Channel Islands. Devon, Gloucestershire and Somerset supplied apples and that more exotic fruit, the banana, was imported via Avonmouth docks near Bristol. Much of this kind of traffic was marshalled into special trains, and once at Paddington was unloaded quickly, since it had to be at the markets by 6 am at the latest. The men who did the unloading were, not surprisingly, paid on a bonus system. Twenty-four gangs of approximately 260 men in total worked in shifts to cope with the busiest influxes; for example, between midnight and 2 am, 12 gangs were employed.

Once the produce was out of the rail wagons, the Great Western company was responsible for the delivery of all fish, poultry, meat and other perishable goods to the markets. In 1908, for example, a complement of 72 teams of horses and one five-ton motor vehicle were used to tackle this work. Other casual workers could be called on in busy periods, bringing the staff up to the thousand mark on some occasions.

Some 700 horses were used, including several four-horse teams, which were employed to haul exceptionally heavy loads. Many of these horses were stabled at Paddington itself. Not suprisingly, the Great Western, always keen to watch its expenditure, had strict instructions with regard to the amounts that its horses should be fed. In a Circular issued in August 1900, the Stores Superintendent at Swindon laid down standard 'provender Mixtures' and the allowance per horse, per day. Differing proportions of oats, beans, maize and hay were specified according to the work done, the geographical area, and the season. The lucky horses engaged in goods work at Paddington received 30 pounds of feed per day in summer, 32 in winter. By comparison, a horse employed on goods work from a country station could only hope to receive 29 pounds of feed per day summer or winter.[24]

By 1900 though, the influence of the internal combustion engine was beginning to make itself discernable. The Superintendent of the Goods Station felt that 'Goods Motors will probably replace horsed vehicles in future, near or far, but at present they have not proved a commercial success'[25]. That future was not far away, and once vehicles with enough power and reliability could be found, the GWR was not slow to acquire them. We shall look at the company's road motor operation in detail in a later chapter.

Summing up his description of the goods station in 1908, its Superintendent, Mr Law, described his job as 'no sinecure'; with the volume of traffic dealt with, and a staff of over 300 clerks and 1,700 other grades to supervise, it is not difficult to disagree with this view. His concluding remarks are worth noting if only to illustrate the 'managerial style' prevalent at the time: '…it has come within my lot…to act the part of Father Confessor, parental admonisher, brotherly advisor, and magisterial chastiser of the frail and unregenerate'[26].

THE ROYAL GATEWAY

OUR description of Paddington so far has been confined to the facilities afforded to the majority of travellers on the Great Western Railway. We now turn our attention to an aspect of the station's life to which that majority were merely spectators. This was, of course, Paddington's role as a Royal Station.

It was to this great terminus that Queen Victoria had travelled on her first rail journey in 1842, and it is worth repeating that it was her use of this relatively new mode of transport that gave it an aura of respectability at that time. Since Windsor was only a relatively short distance from London via Slough, a good number of royal journeys terminated at Paddington. As usual, the Great Western management was not slow to realize the public relations mileage in this, christening the station its 'Royal Gateway'.

In the period covered by this book, Paddington was the scene of much royal pomp and splendour, its cathedral-like interior being an almost theatrical setting for the state occasions which took place there. The frequency of royal visits also meant that the station staff were well prepared for the kind of preparations and work necessary. Arguably the most splendid occasion was the celebration of Queen Victoria's Diamond Jubilee in 1897. On the morning of 21 May the station was gaily decorated with the flags of the 'great European nations'[27] and the 'Stars and Stripes', the decoration being arranged in 'an excellent form in respect of shade and variety'[28]. Large enclosures and balconies constructed for the event were thronged with the 'great and the good' awaiting the arrival of the train.

At 12.30 precisely, the locomotive carrying the Royal Coat of Arms and Royal Standard pulled the train into the station, coming to a halt so imperceptibly that the train seemed to stop without so much as a jerk or a shudder. Press reports at the time also made much of the fact that when the train stopped, the Royal Saloon was exactly opposite the platform and red carpet leading to Her Majesty's carriage. One correspondent wrote: '...the mighty force of the throbbing steam engine had been so nicely controlled that the distance had been judged to a thirty-second part of an inch'[29].

The Royal Train at Plymouth North Road on 7 March 1902. 'Bulldog' 4-4-0 No 3345 Exeter *was temporarily renamed* Royal Sovereign *for the occasion.* (GWR Museum, Swindon)

Although the driver would have driven the train with the greatest of care, his ability to stop the train in exactly the right place depended more on a 'trick of the trade' which has been practiced on many occasions since — a trial trip for the royal train was made some days before the Jubilee celebrations, on the 19th. Once the exact position of the train's final resting place had been agreed, a small white painted stake was driven into the ballast opposite the driver's cab. Thus, on the great day the fireman or driver merely had to stop the locomotive opposite the peg to ensure that the train was correctly positioned. Of course the public could not see the peg, which after all would have ruined the effect!

Once off the train, Queen Victoria was received by the GWR Chairman, Viscount Emlyn, and the Directors, before departing for celebrations elsewhere in the City. Her presence on the platform was the signal for 'a demonstration by the large numbers of visitors assembled of enthusiastic loyalty'[30]. It was later reported that Paddington's Stationmaster, Mr William Rowed, was presented with a gold pin of Crown design, with a diamond setting, bearing the initials 'VRI' as a token of the Queen's appreciation of the arrangements at the station on that day.

Less than four years later, Brunel's station was the arena for a rather more sombre event. On 22 January 1901, Queen Victoria died at Osborne on the Isle of Wight, surrounded by her many children and grandchildren, including the Emperor of Germany. The phrase 'end of an era' has perhaps become something of a cliché in our time, but it is probably true to say that the death of the Queen did cause the population of Britain to feel that despite the tumultuous events of her reign, many more changes would follow the passing of 'that Great Monarch', as Lord Rosebery called her.

Before the Country and Empire could step out into a new world without Victoria, the solemn job of her funeral had to be dealt with, and Paddington was again to play an important role in this drama. Again the station was well decorated, although this time with more restrained crimson hangings. These of course served also to hide the ubiquitous advertising hoardings which had sprung up all over the station. However, Paddington, it seems, was not as bad as some sites, and the *Great Western Railway Magazine* was moved to note that 'the eye is not offended in every turn with advertisement hoardings'[31]. It seems too that although the site was well decorated, the draping was not carried so far as to make the utilitarian surroundings seem too incongruous. This may well have been a reaction to events elsewhere in London, where a morbid hysteria appears to have set in; it was reported, for example, that the 800 street lamps around the Buckingham Palace area were each decorated with large wreaths of laurel leaves.[32] In contrast, the platform at which the funeral train was to arrive was simply decorated with a thick crimson carpet, and on it were arranged two parterres of white flowers.

Another Royal Train, this time in 1903. Churchward 4-4-0 City of Bath *carries the fleur-de-lys insignia of the Prince of Wales.* (GWR Museum, Swindon)

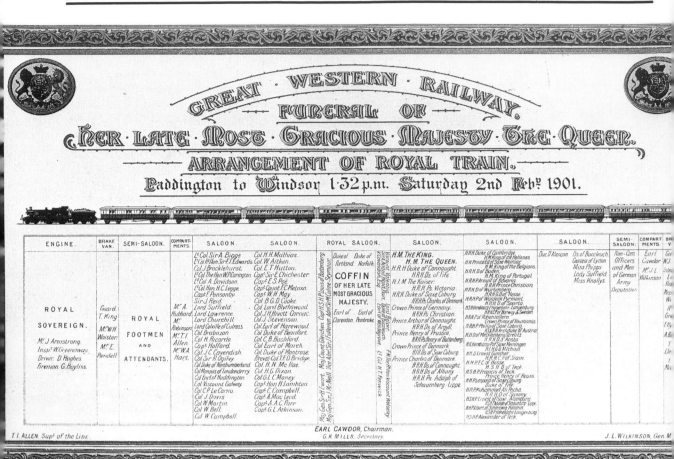

Decorated plan of the train for the funeral of Queen Victoria in 1901. (GWR Museum, Swindon)

The streets in and around the station precincts were packed with people and at around 12.30 a 'portentous hush' fell as the cortège arrived. No music was played, and the great station resounded only to the resolute tramp of the troops' feet. After an enormous procession of the military, the bier carrying the Queen's coffin was brought into Paddington on a gun carriage hauled by eight cream-coloured horses; only then did the band strike up to play Beethoven's Funeral March. After all the distinguished guests had arrived, including the new King Edward and the German Emperor, the music finally ceased. Whilst all the spectators stood bareheaded, the assembled troops stood to attention, the colours were lowered and the train steamed gracefully out. 'London had looked its last on the Queen, and was left with naught but its imperishable memories of her'[33].

Some weeks later the station was host to a rather more cheerful royal visit. The occasion was the arrival of the German Emperor with the new King Edward VII; the funeral drapes had been replaced by crimson and gold hangings, and there was a large turn-out of both staff and public to see the new monarch. Edward, unlike his mother, who scarcely travelled far from Balmoral, Osborne House or Windsor during her reign, was gregarious and mobile, and saw no reason to change his habits when he became King. He was a popular figure and was 'of course a frequent traveller to and from the Great Western terminus, and among all classes of railway staff he has long been regarded with almost proprietary affection'[34].

Management at Paddington allowed around 3,000 staff to assemble in the station, and when the King and the German Emperor inspected the troops, a spontaneous cheer rang out around the great roof of the terminus. As the royal party left, bystanders stretched and strained to get a view. The *Great Western Railway Magazine* concluded: 'London had indeed shown she knew how worthily to greet her King, and to bid farewell to the Emperor who has deserved so well of the nation's gratitude and regard'[35]. Who could have then realized that within 13 years Britain would be engaged in a bloody war with Germany and its leader, Emperor Wilhelm, 'Kaiser Bill'.

Since his mother had not abdicated the throne, Edward did not become King until he was 60 years old. Thus it was, unfortunately, that some eight years after his Coronation, Edward died at Buckingham Palace. Despite the shortcomings of his private life, amongst the public at large he had been a much-loved figure. Yet again, Paddington was the centrepiece for much of the pomp and ceremony surrounding his interment. The arrangements for the funeral were much the same as for that of Queen Victoria, although this time the locomotive chosen to haul the Royal train was one of G.J. Churchward's new 'Star' Class, No 4021, appropriately named *King Edward*.

The reader will not be further burdened with sombre descriptions of state funerals, but instead might be interested to hear of several other 'royal incidents' reported by the *Great Western Railway Magazine and Temperance Union Record*, as it was then known, in November 1895. It was noted that the ticket examining staff at Slough had recently had the privilege of meeting some distinguished first class passengers, who perceived that their exalted social position was such that they did not need a ticket. However, they would 'at any stage meet their liabilities to the company in a manner befitting their exalted station'[36]. One of this privileged group, when questioned, explain that he was the Duke of York, *en route* to Windsor. The article concluded: 'His sham Royal Highness although deprived of...seeing the Queen at Windsor, had the privilege of meeting someone representing her at an institution at Aylesbury, where ladies and gentlemen are boarded at the expense of the country'[37]!

Some years later, another royal occasion was detailed. Like many stations of the period, Paddington was home to what was known as a 'collecting dog' used to raise money for local charities. The Paddington dog, 'Tim', had started his career on the Great Western in 1892, and was owned by Inspector Bush, one of the station staff; in

Front cover of a handbill issued for the funeral of King Edward VII in 1910. (Michael Wyatt Collection)

Waiting for the arrival of General Roberts in 1901; dignitaries from all parts of the empire are present. This picture was originally reproduced in the Great Western Railway Magazine. *(GWR Museum, Swindon)*

1901, 'Tim' was summoned by royal command to Queen Victoria's Royal Saloon on its arrival at the station, and received a sovereign for his trouble. The Queen's daughter, Princess Henry of Battenburg, also contributed along with her children, Princess Ena and Prince Maurice. 'Tim' must have been a familiar sight around the platforms of the great station, and when he died in September 1902 it was calculated that he had raised over £800. There was no rest for the unfortunate hound, however; he was stuffed and placed in a glass case on platform 1 with a collecting box attached!

Royal dignitaries aside, Paddington was also the venue for triumphal scenes when several of the chief figures of the Boer War campaign returned to Britain from South Africa. It is not the place here to describe the history and events of that war, but suffice to say that it had been something of a trauma nationally. The conflict had shown up the inadequacies of the War Office and the Army, as well as showing how ill-prepared the country was for war generally. Although the British eventually gained the upper hand in the hostilities, it was a bloody and hard-fought conflict; the guerrilla tactics of the Boers, and the methods used by the British to subjugate them, had left many people at home feeling somewhat uneasy. There were also accusations of excessive jingoism and propaganda being used to mobilize public opinion in Britain. Indeed, the large military display at the funeral of Queen Victoria which we have already described was seen by some, including the first Labour Member of Parliament, Kier Hardie, as nothing more than a large-scale and tasteless recruiting display for the Boer War campaign.

It certainly seems that no expense had been spared for the return from South Africa in 1901 of Lord Roberts, Commander in Chief. The pillars of Paddington's roof were adorned with banners and shields bearing the armorial device of the Field Marshal, and the back of number 9 platform was decorated with red, white and blue banners. The train, hauled by the 4–4–0 locomotive *Roberts*, which was also decorated with his coat of arms, arrived at number 8 platform which was 'carpeted in crimson'[38]. The Field Marshal was greeted by the Prince of Wales and a strong contingent of the military, not unnaturally to the strains of 'See the Conquering Hero Comes'. Departing the station for Buckingham Palace, the carriages were escorted by the 19th Hussars and ten Indian orderlies, 'splendid fellows whose striking uniforms and stalwart soldierly bearing attracted universal attention and admiration'[39].

Similar scenes occurred with the return of General Kitchener in July 1902. An hour before the arrival of his train, the platforms at Paddington were cleared of all save 'privileged spectators'. Only 1,000 ticket holders were allowed inside the station to see Kitchener met by the Prince of Wales, the Duke of Connaught, Earl Cadogan and the Maharajah of Jaipur, as well as the usual military 'top brass'.

HEADQUARTERS OF THE EMPIRE

WHILST the hustle and bustle of the passengers, parcels and goods work continued down in the great station and its surroundings, another vast army of staff was hard at work in the company's headquarters offices, situated above the Waiting Rooms, Booking Halls and other offices along the main departure platform. There was also more premises in Eastbourne Terrace where six houses had been purchased by the company enabling another 40 offices to be brought into use. To understand something of the working of this complex, a brief description of the various departments which made up the company's internal structure may be enlightening.

Some idea of the enormous extent of the Great Western network has already been given in the introduction to this book, so it is easy to see that the sheer size of the undertaking required a considerable bureaucratic machine to manage and control it. At the very top of the organization was the General Manager's Office; this of all departments had perhaps the most influence over the running and development of the company, and the General Manager himself was perhaps the most powerful man on the GWR. His 'Chief Executive' role meant that he was indeed the 'Captain of the Ship', and was responsible for developing the broad strategic policies of all departments. As we have already seen, the Great Western in its 'Golden Age' was very fortunate in having dynamic and forceful General Managers in both James Inglis and Frank Potter to direct and supervise operations.

Having noted their strategic role, however, it would be as well to remember that they nevertheless kept their eye on the less important issues, and no project of any real size or significance could be carried out without the sanction of the General Manager[40]. As well as its Executive role, the General Manager's Department also contained offices pertaining to the Company Accountant, Solicitor and Secretary, and also dealt with Railway Clearing House, Board of Trade and Parliamentary matters. The publicity section, which will be described in a later chapter, was also part of this department.

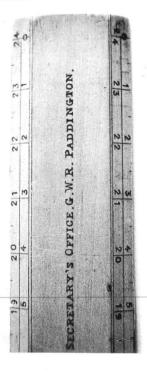

Part of a 12-inch ruler from the Secretary's office; the bottom shows that over the years it has been less than well treated!

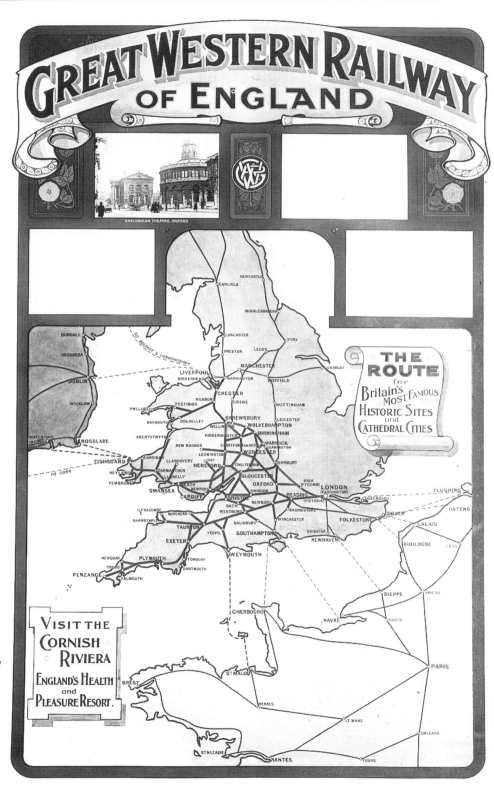

This photograph taken by the company photographer shows 'work in progress' in the advertising department; the author has not been able to ascertain whether the poster was ever finally issued. (National Railway Museum, York)

Returning to the Great Western company structure, four great divisions were responsible to the General Manager: the Superintendent of the Line's Department, the Engineering Department, the Chief Goods Manager's Department, and the Locomotive Department.

The Superintendent of the Line's Department, known as the 'Traffic' department within the company, dealt with just that; it was this office that ensured that the railway actually worked. All aspects of operations were watched over, including staff appointments, wages and hours, passenger fares, tickets and rates, and the preparation of timetables for both public and company servant use. It was this department which also ensured the correct distribution of carriage and wagon stock for train service requirements, a critical role in such a busy and complex operation.

The Engineering Department had a different yet equally important responsibility; it maintained and renewed the company's permanent way, bridges, tunnels, stations and other structures, and also, especially in the 'Golden Age' period, planned, designed and supervised the construction of new lines and facilities for the railway.

The Chief Goods Manager had considerable influence and power, which was not surprising since almost 50 per cent of the company's revenue depended on the goods services which he administered. In fact, on most railways at this time the largest revenue-earning division was invariably the Goods Department; this importance was recognized by the fact that the Chief Goods Manager was subordinate only to the General Manager, and had an advisory seat on the GWR Board itself. It might be worth noting here that although the Goods Department was responsible for the collection and delivery of goods, and its safe stowage and loading, the actual running of the trains was the province of the Superintendent of the Line's division.

The final department was the Locomotive Department. If we may return to the maritime metaphor, if the General Manager's Department was the ship's 'bridge', the Locomotive Department was the 'engine room', providing the motive power and the means to keep the Great Western system running. The production and maintenance of locomotives, carriages and wagons was the main concern of the Locomotive Superintendent, giving the post some not inconsiderable stature. An additional factor was that of all the departments thus far described, this great empire was the only one not to have its headquarters at Paddington. The centre of this operation was some 77 miles away at Swindon, giving the division a large amount of independence, and this played a key role in the development of the GWR during this period. In Part Two we will look in greater detail at the workings of what was to many an alternative headquarters of the Great Western.

Thus it was that, with the exception of the Locomotive Department, most of the administration for the other groups was

This view of 'Badminton' Class Grosvenor *is of interest not only because of the engine itself, but also in that it shows in the background, above the station canopy, some of the large number of offices in the precincts of Paddington.*

carried out in the Paddington offices. Pressure of space was always a problem, some rooms accommodating upwards of 50 clerks. In total, some 1,500 were housed in and around the station. In the main offices there were four corridors, the longest two about 850 feet in length with around 140 individual rooms. One drastic solution to the office space shortage was to add another storey to the main office block itself, which was done after 1905.

For the vast majority of staff, the work must have been boring and repetitious; in some departments, typewriters and comptometers had been introduced, but in the period before the First World War a large amount of copying and calculation was still done by hand.

A glimpse into a clerk's life at this time can be obtained by a look at a rule book for the period [41]. This example comes from the Chief Goods Manager's Office, although life cannot have been greatly different elsewhere at Paddington. Staff were expected to work from 9 to 5.30 on weekdays, and 9 to 1.00 on Saturdays. It was also noted that to avoid inconvenience to the ordinary travelling public on through trains between suburban stations and the City, 'members of staff who reside in the suburbs are required to strictly comply with special notices…as to the use of certain through trains' [42].

Someone in Plymouth had obviously incurred the wrath of Paddington, as the tone of this letter shows!

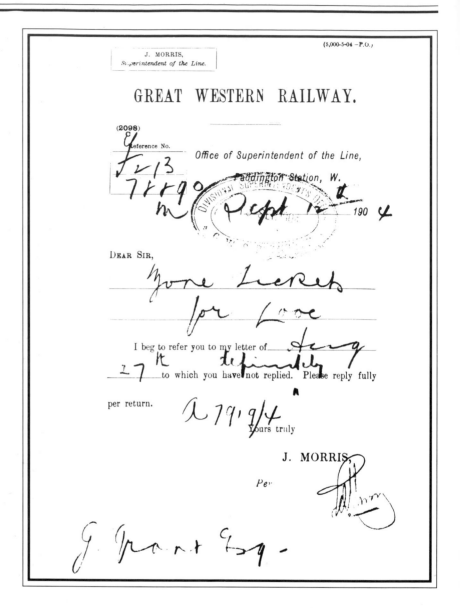

To those of us who despair of quick replies from large organizations, it is worthy of note that in 1914 the GWR required that 'every letter shall be dealt with on its day of receipt'[43]; furthermore, 'care must be taken that every letter sent from the office is nicely composed, clearly written or typed and in no case must a brusque or discourteous tone be adopted'[44]. Discipline was, needless to say, tough in such offices. Speaking to the GWR Lecture and Debating Society in 1905, Mr W. Dawson outlined some 'golden rules' for those in authority, one of which was that it was useful to discuss methods of work with men, but 'never discuss whether your absolute commands shall be obeyed'[45]. He concluded his lecture with the advice to 'keep an iron hand in a velvet glove'[46]. The Goods

Department rule book also warned staff to 'avoid loud conversation or discussion of extraneous matters likely to distract others'[47].

The staff guidelines laid down in the rule-book also highlighted one of the most significant weaknesses in the Great Western administrative machine; it notes that 'no section or department must undertake duties which appertain to another'[48]. The separate departments were just that — separate. This was largely due to the company's recruitment policy; when clerks were appointed at the age of 14 or 15 they had little or no choice as to where they were to work. The general procedure was that after the production of birth and medical certificates together with three testimonials, the prospective clerk sat an examination. If successful, a post was allotted as a vacancy occurred regardless of the ability of the applicant, or his wishes. This meant that the clerk might be appointed to the General Manager's Office, or alternatively some minor backwater, where opportunity for advancement was less likely. The Traffic department, for example, had a whole variety of posts, whereas in some of the smaller offices, prospects were far bleaker.

The frustration felt by some good men led to their leaving the service, and also conversely led to less able men maintaining the same post for almost the whole of their railway career. This is not to say that there were no opportunities for advancement — Felix Pole, for example, started as a Telegraph Clerk at Swindon station in

No 3352 Camel *prepares to leave Paddington: this 'Bulldog' Class engine was built in 1899 and had its numberplate rather incongruously fixed to the side of the smokebox.* (Brian Arman Collection)

A GWR telegraph 'sender' apparatus; the wooden knob shows considerable wear from the thousands of messages which must have been transmitted on it.

1893, and by 1921 he had risen to the heights of General Manager!

From the company point of view, the sharply drawn lines of the various departments were a handicap; the cumbersome bureaucratic organization did work, but it was not helped by this lack of inter-departmental knowledge, and the relatively uncommon transfer of men from one department to another led to the evolution of a rather parochial system. Each section was highly defensive of its own interests and suspicious of other groups, often to the detriment of the system as a whole.

One development which went some way to addressing this problem was the provision of better telegraph and telephone equipment during the 'Golden Age'. It is obvious that one of the most important single factors in ensuring the smooth running of such a big organization as the Great Western is good communication. It was not until the beginning of the new century that the company began to realize the importance of both the telegraph and the relatively new innovation, the telephone. In 1898, the Telegraph Office was situated off number 1 departure platform, in cramped accommodation with few telephones and what was known as 'single needle' telegraph equipment. Then, in the light of the other changes happening elsewhere on the railway, the whole communication system of the company was upgraded. A new, better lit and ventilated room was obtained, and improved telegraph equipment of the 'Duplex' and 'Quadruplex' type was installed ('Duplex' meant that two telegrams could be signalled each way, 'Quadruplex' allowing two messages to be sent and two messages to be received simultaneously). The telegraph system was a vital artery in the business of the company; each day around 7,000 messages were sent and received concerning all aspects of the railway's business.

For example, it would take around two minutes for a message to be transmitted from Plymouth to Paddington; when such a message was received, it was dispatched to the relevant department at Paddington by means of a pneumatic tube system, similar to that used in many shops until recently. The 15 most important offices were connected to this system, and it is interesting to note that the furthest office, in the Goods Depot, could be reached in 30 seconds, much faster than sending a messenger!

One of the most important moments of the day was at 2 minutes to 10 in the morning, when all telegraph work on the whole GWR network was halted. At that moment the correct Greenwich Mean Time was transmitted, allowing station staff from the smallest wayside station to the biggest junction to synchronize and wind their clocks. It was obviously extremely important that all timepieces on railway property told exactly the same time, and the general public came to depend on the accuracy of GWR timepieces; it was noted in 1913 that 'nowadays nearly everybody carries a watch and sets it to GMT ascertainable from either the railway or the Post Office'[49].

The newer innovation of the telephone was adopted by the company on a more gradual basis. In 1909 Paddington was served by a small exchange in the GWR hotel, which had 25 lines to the local telephone exchange, and two smaller switchboards situated in the Goods Office and the Telegraph Office respectively. On the main switchboard, the three lady operators presided over some 260 extensions, and dealt with around 600 enquiries per day. Speaking to the GWR Lecture and Debating Society, Mr C. Gibbs argued: 'In these days every small tradesman has a 'phone to carry out his business, and surely the biggest trader of all, the railway company, should do likewise'[50].

The Great Western was not, in fact, to be left behind, for the development of the telephone marked a new era in communication, and its importance with regard to business was not lost on the Paddington management. By 1913 a new switchboard had been brought in to replace the three smaller installations. With six operators and the possibility of 1,000 extensions, it was 'a model of up to date equipment and management'[51]. It was suggested at the time that there had been some reluctance amongst the staff towards the use of the telephone, but in a short time the 'mere suggestion of withdrawing it is met with voluminous objections'[52]. The new switchboard was designed 'in house' by the company's Signal Engineer at Reading, and was installed by the Western Electric Company of Woolwich.

Although well-worn, this handbill is worthy of inclusion since its date is of interest — the privileged minority attending the Regatta would have little to celebrate in the following four years of the Great War.

The general public was also able to have access to the telephone network through four public telephones installed at Paddington in 1908. It was clear that the public was as enthusiastic about the idea of telephones as the company, for in the first 12 months of their operation over 36,000 calls were logged, with the highest weekly total being 800. Those who regularly use the telephone kiosks at Paddington today will be pleased to hear that in 1909 the boxes were cleaned out, and earpieces and mouthpieces disinfected, four times a day, a level of service British Telecom would do well to emulate!

* * *

Before concluding our description of the Great Western's premier station, it might be interesting to contemplate a GWR service from Paddington which was not bound for the sunny shores of Cornwall, or Birmingham, the North or Wales. In June 1909 a small leaflet entitled 'The Sights of London'[53] was issued. This described tours by a 'Sight-seeing Motor Car'. Departing from the arrival platform at Paddington at 10.30 am and 2.30 pm, a GWR 'Motor Char-a-banc' which, the leaflet noted, was covered and had windows which could be closed in case of rain, took the visitor on a two-and-half-hour circular tour of the capital's sights including Buckingham Palace, Piccadilly Circus, the National Gallery and so on. The trips were 'personally conducted' by a competent guide. The leaflet also noted that in the days of the horse bus such a tour would have been impossible — however, it was now possible through the 'Characteristic Enterprise of the Great Western Company'.

As we continue our journey through the Great Western Railway during its 'Golden Age', we shall certainly encounter many more examples of such 'Characteristic Enterprise'.

PART TWO

SWINDON, HEART OF THE EMPIRE

SWINDON, some 77 miles from Paddington along Brunel's 'billiard table' main line, was one of the busiest and most important places on the Great Western network during the era covered by this book. To many, the town will always be associated with all things 'Great Western', and it is probably true to say that even at that time few people, apart from those with relatives living in the town, would have visited it for anything other than 'Great Western' business. As Ken Ausden noted, although it expanded rapidly, like many other industrial areas founded around the same time, its popularity never quite matched its growth rate![1]

This chapter, then, is the story of a place entirely dominated by the subject of our book, the Great Western Railway. Although Swindon certainly shared many characteristics with other settlements dominated by one industry or trade, it was the very distinct nature of that industry which marked Swindon out from the crowd; the town was acknowledged as the place where they built railway engines, arguably the best in the world! Even today, with the works closed and the town's importance as a railway centre cruelly diminished,

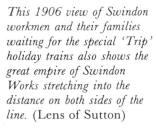

This 1906 view of Swindon workmen and their families waiting for the special 'Trip' holiday trains also shows the great empire of Swindon Works stretching into the distance on both sides of the line. (Lens of Sutton)

Swindon still finds it hard to shake off its 'Railway Town' image.

The 'Golden Age' evident in the general development of the Great Western in the period before the First World War was also reflected in events and developments at Swindon. The year 1914 marked a high point in GWR activity in the town; around 14,000 people were employed in the company's Locomotive, Carriage and Wagon Works, a figure never to be exceeded. Physically the works had grown almost to its greatest extent, although the crowning feature, the great 'A' Shop, where so many famous locomotives were constructed in the inter-war years, was not fully completed until after the Great War. The late Victorian and Edwardian period saw an enormous outpouring of innovation and growth, masterminded for the most part by George Jackson Churchward, the company's Locomotive Carriage and Wagon Superintendent.

Under his direction, the powerful locomotives and modern rolling-stock needed to serve the improved GWR were produced, providing a solid foundation on which the many other developments occurring elsewhere on the system could be based. If Paddington was the administrative heart of the company, then Swindon was its technical and mechanical nerve centre. This was not only in the field of locomotive and rolling-stock design, but also applied on a more mundane level — almost everything needed to run the railway was made and supplied by Swindon Works, from the smallest nut and bolt to larger items such as tools, lamps, station fittings, notices and so on. All were manufactured in the Works, and were dispatched to the far reaches of the great Western system from the General Stores, a considerable empire in itself!

The 1930s have been called a 'Golden Age' at Swindon, when C.B. Collett's 'Castle' and 'King' designs were being produced in considerable numbers. But it must be said that the pre-First World War period could not be matched, the inter-war years being marred by the delibitating effects of the General Strike and the Depression. In the later period, too, the coming of new industries to the Swindon area showed, albeit in a small way, that the Great Western's pre-eminence as the dominant employer in the town was not likely to be a long-term certainty.

It should be said that in creating a portrait of Swindon in the years before the Great War, it would be easy to concentrate on the achievements of G.J. Churchward, and the many fine locomotives which emerged from the company's Works during the era. But important though these engineering breakthroughs were, the author feels that there is rather more to the story. The revolution in locomotive design has already been the subject of much analysis by many distinguished railway writers, and this is not the place to repeat such discussion at any length. Instead, the reader will be given a description of the Works during the period in question, and its relationship with the town which depended almost entirely on the fortunes of those Works and the Great Western Railway in general.

INSIDE SWINDON WORKS

IT is difficult to convey adequately the enormity of Swindon works. To say that the factory covered an area of nearly 200 acres does not really do justice to the sheer size of the place. The main part of the complex developed originally in the 'V' between the Bristol-London main line and the Gloucester branch line. In the period before the First War, however, it covered a far more substantial area east of the Gloucester line as well, where the Carriage & Wagon Works was based. To the west, the Works extended to the Rodbourne Road, although in the years after 1900, new important development took place further west of that point.

Perhaps a more telling indication of the physical extent of the factory was that office staff were issued with bicycles to enable them to get from one side of the Works to another. However, such were the distractions that it was not unknown for an office boy to take a leisurely route round the highways and byways of the place in order to gape at the new engines being built, even if it meant a telling-off from the Foreman or Chief Clerk at the end of it! Several of these bikes have been preserved, and, needless to say, like most items of company property the magic initials 'GWR' are indelibly stamped on the bike frame.[2]

Inside the works, new locomotives, carriages and wagons were constructed for the railway, along with the never-ending task of maintaining existing stock. But this was by no means the end of the story; other less glamorous items were also made and repaired at Swindon, including tools, furniture and other fittings. To a large extent the Works was self sufficient, and it was the proud boast that all that was needed was iron, timber and a few other necessities to produce almost anything it needed to exist. This self-sufficiency also extended to the supply of its own gas, electricity and water, and these will be described in due course.

Part of the aura of the factory was that it was surrounded for the most part by high brick or stone walls, which added to the exclusive nature of the Works. Presumably the fortress-like walls led to the expression 'inside'; this did not mean a stretch inside the local jail, as many outsiders mistakenly thought, but was local slang for being employed in the Works. Over the years, its independent and exclusive nature led to the Works being somewhat distant from other parts of the Great Western system; indeed, it is not unfair to suggest that both management and workforce felt that they were a 'cut above' other areas and departments on the GWR. One expression which perhaps summed up part of this attitude was 'Paddington answers to Swindon, and Swindon answers to God.'[3]

The sense of unity and brotherhood with other staff on the system felt by many GWR employers does not seem to have been so strongly felt at Swindon; it was certainly true that for many years the Works maintained an aloofness which bordered at times on narrow-minded insularity. This negative side of the 'Railway Town' image is seldom reflected in literature on Swindon; however, it was true to say that even up to the Second World War, if you did not work 'inside', or have relatives working there, you were something of a second-class citizen in the town. Without such connections, it would have been difficult to be totally integrated into the community, particularly in the period we are examining.

Returning to our description of the Works itself, the feeling of a vast independent empire was heightened by the fact that access to most parts of the site was through numerous tunnels and subways running under the tangle of rail lines surrounding the establishment. It was possible to walk for some considerable distance around the Works by means of three passages and tunnels linking the various workshops. Perhaps the most impressive entry was gained through what was rather enigmatically known as the 'Tunnel Entrance', situated in Bristol Street opposite the Mechanics Institute; this was a favourite spot for local photographers to record the large outpourings of men both at lunchtime and at night when the Works finished for the day. The gates were presided over by the Watchmen, who kept undesirables out and the workforce in; when the final hooter had blown in the morning, the great doors were shut tight to the outside world until lunchtime. The Watchmen were often workers who had been injured in industrial accidents in the Works, and had been moved to lighter duties.

Once inside the gates, the visitor walked down a long dark tunnel under the main line, before emerging blinking into the sunshine in front of the Works General Offices, at the very heart of the Swindon Empire; readers may find it useful to refer to the map reproduced here, as various important features of the complex are described. The Offices were the administrative nerve centre of the whole operation, and although there were other offices for the Locomotive Works Manager and the Carriage Works nearby, the vast majority of important decisions were made in the main Office building. The General Offices had formed part of the core of the original works opened in the 1840s, and had housed offices for Brunel, Gooch and Sturrock, although in later years Brunel's Office suffered the

One of the subways off the main tunnel entrance seen in 1986. The building in the foreground was once the drawing store for the Locomotive Works.

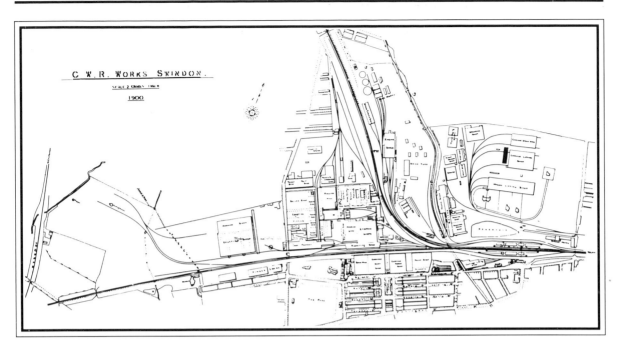

Plan of Swindon Works, 1900. (GWR Museum, Swindon)

indignity of being converted into a gentlemen's lavatory. Whether the Great Man would have approved is debatable!

Much alteration had taken place since the earliest days of the operation at Swindon, and in 1904 the building was substantially modified when an extra storey was added, and a purpose-built L-shaped Drawing Office was created. It was in this spacious and lofty area that many of the classic GWR designs were produced. At the time, the office facilities were seen as some of the most up-to-date in the country; an adjunct to this complex was a photographic studio, from which many of the superb photographs chronicling the railway's progress emerged.

Below the Drawing Office, rather more mundane if no less important work was done; the offices housed the Locomotive, Carriage & Wagon Superintendent and his staff, the Store Superintendent, Carriage Department Accounts, and the Locomotive Mileage Office. Large numbers of clerks maintained the vast administrative organization needed to keep the Works in motion; one of the more interesting rooms in the block, it was reported, was the one housing the mechanical appliances used for clerical work, adding machines and addressographs. This was a far cry from today's automated office systems; most records were kept in great bound ledgers, and material was laboriously copied by the large numbers of staff.

Nonetheless, by the standards of the day the offices were modern, being electrically lit and steam heated; telephones had been installed as early as 1885, and with the size of the Works one can assume that this feature was more of a necessity than a luxury. A memorandum

Churchward's spacious Drawing Office, seen in 1910. (National Railway Museum, York)

to the offices of William Dean, Locomotive Superintendent until 1902, records that the installation of telephones to his Office, the Carriage Department Manager and the Enquiry Office cost the company the sum of £83 11s 4d![4]

The eastern side of the Works was concerned mainly with locomotive maintenance and construction. At its most simple, the factory functioned through a large number of workshops of varying sizes, which manufactured or repaired component parts which were subsequently assembled into new or rebuilt locomotives in the Erecting Shops. To distinguish the various different shops, those on the locomotive side were allocated letters, and those on the carriage side individual numbers. It should be remembered that in such a large establishment there were a huge variety of skills involved; in a later publication on the Works, it was noted with some regret that in latter years the number and variety of trades had sadly diminished. Some occupations such as 'Caller up, Chaff cutter, Cooper, Ding Separator and Shingler' had long gone, but were amongst a host of other trades practised in the years before the First World War.[5]

The basis of much that was done in the Works were the 'Hot' shops. Two foundries produced castings in both ferrous and non-ferrous metals, while larger components were stamped and forged into shape in the Steam Hammer Shop. Alfred Williams, the poet and writer, worked in a similar workshop in the Carriage Works, and his book *Life in a Railway Factory*, published in 1915, gives a vivid description of what working conditions must have been like during the 'Golden Age'. Metal ingots were first heated up to the correct temperature in a furnace, then stamped and shaped by the great hammer head to the correct profile. The hammer driver was a skilled craftsman, since he only had a limited amount of time in which to complete the forging before the metal became too cool. Great dexterity and experience were needed to judge the kind of blow needed to mould the metal; too heavy, and the valuable forging could be put out of shape. Williams wrote that he found the whole process mesmeric, although the heat, noise and vibration made it one of the most unpleasant places in the factory to work. To make matters worse, the men of the Hammer Shop worked 12-hour shifts, with only a few pauses for meals.

Similar hot and dirty workshops catered for the manufacture of other fittings such as springs and wheels, while large blacksmiths' shops made and repaired a host of smaller parts and components. Perhaps the most skilled craftsmen were those working in the fitting and machine shops; it was these men who took the rough castings and forgings already described and machined and assembled them into a form ready to be fitted to the locomotive. Various workshops specialized in particular items — 'W' Shop, for example, was used principally for the production of engine valve gear, superheater apparatus and other locomotive and tender fittings.

During the 'Golden Age', much money was spent on new equipment for this and similar shops, 'R' (Machine) Shop was considered to be well up-to-date, its equipment during the 'Golden Age' being augmented by the introduction, on a very large scale, of labour- and time-saving devices of extremely ingenious design. Many of these machines were semi-automatic, and were used for repetitious work such as the production of nuts, bolts and stay-bolts for boilers. Although, of course, these machines did save the company time and money, they were greeted with less enthusiasm by the men, whose numbers were ultimately reduced by the automation of these processes.

A huge assortment of equipment filled these buildings — lathes, slotting and shaping apparatus, milling machines, drills, punches and shears, grinders and planes — and many were powered by stationary steam boilers via a complicated tangle of shafting and belting which filled the shops in many parts, from floor to ceiling. Alfred Williams wrote that 'the interior is like peering into a dense forest where all is tangled and confused and everything is in a state of perpetual motion'[6]. During our period, with the electrification of the Works, great efforts were made to increase the number of machines directly powered by electricity.

Another specialist trade was practised in 'P2' Shop. Here steam cylinders of all types and sizes were fitted and machined. This job was all the more difficult when one remembers that cylinder components weighed around 6 tons each when fitted; special large borers, planers and drills were provided, and the output of the shop was recorded in 1914 as being over 250 pairs of cylinders per year.

Although the fitting and machine shops were much less dirty places to work, danger still lurked in the mass of belting and machinery. Accidents were not uncommon, especially since by

GREAT WESTERN RAILWAY.

RULES AND REGULATIONS

TO BE OBSERVED BY

WORKMEN EMPLOYED IN THE WORKSHOPS

OF THE

LOCOMOTIVE, CARRIAGE AND WAGON DEPARTMENTS.

1. Every applicant for employment must be in good health, and will only be temporarily engaged until a satisfactory character has been received from his last employer for whom he has worked six months. He must produce his Certificate of Birth, and must sign a declaration that he has read a copy of these Rules, and that he undertakes to observe and be bound by them as a condition of his employment.

2. The usual hours of work are as follow:—

Monday to Friday
6.0 a.m. to 8.15 a.m.
9.0 ,, ,, 1.0 p.m.
2.0 p.m. ,, 5.30 p.m.

Saturdays
6.0 a.m. to 8.15 a.m.
9.0 ,, ,, 12. 0 noon

totalling 54 hours per week, or an average of nine hours per day.

Rule book, Swindon Works, c 1910.

today's criteria safety standards were still fairly low. The rule book issued to the workforce laid down a series of regulations to try and combat the steady number of minor accidents and mishaps; for example, rule 52 noted: 'Sticks and brushes are provided for the purpose of removing drillings, turnings, etc from tools or machines, and any workman removing them with his fingers will be considered guilty of serious and wilful misconduct, and render himself liable to instant dismissal'. Rule 33 added: 'It is most important that workmen employed on lathes and other machines should wear close-fitting jackets'[7].

It is not coincidental that the Trimming Shop in the Carriage Works had one section which made up artificial limbs for Great Western men unfortunate enough to lose their own in the service of the company; an interesting, if grisly, order book for the department has survived, which shows that although the majority of artificial hands, arms, legs and feet were supplied to victims of shunting accidents, Swindon Works staff also had need of the services of that department. In a survey of the Trimming Shop, the *Great Western Railway Magazine* proudly boasted that since its inception in 1878, over 4,000 artificial limbs had been produced — an indictment of the company's safety record rather than a measure of the productivity of the Trimming Shop, one might argue!

'K' Shop, situated in one of the buildings forming the original core of the Works, was home to another skilled group of craftsmen, the coppersmiths. It was here that the decorative features which distinguished GWR locomotives from the 'crowd', the copper chimney caps and the brass safety valve covers, were produced. The latter were made by cutting a brass sheet to the right pattern using a template, then bringing the edges together and brazing them to form a tapered barrel; the cover was then beaten out by hand or by pneumatic hammer to the correct profile, then refined by a boxwood mallet or a steel-headed tool. Finally, the cover was planished with a bright-faced hammer to remove any marks; this was the most delicate part of the operation, since any heavy-handed slip could ruin the effect, not to mention the product of hours of work. One further touch was a polishing lathe, to buff up the brass to a bright finish.

The 'tinkers', as the coppersmiths and tinsmiths were known, did a diverse number of other tasks. Some specialized in the production of the intricate copper piping fitted to locomotives, while others made a huge number of tin articles like lamps, cans, machinery guards, dishes, oilers, and so on. A galvanizing plant also produced treated articles like water troughs, roof guttering and mangers for horse stables!

One further craft which played a key part in ensuring the success of Great Western locomotives in the 'Golden Age' remains to be outlined and that was boilermaking. Although there may have been less subtlety in what this group of craftsmen did, their role was to produce what both Dean and Churchward realized was fundamental for a good locomotive fleet — a strong, powerful, free-steaming boiler.

In a recent book, Denis Griffiths contended that part of Churchward's genius lay in 'deriving a standard range of boilers' which, he continued, 'set the pattern for GWR locomotive appearance until the railway ceased to exist'[8]. The Boiler Shop therefore had the onerous task of manufacturing boilers to the Superintendent's onerous standards. The shop was divided into three sections — the 'V' (Boilersmiths) section, where locomotive boiler construction and repair work took place; the 'L2' (Tank) Shop; and the 'P1' (Boiler-mounting) Shop. Also close by was the 'Q' (Angle-iron Smiths) Shop.

Alfred Williams noted that by and large the boilersmiths were an exclusive order, and guarded their skills jealously. Two distinct groups were apparent — the platers, who prepared the plates making up the boiler, marking them off, and cutting and bending them into shape, and the riveters, who fixed the whole assembly together. In the earliest days much of the work was done by hand, but by 1900 machinery had made the job of building safe, robust boilers rather

An atmospheric photograph of a boiler being lifted to enable riveting to take place in 'V' Shop. On the right is a brazier for the heating of the rivets, a job usually done by apprentices. (National Railway Museum, York)

easier. Large flanging hydraulic presses, and other rolling and pressing machines, were used extensively in construction; the Boiler Shop also had the benefit of powerful cranage, which enabled the large, bulky boilers to be moved easily around the workshop. The largest, built by Fielding and Platt, was capable of lifting 30-ton boilers.

The most notable feature of the Boiler Shop, however, was that it was by far the noisiest place in the factory. Quite apart from the mechanized processes already mentioned, there were also three hydraulic riveting machines in operation. Enormous drills were used to make rivet holes, and there was also a large device capable of planing metal plates of up to 18 feet by 10 feet in size, on two sides at a time. Coupled with this there were a host of small hand-held power tools used for grinding, hammering, drilling, punching, shearing and riveting, to say nothing of the more mundane hand tools used by the men.

With anything up to 80 or so boilers being worked on at any one time, it was not surprising that the din was temendous; Alfred Williams wrote that the heaviest artillery was feeble compared to the noise generated. He described the experience of actually being inside a boiler whilst it was being worked on: 'Do you hear anything? You hear nothing. Sound is swallowed up in sound. You are a hundred times deaf'[9]. It was fairly common for men to have to work inside locomotive boilers in this fashion, so it is not surprising that amongst the 400 or so boilersmiths employed in the shop, premature deafness was common. Sign language and intuition allowed the men to communicate and do their work — they did not waste time shouting at each other. One story common in the shop was that even though the Foreman might be a little deaf, his hearing miraculously improved if an apprentice was cheeky, and the youngster often got a clip round the ear for his trouble!

It is not an understatement to say that the quality of workmanship in the Swindon Boiler Shop was second to none, and it enjoyed a high reputation both inside and outside the company. In completing our look at this department, it only remains to mention 'L2' Shop, situated nearby, where tender, side and saddle tanks were built and repaired; on a railway with so many tank locomotives, this was clearly an important shop.

The final stage in our survey of the Locomotive Works is the Erecting Shop. It was here that all the different pieces of the locomotive 'jigsaw' were assembled, all the endeavours of the separate trades and crafts we have so far described were combined, and the engine was finally completed. It was during the 'Golden Age' that great improvements were made in this area, with the construction of new, efficient modern workshops to replace the cramped Broad Gauge era facilities.

At a Swindon Engineering Society lecture some 50 years after our period, A.W. Millard remarked on the changes which had taken

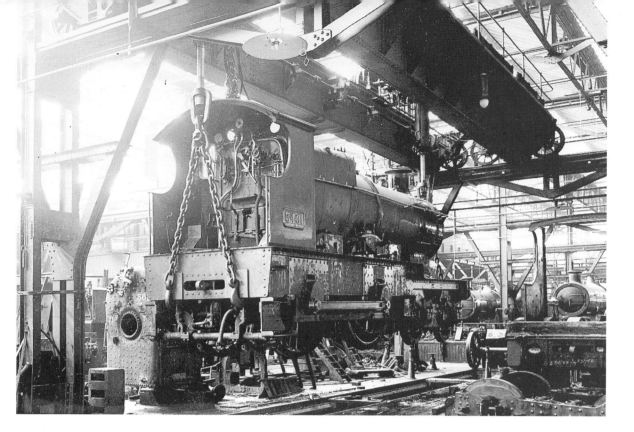

No 3401 Gibraltar *in the new Erecting Shop at Swindon. This locomotive was rebuilt from an 'Atbara' Class to a 'City' Class in 1907. This 1912 view also shows the untidy nature of the workshops, with jacks, ladders and all manner of tools dumped all over the floor.* (GWR Museum, Swindon)

place around the turn of the century. He noted that in the past an erector and his apprentice were mainly responsible for the engine under construction. 'As a craftsman, his general knowledge of engine parts created a feeling of personal responsibility. With plenty of work and supplies arriving to meet the demand, he was quite satisfied that the time of three months for erecting was justified'[10]. With the coming of Churchward, new methods were slowly introduced; these included the standardization of parts, and the mechanization of some processes, which meant that the old 'personal touch' added by the craftsmen was reduced in importance. Good though the old method was in many respects, it did lead to varying degrees of workmanship and accuracy; what was now needed was the application of modern factory processes which would enable Churchward's locomotives to be both robust and reliable.

A description of the new Erecting Shops will be given later, but for the time being the following very brief summary must suffice, taken from over 20 pages given to the subject by E.T.J. Evans, a member of the Swindon Engineering Society, when he lectured to that learned body in December 1910[11].

The first step, Evans says, was that the Foreman of the Erecting Shop was supplied with drawings by the Works Manager; the detail shown in these varied, and it was not unknown on new designs for the Works Manager, Locomotive Superintendent and Foreman to alter or modify features as they went along, experience also playing an important role in locomotive construction. The locomotives frames were fabricated first, with great care taken to ensure that the

The company did not encourage shirking, particularly when using the Factory facilities!

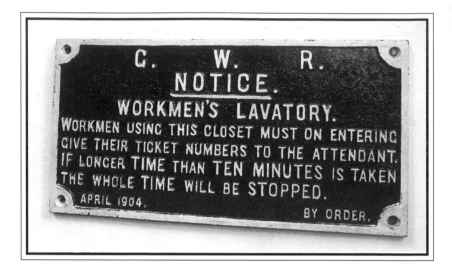

whole assembly was square. The cylinders were fixed next, followed by stiffeners, cross stays and buffer beams. Whilst this was in progress, scrupulous care was taken to make sure that none of the parts were out of true; this was done using plumb-lines, spirit levels and gauges.

The boiler was then lowered on to the frames and, whilst other jobs were in motion, what the engineers of the time called 'Magnesia Boiler Coating' was literally plastered on by hand (it has since transpired that this mixture contained asbestos, and given today's exacting safety standards over this deadly substance, the thought of workmen putting this material on by hand is quite alarming). Steam was pumped into the boiler to speed the drying process of this boiler covering.

Once the axle-boxes and springs were completed, the locomotive was 'wheeled'; an overhead crane with two crabs literally lifted the locomotive up, and then lowered it back down on to the wheels, placed over the workshop pit. This process was a slow and precise operation, requiring that everything was correctly in position. The engine valve gear was then completed, and all pipework and fittings added, a complex job which included the completion of injectors, vacuum brakes, blast pipe and so on.

The cab and its fittings complete, the painters started their work. Unlike many railways, the Great Western did not have a separate Paint Shop for its locomotives, the work being done *in situ* in the Erecting Shop. The engine was first rubbed down with pumice and water, then a lead primer was applied; this was followed by coats of green, black and 'Indian red', the distinctive colour used on GWR locomotive frames in the years before the Great War. The final touch was a number of coats of varnish which protected the paintwork from the elements. Nameplates and numberplates were then added, and, after being weighed and balanced, the engine was given a trial run (usually to Dauntsey or Chippenham on the old main line) before finally entering traffic.

Even from this brief and somewhat fragmentary description, it is to be hoped that the reader will be left in no doubt that the whole process of building Great Western locomotives at Swindon in the 'Golden Age' was anything but a slapdash affair. Even with the advent of more modern equipment in this period, the process was not a quick one. Neither were Great Western engines cheap, 'Star' Class 4–6–0s costing over £3,000 each. The company got its money's worth from such engines, though, for by the 1950s, when some were withdrawn, many had run well over 1 million miles.

We have so far concentrated on the locomotive side of operations, and must now look at the Carriage & Wagon Works. It can truthfully be said that over the years rather less attention has been paid to this aspect of the company's operation at Swindon; perhaps the production of these more mundane items of rolling-stock has not inspired writers to concentrate on, or emphasize the importance of, that department. It is also true to say that the craftsmen employed in the Carriage Works were as skilled as their locomotive brethren, if not more so.

The construction of a Great Western coach depended, like its locomotive counterpart, on the combination of various workshops in producing the raw materials and components to make the completed carriage. In general, the final erection of coaching stock was done in workshops south of the main line, in the block facing Bristol and London Streets, whilst, with some exceptions, the production of component parts and the whole process of freight wagon construction was done in the area east of the Gloucester branch line. The imposing frontage of the Carriage Works is still *in situ* today, and was originally constructed from stone extracted from Foxes Wood Quarry, next to Brunel's main line just outside Bristol. Old

London Street in the early 1900s, showing the trees in front of the Carriage Shops. Beyond the cottages of the railway village, the towers of the Mechanics Institute can be seen. (GWR Museum, Swindon)

photographs show a line of trees next to the Works frontage, presumably placed there to deaden some of the noise from within; although apparent in turn-of-the-century views, they are no longer in existence.

The first stage of the carriage and wagon process was the Sawmill, situated at the west end of this block; its role was the receipt of timber and the cutting of tree-sized sections into a more managable form. An up-to-date Sawmill was constructed in 1908, situated on the south side of the main line, and featured a Ransome horizontal band saw which could cut Baltic oak at a rate of 50 feet per minute. A large overhead crane enabled timber to be handled easily, and was useful in that it could also run outside the shop. The Sawmill also had a large wood planer, which incorporated a device by means of which the shavings could be recycled and re-used as fuel elsewhere.

In general, all the metal parts for carriages and wagons were produced in the area north of Swindon station. Here were similar shops to those on the locomotive side; 18 Shop, for example, was known as the Stamping Shop, where metal fittings for rolling-stock were forged and stamped out using hydraulic presses capable of producing pressings at anything from 25 to 200 pounds pressure. Here too were steam and 'drop' hammers used to make items such as buffer components, bogie parts, brake levers and rods. It was reported that 18 Shop could produce as many as 120 sets of ironwork per week (there being 100 items per set). Over the years, Great Western management had ensured that the most up-to-date forging and stamping machinery had been installed, ensuring that the items produced were of the highest quality.

An old veteran returns home: this 1881 Dean Family Saloon is probably one of the earliest surviving GWR coaches, and illustrates clearly the 'old order' as compared with the more modern Churchward stock illustrated elsewhere in the book. The carriage is seen under restoration in Swindon in 1989. (Courtesy Bill Parker)

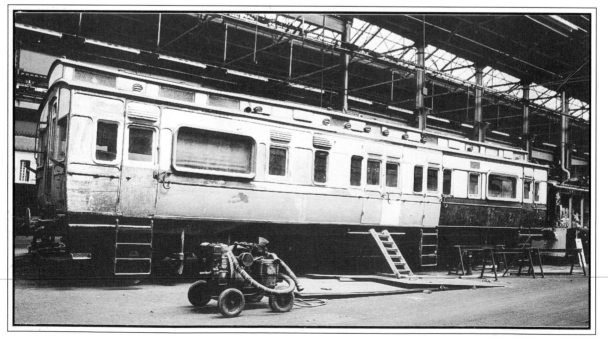

The Carriage Erecting Shop in the early Dean period. With the large amount of timber present, and gas lighting, the company's concern over fire precautions was understandable. (Swindon Reference Library)

In 13 Shop, the more substantial frames of both carriages and wagons were assembled, with the assistance of portable riveting and drilling equipment, hydraulically powered, which was largely introduced in this period. Near the Frame Shop, 15 Shop dealt with brake and other miscellaneous fittings, including axle-boxes, drawgear, axles and boxes for road vehicles, platform trolleys and rail and other loading gauges. It was here too that the ticket-issuing machines used all over the GWR system were made and repaired.

Numerically next was 16 Shop, the Wheel Shop; clearly the repair and manufacture of carriage and wagon wheels was of the utmost importance, since they made a critical difference to the quality and safety of travel in Great Western stock. For many years, carriage wheels had been fitted with wooden centres; 'Mansell' wheels, as they became known, gave smooth running but in the Churchward era were slowly but surely being replaced by metal wheels. The withdrawn Mansell wheel centres were not wasted, however — they were re-used as wood block flooring throughout the factory. The demolition of the old 'A' Shop in early 1987 revealed many segments of these wheels still *in situ* and, for their age, in remarkable condition. Wagon wheels were of a steel construction, and had an eight-spoke centre. Both these and carriage wheels had their tyres turned on

The company's penchant for marking all its property with its initials even extended to carriage blinds, which had the GWR monogram woven into the fabric.

F.W. Marillier, Carriage & Wagon Works Manager, 1902–1920. (GWR Museum, Swindon)

purpose-built lathes after being shrunk on to the wheels; the whole assembly was then tested on a wheel-balancing machine, to ensure the smoothest running.

Crossing back over the main line, next to the Sawmill was 4 Shop, the Carriage Body Shop; it was here that the coach was assembled. The true craftsmen came into their own here as the skeleton of the coach body was built, the high standards of workmanship matched by the raw materials. In Dean's era, clerestory carriages were built with Polish Stettin oak for the framework, and Honduras mahogany for external panelling; in the reign of Churchward, change was afoot, due partly to the rise in the price of timber, and partly to increased concern about the dangers of fire. There were two particularly calamitous fires on the Midland Railway in the period before the First World War which made designers reconsider their use of materials; Michael Harris, in his survey of GWR coaches, notes that after 1910 the use of mahogany for body panelling was gradually discontinued, being replaced by the less flammable steel body panels[12].

Once the body was completed, including doors, seat frames and partitions, it was wheeled into No 8 (Paint) Shop; next door was the Trimming Shop, where all the 'soft fittings' for the coaches were made. This included seats, seatbacks, carpets and blinds, as well as cushions, towels, overalls, aprons, signalling flags and a host of other items; when the versatility of the Works and its self-contained nature are discussed, what better workshop than this to take as an example? Once fitted out, the coach would return to the Paint Shop to be painted, but as was the case in all things Swindon, this was no hurried process. The finish was as follows: 'red lead, filling, then stained and rubbed down, lead colour, ground colour, lake, subsequently signwriting, lettering and the Company Crest applied'. After lining, no fewer than four coats of varnish were applied; after such a laborious process, it seemed a terrible shame to put the coach into service and get it wet and dirty too quickly!

Before concluding our brief survey of the Carriage & Wagon Works, two further workshops merit a mention; the Carpenters and Cabinetmakers Shop was termed the 'utility' shop of the department; indeed, it could turn its hand to almost any task, and the variety of items produced here was endless. Many of the objects so eagerly sought after by railway enthusiasts and collectors today were churned out here, including ticket-issuing cases, label racks, tables, chairs and benches, platform seats, direction and notice boards, trolleys, crates and furniture of all kinds.

The Road Wagon Shop (17 Shop) was responsible for the building and repair of the many and various road vehicles owned and used by the Great Western; the company ran about 3,600 horse-drawn vehicles, so the workshop was both a busy and an important place. It was estimated that around 5,000 wheels passed through the shop for

An early view taken in the 1880s which shows some of the other items made by Swindon craftsmen in the Carriage Works. Road wagons, station seats, sack trucks and wheelbarrows can be clearly seen in this view. (Swindon Reference Library)

repair each year. In the 'Golden Age', the newfangled motor vehicle began to assume importance, and the shop also assisted in the repair and maintenance of these as time passed.

The last facet of the Works to be discussed in our survey were the essential services which needed to be provided to prevent the Works from grinding to a halt. One establishment which played a key role in the running of the GWR operation at Swindon was the General Stores, situated on the north-east side of the Gloucester branch; this was an empire in itself, keeping and supplying the Works with a host of items from brushes to bolts, furniture, paint — in fact, almost anything. The Stores also supplied stations on the GWR network as a whole through a series of travelling stores vans, which traversed by system on a regular basis. As a result, a stationmaster hundreds of miles away in Cornwall had to send his requisition for stores to Swindon and, in due course, they arrived from the heart of the GWR network.

On a more rudimentary level, the whole site had to be provided with more basic necessities — water, gas and, latterly, electricity. An adequate water supply had always been something of a problem in Swindon, even in the earliest days of the Works, when water had been pumped from the local canal. The water consumption of the undertaking during our period must have been enormous; notwithstanding the large amounts used by the boilers and other machines, most of the 14,000 men washed their hands and used the 'facilities' at least once a day! After struggling to use local supplies, the company drove several unsuccessful trial wells on the Works site. In one instance, in the North Yard, salt water was struck, giving rise to a mischievous rumour amongst the workforce that a tunnel had been dug to Weymouth, a favourite destination for many of them during the 'Trip' holiday!

The Great Western was forced to look further afield for water, and eventually developed a suitable borehole at Kemble, some miles north of Swindon. By the early 1900s, demand had increased to the extent that the regular trains of tank vehicles and old locomotive tenders from Kemble were not enough; in 1902–3 a new pumping station was built at Kemble, and from there water was pumped down a 15-inch main to the Works. This still supplied the factory right up until its closure in 1986.

A new Gas Works had been built in 1876, and this was modernized in both 1888 and 1896; further improvements were made before the First World War, including the provision of a new gas-holder of a million cubic feet capacity in 1907. Gas consumption rose considerably, not least because it was used to power generating equipment in order to provide electricity for the Works. The company had pressed ahead with its own arrangements for the supply of electricity, since at that time no municipal supplies existed; the decision was a far-sighted one, and assisted in ridding the Works of a great deal of old-fashioned equipment.

Developments in the Golden Age

HAVING given the reader a portrait of the Works in the period before the First World War, we will now look at the ways in which the growth and development of the period manifested itself at Swindon. One notable feature of the Works was that it was able to expand comprehensively in the late Victorian and Edwardian period because it had escaped relatively lightly from the trials and tribulations of the era of depression and torpor suffered by the Great Western Railway before its 'Great Awakening'. During those dark years, Swindon had managed to maintain a steady, if unspectacular, progress. Several reasons for this are apparent; as D.E.C. Eversley argued, the attitude of successive Locomotive Superintendents was all important. Gooch, Armstrong and Dean were all 'Company Men' in the strongest sense of the term, but were also all too aware of the consequences of large-scale redundancies in a one-industry town such as Swindon[13]; this was apparent in the decision to concentrate much of the Company's locomotive, carriage and wagon work in the town. In this respect, the siting of the Carriage Works at Swindon in preference to Oxford was also an important step, although opposition from Oxford Colleges must have played an important role in assisting the company's decision.

Another factor was that despite the financial problems faced by the company as a whole, locomotives and rolling-stock still had to be repaired, ensuring at least a fair amount of work for the factory. The end of the Broad Gauge in 1892, and the subsequent conversion and scrapping of much rolling-stock, was another factor in maintaining a steady workload. All this meant that Swindon Works was in a reasonable condition to see, from 1895 onwards, a period of growth which was to ensure its true place as the heart of the Great Western system.

Without doubt, the architect of much of this expansion was George Jackson Churchward, one of the most significant figures in the history of the Great Western. Born in 1857, he started his career on the South Devon Railway, before moving to Swindon at the age of 19 to work in the Drawing Office. In 1885 he became Manager of the

RIGHT *The view from Churchward's window in Newburn House. The reader should spend some time looking at the wide variety of locomotives, and should also notice the dog in the kennel in the garden!* (National Railway Museum, York)

BELOW *The Severn Valley Railway is the home for this Churchward 'Toplight' carriage. Typical of those built at Swindon during the 'Golden Age', the crimson lake livery is that carried in the years just prior to the Great War.*

Carriage & Wagon Works, working closely with William Dean to produce a series of luxurious and comfortable coaches for the company. In March 1896 he was appointed as Assistant Manager of the Locomotive Works, a position which was, in effect, second in command to William Dean, the Locomotive Superintendent. From this point there was a clear period of innovation and growth, which further accelerated when Churchward was appointed as Dean's successor in 1902.

It appears that although Churchward took over officially in that year, there was a period of transition when the influence of both men was prevalent, a situation which has been discussed at length in various publications, and by numerous distinguished railway historians. It is hopefully enough to say that with his official appointment in 1902, Churchward started to press forward with new innovatory designs. It is also true to say, however, that

Churchward's position and role within the company as a whole was somewhat different from that of his predecessor. In the last years of his tenure, William Dean's health had deteriorated, largely due to the strain of dealing with the conversion and scrapping programme necessitated by the abolition of the Broad Gauge. In latter years it was also clear that the management at Paddington was less than happy with some of the experimental non-standard designs which were emerging from the Works. Examples of these include the 4-2-4 tank engine No 9, built in 1884, and the 'Crocodile' 4-6-0, No 36, built in 1896, which, although powerful, was not continued with.

With the accession of a new man, the Great Western Board stepped in to reduce the independence of Swindon, and a memorandum to Churchward was issued by Paddington in April 1902. In it the company sought to restrict the remit of the Locomotive Superintendent, and bring him into closer contact with

Paddington. In the past the post had carried a great deal of power as well as responsibility, and the salary paid to Dean, for example — £3,500 — reflected this. The new instructions required that Churchward should keep in close contact with the General Manager and the Chief Civil Engineer with regard to any major change in the design of engines or rolling-stock. The suggestion was also made that he should consider suggestions made by officers of other departments. Relating to earlier comments about some of Dean's designs, it was noted that Chief Officers should be consulted in detail about any new locomotives, before money was allocated for their construction[14].

How much notice Churchward paid to these instructions is difficult to judge with any certainty; what can be said, though, was that the series of improved standard designs which emerged from Swindon during the Great Western's 'Golden Age' were the result not only of Churchward's genius as an engineer, but were also a response to the needs of the company as a whole. Demands for larger and more powerful engines came as the company surged into the Edwardian era; as new lines and services were introduced, there was a need for quicker train speeds and shorter journey times. The increased popularity of the company's services led also to larger trains being run, with heavier and more comfortable carriage stock, which again required more powerful locomotives to haul them. It soon became apparent that the barely adequate nineteenth-century locomotive fleet was in need of renewal. Even Dean's relatively new 4-2-2 and 4-4-0 locomotives designed just prior to 1900 did not have enough power to cope with the work now asked of them by the traffic department.

To produce the new and larger engines required, it needed more than just Churchward and his design team to produce plans and specifications — new premises were also necessary to replace and augment the rather cramped accommodation already in use at Swindon. A considerable amount of land west of the area, used for the scrapping of Broad Gauge stock in 1892 and 1893, was purchased by the Great Western after 1895. A significant event, too, was the authorization by the GWR Board of £68,000 between 1896 and 1899 for new tools and equipment; as well as this, other preparations, such as the improved supply of gas, water and electricity, were also made, as we have already seen.

Many of the new locomotive designs which were to emerge from Swindon Works before 1918 were completed in a new modern workshop designed by Dean, Churchward and their team in the early years of the new century. The new facilities were situated just to the west of Rodbourne Road, and cost around £33,000 to construct. Authorization was given by the GWR Board for work to begin in 1900, and the building, which was to become the first part of the great 'A' Shop, was not fully completed until 1904.

It was a striking contrast to the Broad Gauge era workshops to the east. Constructed entirely in steel and brick, it had a large number of windows which must have made the new Erecting Shop both more efficient and a rather better place for the men to work in. The working space itself, covering some 230,000 square feet, was divided into two; on the north side was a large Machine Shop, whilst on the south side was a spacious Erecting Shop consisting of four large bays, accessed by traversers. Powerful overhead cranes were provided to lift heavy components or even engines from one part of the workshop to another, without interfering with any of the other roads. In addition to these cranes, a small overhead crane was used to assist in hydraulic riveting, which was done on one side of the shop.

Photographs show the airy and spacious nature of these new premises, but impressive though they were, it soon became apparent that they were not large enough to cope with the newest engines being designed by Churchward. As one writer noted, the force of change at Swindon had become almost unstoppable, since each new development seemed to follow logically from the last. Churchward's newest 4–6–0 locomotives were considerably heavier than earlier designs; the new cranes which had been installed in the Erecting

One of the great rolling presses used in the Boiler Shop; apart from a ghostly shape in the background, no workmen are in evidence. (National Railway Museum, York)

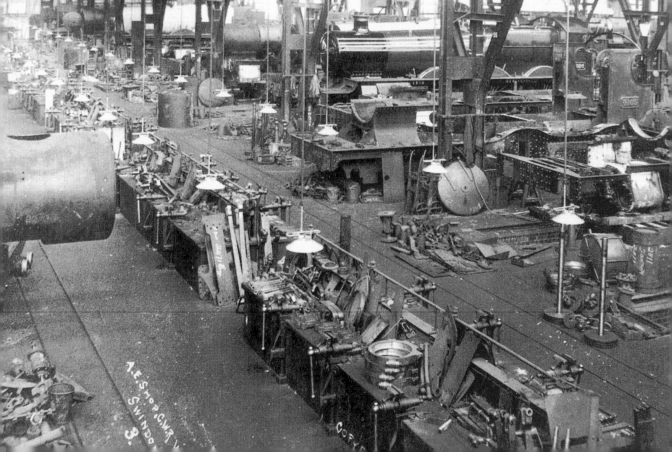

The Swindon photographer, Hooper, took numerous interesting photographs inside the Works during the 'Golden Age'. This view of the new Erecting Shop shows a 'Saint', a '45xx' 2–6–2, and a 'Metro' tank in various states of undress!

Shop could only lift a maximum of 50 tons, a weight easily exceeded by the new 'Saint' and 'Star' engines.

Plans were therefore drafted to build a far larger workshop further west of the newest 'A' Shop extension. However, by 1910 the climate at Paddington had changed, and the GWR Board was no longer prepared to give Churchward *carte blanche* to spend money on innovations or improvements unnecessarily; as the reader will discover in later chapters, the company's investors did not all welcome the vast amounts of money being spent by the Great Western in its attempt to be the most up-to-date railway in the country. Like every other department, Swindon now had to fight for any large amounts of investment. In the case of the proposed extension to 'A' Shop, the Board commissioned an independent report to determine whether the planned extensions were really necessary; in the event, the leader of the enquiry, Sir William Plender, submitted three lengthy reports between 1912 and 1915, with regard to locomotives, carriages and wagons.

His first report was on locomotives, and in it he declared that he was 'satisfied that some rearrangements and extensions of the existing works are necessary to relieve present congestion and meet the current and growing need of engine accommodation efficiently and economically'[15]. A warning note was sounded, though, when a recommendation was made that any extensions should be made for the purposes of locomotive maintenance and repair, rather than for the building of new stock; new work was to be catered for in slack periods during the repair cycle. Even with this limitation, Churchward pressed ahead with the new plans. These workshops were to be of an enormous nature, adding another 257,000 square feet to the existing Erecting Shop. The outbreak of war in 1914 slowed work on this great project, and it was not finally finished until 1020. When finally completed, the 'New' Shop, as it was always known to the men, covered a staggering $11\frac{1}{4}$ acres, and cost £420,000, a large amount even by today's standards.

Although not finished until after what we are referring to as the Great Western's 'Golden Age', 'A' Shop is nevertheless indicative of the innovatory enterprise at work at Swindon during the period. During those years, the Works had emerged strongly from the nineteenth century, and had been thoroughly modernized. New tools and equipment, new working practices, and finally new premises had enabled the Great Western to turn out precisely the kind of new locomotives, carriages and other vehicles needed to run the new improved services being introduced at the time.

It is hoped that the preceding description of Swindon Works has given the reader something of a taste of the atmosphere of the place in the 'Golden Age', and an impression of the work done there. Seeing this vast operation, it is not difficult to see why Swindonians were so proud of it, and why they felt sure that they were the most important part of the Great Western system.

Another Hooper view shows a 'Star' in the background, and much miscellaneous clutter around the workshop floor.

THE
CHURCHWARD
REVOLUTION

THOSE with even the most general interest in the Great
Western Railway will have observed that the aspect of its
development which has most attracted the attention of writers
in the past has been the question of its motive power. With this in
mind, this section of the book is in no way a comprehensive survey of
the events in this field during the 'Golden Age'; however, no survey
of the period could be complete without some reference to the
development of Great Western locomotives by Churchward at
Swindon.

As was noted earlier, new engines and rolling-stock were produced
largely as a result of the demands placed on Swindon by the
management at Paddington in response to the tremendous forward
strides being made by the company in the building and operating of
new lines and services. Speaking to the GWR Lecture and Debating
Society in 1904, G.H. Burrows, one of Churchward's team, argued
that 'the non-stop long distance runs and the high average speed at
which modern express trains run have necessitated the designing and
production of engines of a very high standard of excellence'[16].

Various distinguished railway engineers and historians have
analysed the nature and significance of the reign of G.J. Churchward
in some considerable detail, so it is not intended that a full
description of every locomotive type produced during the era be
attempted; if the author omits a particular favourite of the reader,
then apologies are tendered in advance! What this section will
hopefully do is to illustrate some of the factors which made these
advances possible, as well as the broadest outline of events.

By 1900, most passenger traffic on the Great Western was handled
by Dean 4–4–0 and 4–2–2 tender locomotives, with a large amount
of goods work being done by 0–6–0 tank and tender engines. Even
though Churchward did not actually take over from Dean until 1902,
there is some evidence that by early 1901 he had devised a range of
standard engine types which would serve most of the railway's needs
for the foreseeable future. This was perhaps the essence of
Churchward's genius; he planned and introduced a fairly limited

number of basic designs which could be adapted to suit all the projected increases and developments in traffic on the railway.

Standardization was also apparent in the way in which the locomotives were to be constructed. Harry Holcroft, who worked in the Drawing Office under Churchward, notes that in the standard scheme there were four standard boilers, three driving wheel and two carrying wheel sizes, two cylinder blocks, and very similar valve gear. This kind of standardization was not new — it had started back in the days of Daniel Gooch — but it was brought fully into play in the Churchward era. On a more general level, the main requirements fulfilled by new designs were a free-steaming boiler and, just as important, the free movement of steam from there to the cylinders themselves.

In all, some 888 'standard' Churchward-designed locomotives were produced between 1902 and the engineer's retirement in 1922; some measure of their success may be ascertained by the fact that, of this total, 586 were still in use in 1950. It would be easy to put down much of the success of the motive power built in the years before the First World War to the genius of Churchward himself — his skill as an engineer is without doubt — but there were other factors which contributed to the outpouring of innovative designs at this time.

Much of the credit for the important work done in the 'Golden Age' must also rest with the team of men assembled by Churchward himself. There is no doubt that he was astute in his choice of staff for his department, and he ensured that there were young, enthusiastic and talented people in the Drawing Office, Laboratory and Test House, as well as in other parts of the Locomotive, Carriage & Wagon Department. He was keen to encourage new ideas and, as Holcroft reveals, his method of work assisted him in this. He describes how 'working committees' were set up, consisting of draughtsmen, who drew up the proposals, the chargeman or foreman of the gang working on the project on the factory floor itself, Churchward and several of his assistants. The involvement of those practically involved in the task, such as foremen or other specialists like pattern-makers, meant that many practical problems were avoided at a very early stage[17]. Churchward alluded to this method in remarks he made to the Swindon Engineering Society in 1910, when he argued that, when struggling with a particular engineering problem, a committee rather than individual approach often worked, since 'with a committee of three or four, just as clever as themselves, it would be surprising how much quicker they would be able to solve the problem'[18].

By all accounts, 'the Old Man', as he became known, was a good leader of men and, unlike Collett who succeeded him, was often seen around the Works talking to all sections of the workforce. Although well liked by the men, he also had the reputation of being tough on those whom he felt were not carrying out their work in the correct manner, be he a labourer or foreman! The varied group of engineers

GWR Apprenticeship Indenture. (GWR Museum, Swindon)

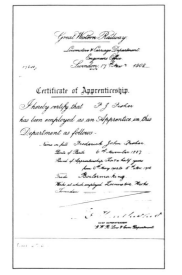

The varied type of lectures held by the Engineering Society can be seen in this 1896–7 programme.

Programme for Winter Session.
1896-7.

DATE.	SUBJECT.	NAME.
*Thurs. Oct. 22	" Röntgen's Rays ; or the new Photography."	Prof. J. Wertheimer, B.SC., B.A.. F.I.C., F.C.S., Principal of the Merchant Venturers' Technical College, Bristol.
‡Thurs. Nov. 5	"Notes on Locomotive practice on the L. & N.W.R."	Mr. J. W. Cross, Stud. M. Inst. C.E.
‡Thurs. Nov. 19	" The Design and Formation of Rolls."	Mr. E. W. Ellis.
‡Thurs. Dec. 3	" Bogies and Radial Wheel Bases as applied to Railway Rolling Stock."	Mr. A. G. Cresser.
‡Thurs Dec. 17	" Applications of Electricity in Workshops. "	Mr. F. L. Wait, Wh. Ex.
‡Thurs. Jan. 14	" Hydraulic Stamping and Forging Machinery."	Mr. L. R. Thomas
‡Thurs. Jan. 28	" Notes on the Inspection of Materials."	Mr. F. W. Carlton
Tues. Feb. 2	" CONVERSAZIONE."	
‡Thurs. Feb. 11	" A Study of Lubricants from Engineering and Chemical standpoints.	Mr. T. H. M. Bonell, Wh. Sch.
‡Thurs. Feb. 25	" Machinery and Light Railways on Indian Tea Gardens."	Mr. F. Adamson West, Assoc. M. Inst. C.E.
‡Thurs. Mar. 11	" Some useful lifting appliances."	Mr. C. E. Blyth.
†Thurs. Apr. 1	ANNUAL GENERAL MEETING.	

The Meetings will be held in the Institution at 7 p.m.
* Large Hall at 8 p.m. † Lecture Hall at 7.30 p.m. ‡ See Notice Circulars.
CHAIRMAN   MR. A. E. LEADER.

Visits to places of Engineering interest will be arranged during the Session.
E. G. IRELAND, Hon. Sec.

employed by Churchward is a testament to his skill as an administrator; not all of them came from a purely Great Western background, and staff were brought in from outside in some cases. One example was C.B. Collett, Assistant Works Manager, who succeeded Churchward after his retirement. He had previously worked for Maudesley, the Marine Engineering firm.

Many of the figures prevalent in the early years of the twentieth century went on to be key figures in either the Great Western itself, or in other British or overseas railway companies. Examples were E.T.J. Evans, F.W. Marillier, W.A. Stanier, F.W. Hawksworth, J.W. Cross and G.H. Pearson. Another more senior figure was W.H. Waister, whose considerable practical company experience (he was 55 in 1902) proved invaluable as 'Outdoor Assistant' to Churchward.

One further advantage held by Swindon was that it made efforts to ensure that the supply of well-educated and well-trained engineers would continue. With the accession of Churchward, production at Swindon in all departments increased dramatically, so more staff at all levels were necessary. Up until that point most training had been essentially gained by practical experience alone; this was the basis of most apprenticeships and, although not a bad method, was rather primitive, bearing in mind the high standard of workmanship which was becoming the norm at Swindon.

Thus the establishment of a 'Technical School' on Victoria Hill, which took over much of the work originally done by the Mechanics Institute, was an important step. There, many members of the workforce attended evening classes to obtain the more academic qualifications needed to further their careers. Another development came in 1903 when, with the full support of the GWR Board, a scheme allowing apprentices to attend full-time classes on two afternoons a week was started. Fifteen students were allowed in the first year, reducing to only six in the third and final year of the course; competition was, needless to say, fairly stiff, but it did ensure that a stream of well-educated engineers for all departments was available.

One further source of assistance was the 'Swindon Engineering Society', which has already been mentioned; in its ranks were the cream of the young talent Churchward was nurturing. Started in the late 1890s as the Junior Engineering Society, regular meetings were held at which papers on a huge variety of subjects were given by Society members and, on occasions, guests. As an example, the 1910 session included discussions on Heat Treatment of Carbon Tool Steel, Cylinder Lubrication, Cranes, and the GWR Road Motor Department.

Churchward was the Society's President, and in that year he reminded members that he 'preferred to see discussions narrowed to some extent to the business in which they were engaged'[19]. This was a reference to some of the more wide-ranging papers given on subjects which were not specifically related to the Great Western itself. This minor criticism apart, it is not difficult to see that the

One of the 'Frenchmen', 4–4–2 compound No 102 La France. (GWR Museum, Swindon)

Society must have been instrumental in stimulating discussion and debate about the very matters in which Churchward was so interested.

As well as tapping the talent of his own workforce, Churchward was also not afraid to look elsewhere for ideas and inspiration. A comprehensive library was assembled in the offices at Swindon, which reflected railway developments the world over. Great Western staff were also sent abroad to report on railway practice elsewhere; one such trip was undertaken by H.C. King, the Locomotive Works Manager, who with five other members of staff travelled extensively in the United States in 1905.

G.J. Churchward was certainly not afraid to incorporate ideas and designs from other railways, and perhaps the best example of this was the purchase of three French locomotives in the early 1900s. This action was part of a process of experiment which proceeded in several stages. Having devised a projected range of motive power for the future, and having done considerable research into the best methods to be adopted, Churchward then produced various prototypes on which further tests could be carried out, as we shall see shortly.[20]

When the first of Churchward's new designs, 4–6–0 No 100, appeared, it caused a fair amount of debate, since it owed more to American design than anything which had been previously built by the Great Western Railway. Its angular lines might well seem modern-looking to enthusiasts in the 1990s, but, as Alan Peck noted, they were not appreciated by many at the time. It had 18-inch outside cylinders, with a 30-inch stroke, and improved vacuum brakes, a development necessitated by a fatal accident at Slough which had highlighted the inadequacies of the old steam braking system. Dean remained in office for three months after the outshopping of No 100, although it seems unlikely that he had much to do with its design and construction; as a mark of respect, however, the engine was subsequently named *William Dean*.

The true extent of the changes brought about by G.J. Churchward did not become apparent until 1903; in that year, three prototype standard designs appeared. The first was No 98, a two-cylinder 4–6–0 passenger engine which was to be the forerunner of the 29xx 'Saint' Class. The second was No 97, which was a 2–8–0 goods engine with the same 'Standard No 1' boiler as No 98. This was to be the forerunner of the '28xx' Class, and will be described in further detail later in the book. The final standard prototype was No 99, which was a 2–6–2 'Prairie' tank locomotive; this was fitted with a 'Standard No 2' boiler, and it was anticipated that it would be used for mixed traffic purposes, since it was fitted with 5 ft 8 in wheels. In later years, an assortment of other designs of a similar nature were to be turned out of the workshops. In 1904, a similar prototype, No 115, was built, which was a smaller version of No 99, with 4 ft 1 in wheels and a smaller No 5 boiler.

The level of standardization already mentioned was apparent in

No 99, Churchward's prototype 2-6-2, seen outside the Works not long after construction. (GWR Museum, Swindon)

the construction of these three designs; all cylinder castings were alike, and most of the Stephenson valve gear was common to all the engines. Once these prototypes were produced, they were put into traffic and rigorously tested under everyday conditions. The next stage of Churchward's work involved the testing of the French locomotives already mentioned. There had been much discussion as to the merits of compounding — that is, the combination of both high- and low-pressure cylinders on a steam locomotive. To compare the performance of such locomotives, Churchward purchased a 4-4-2 de Glehn locomotive from the Société Alsacienne. Speaking at the half yearly shareholders meeting in 1903, the Company Chairman, Earl Cawdor, reported the purchase of the engine, arguing that 'we want to be satisfied whether they can teach us anything...I do not care whether it is from the French or the Germans if we can learn something or other'[21].

The engine arrived at Poplar Docks in London on 19 October 1902 in a large number of packing cases; after being shipped to Swindon on a special train, it was reassembled in the factory before entering traffic in February 1903. For the purposes of comparison, Churchward had a two-cylinder simple 4-4-2, No 171, constructed. This was largely similar to the prototype No 98, and could be

FAR RIGHT *One of the 'Albion' Class two-cylinder 4-4-2 locomotives, which were matched against the French compounds. This example was No 187* Bride of Lammermoor, *seen at Plymouth in 1912.* (Alan Parrett Collection)

converted to a 4–6–0 at a later date, as happened after July 1907.

Both locomotives acquired names, the French compound becoming No 102 *La France*, and No 171 becoming *Albion* in February 1904. In the space of two years, much was learnt from comparative trials. The French locomotive ran well, but was designed for conditions different from those experienced on the GWR; it was noted, however, for its smooth running at high speed, and was used on many of the most important trains run on the Great Western, including the 'Cornish Riviera Limited'. It did, however, prove slightly more difficult to drive, although there was little to choose between the GWR and French examples for economy.

That the purchase of the French compound had been useful was proved by the fact that Churchward took the unprecedented step of asking the GWR Board for permission to buy two further locomotives. Two larger engines of the type used on the Paris-Orleans Railway were this time purchased, and arrived in 1905; these were named *President* and *Alliance* respectively, and had larger boilers and cylinders than No 102. For further comparison, a further 19 examples of the '171' Class were built at Swindon; 13 were constructed as 4–4–2s, the remainder being turned out as 4–6–0s. It was soon found that the 4–6–0 type had the distinct advantage of much better adhesion, which could be extremely useful for trains running on the steeply graded South Devon section of the West of England main line.

BELOW *Churchward's pioneering 4-4-2 No 40, later named* North Star. (GWR Museum, Swindon)

By 1906 enough research had been done to allow Churchward and his team to draw some conclusions from the results, both theoretical and practical, which they had obtained. In the end it was decided that, although giving smoother running, there was little to be gained by the Great Western adopting compounding for its express passenger locomotives; the Swindon designs were as powerful, and just as economical as the French locomotives. As Holcroft observed, it was seen, however, that the idea of 'divided drive', where different sets of cylinders drove different axles, did have merit in producing smoother running and less wear.

The time and effort spent in these comparative tests was, as Alan Peck remarked, fully justified by the locomotives which then followed. In April 1906, the first of what was to become the 'Star' Class, No 40, emerged from the Swindon Factory. Like No 171, this was to be something of a mobile 'test bed', but once in service it began to show how worthwhile all the comparative testing had been. It combined all the best features of both the French engines, and the most up-to-date Great Western ideas. Unlike subsequent members of the class, it was fitted with 'scissors' valve gear, which was replaced by Walschaerts motion in due course.

Built as a 4-4-2, the locomotive was named *North Star* in September 1906, a fitting choice of name for such a pioneering locomotive; it was rebuilt as a 4-6-0 in 1909, and was eventually converted to a 'Castle' Class engine in 1929. Ten 'Stars' were built between February and May 1907, and the Great Western went on to produce over 70 examples of the class.

To many, the production of the 'Star' Class was the culmination of all that had been going on at Swindon during the 'Golden Age'. The class was more than capable of handling the ever-increasing loads on the new services, and to many enginemen, even after the introduction of the more powerful 'King' and 'Castle' designs in the years after the Great War, the 'Star' Class was still the best. It is also true to say that those more modern designs were largely refinements and enlargements of the basic 'Star' design; indeed, some historians have argued that to a large extent, Churchward's locomotive development policy was continued by his successors Collett and Hawksworth right up until the end of the Great Western in 1947, which says much for the strength and solidity of his designs.

We have not had the space in this brief survey to look at all the various types of engines produced at Swindon in the years before the Great War, including such designs as the famous 'City' 4-4-0s and their less successful 4-4-0 counterparts, the 'Counties'. Some of the admirable books listed in the Bibliography will hopefully be of interest to the reader wishing to delve further. K.J. Cook, who himself had a distinguished career at Swindon, provides a fitting conclusion to our brief survey of the 'Churchward Revolution'; he noted, in a lecture to the Institute of Locomotive Engineers, that it would be 'improbable that ever again will one man make such a contribution to locomotive design or that a policy laid down by any other designer will remain satisfactorily extant for so long'[22].

One of the less successful Swindon designs of the period, the 'County' Class. No 3477 County of Somerset *was built in 1904, and is seen at Weymouth about eight years later. The class had a reputation amongst enginemen for their rough riding.* (Alan Parrett Collection)

SWINDON: TOWN AND FACTORY

HAVING spent a great deal looking at the company's Works at Swindon, it now only remains to look at the social aspect of the Great Western's involvement with the town; as was noted earlier, both town and Works were inextricably linked.

When the Railway Works opened in 1843, there were two separate communities in Swindon, 'Old' and 'New'. Up the hill was the core of the old market town which had, to all intents and purposes, been decaying until the coming of the railway in the late 1830s. With a rapid influx of skilled and unskilled labour from outside the district needed to man the Works, the Great Western was forced, rather reluctantly one assumes, to arrange for the building of accommodation for its workforce. Thus, 'New Swindon' was established on an area of flat land near the Works. Initially some 300 cottages were built by the London firm of J. & C. Rigby to the design of the architect Digby Wyatt with some assistance, it is said, from Brunel himself. The 'Railway Village' houses were of a high standard of construction compared to much industrial housing of the period, and satisfied the urgent need for the housing of the staff of the new Works. The full story of this early pioneering railway community has been told elsewhere, and strictly speaking does not form part of our tale. Suffice to say that the 'Company's Houses', as the cottages became known, formed only the core of a much larger settlement which evolved as the Works itself grew.

With the gradual expansion of the company's operation at Swindon, a wide expanse of green fields around the centre of New Swindon gave place to thickly populated streets, and a sea of red brick advanced across what had been largely agricultural land. The communities which grew up around the Factory were occupied almost entirely by railwaymen and their families, for although a small proportion of the workforce did come from outlying villages like Purton, Lydiard, Wroughton and South Marston, the majority travelled only a relatively short distance to work. For those travelling any distance, it meant an early start, for work began at 6 am. For those living in town, if they were not already awake, at 5.20 am the

One of the two 'Magneta' time-clocks introduced in the Works in 1912, and which powered electric clocks all over the Factory. This example is now preserved in the GWR Museum.

sound of the Works hooters made sure that they were! They sounded again at 5.50 and 5.55 before one final blast at 6 am. The hooters were in fact ships' hooters, and for many years played a vital part in the timekeeping of the town; the sound was hard to ignore, its strength being such that with a following wind they could be heard some 25 miles away in the Cotswolds!

Alfred Williams evocatively described the scene early in the morning as men were arriving for work. In general, he wrote, most men left it until almost the last moment to arrive, and at 5 minutes to 6 the streets leading to the entrances were packed with a dense crowd of men and boys, all off to their daily toil: 'It is a mystery where they all come from. Ten thousand workmen! They are like an army pressing forward to battle. Tramp! Tramp! Tramp!'[23]. The streets must have had an eerie air of calm when the Works doors clanged shut, and the dust had settled.

In the 'Golden Age', the red brick terraces were largely completed, and linked by the newest innovation in the town, the electric tram, were the two areas most closely linked with the railway, Gorse Hill and Rodbourne. Each had a different character. Gorse Hill, situated north of the station, near the Carriage & Wagon Works, was occupied mainly by workmen from that department. Rodbourne, however, was built within striking distance of the Locomotive Works, and one of its longest roads, Redcliffe Street, ran the entire length of the great new 'A' Shop, separated only by a lofty red brick wall. There was always a fierce rivalry between the two districts, reflecting the rivalry between the 'Loco' and 'Carriage' departments generally — never the twain should meet!

Working for the Great Western in Swindon did have its advantages; it meant that the workman and his family had access to two of the most important social institutions in the town, the Mechanics Institute and the Medical Fund. Contrary to popular belief, these facilities were not provided by a benevolent company anxious to look after its workforce, but were the results of the efforts of far-seeing and hardworking members of the railway community itself. The company's assistance and influence was undoubtedly a critical factor, but in both cases it was the people of Swindon who provided the impetus for the provision of these facilities.

The history of the Mechanics Institute is a case in point. Founded as early as 1843 by a group of men from the Works who, with the assistance of some friends, set up a library, it grew from occupying a room in the Factory in its earliest days, to the eventual occupation of substantial purpose-built premises in the heart of the railway village. In the years before the First World War, the Mechanics Institute housed a large theatre, which put on not only local but also national musical and theatrical events; it also had a superb library which contained a wide selection of books, periodicals and newspapers. A host of smaller rooms were provided for a whole range of other social, educational and cultural activities.

The Institute also administered the running of the 'Trip' holiday. Similar to the 'Wakes Week' phenomena in northern industrial towns, 'Trip' was an annual event. For the company's part, it provided a free ticket for each worker and his family to the location of their choice. The first such event was held in 1848, when 500 people were taken to Oxford. By 1900 thousands went on a series of special trains to different locations, which often departed from inside the Works rather than the station itself. 'Trip' holidays were unpaid by the company, but many stayed away in lodgings at the seaside, although few could actually afford to stay for the whole week. Favourite resorts were Weston-super-Mare, Barry and Weymouth; the latter was so popular with Swindon folk that in 'Trip' week it was renamed 'Swindon by the Sea' by the local traders! Whilst so many of the 14,000 workforce were on holiday, Swindon itself was very quiet, and many traders did not bother to open since business was so poor.

Another event which the Mechanics Institute ran was the 'Children's Fete'. This was held in the Great Western Park in Faringdon Road, and for the price of admission a child was given a slab of cake, which was naturally made to a secret recipe, and two tickets for a ride on the roundabouts or other attractions available that day. Up to 20,000 children might attend, so some special method had to be arrived at for cutting the cake; in true GWR fashion, a member of the staff invented a cake-cutting machine which must have been a great help![24]

Men leaving the Works after the sounding of the hooter. As this picture shows, even the trams had to stop due to the sheer numbers of men. (GWR Museum, Swindon)

*A beautiful period photograph,
taken in the waiting room of
the GWR Medical Fund.
Some of the doctors and other
staff employed by the Society
can be seen in the background.*
(GWR Museum,
Swindon)

The second facility provided for the workforce was the GWR
Medical Fund. Set up in 1847, it had originally been formed to
provide for the supply of a doctor for railway village residents, but
the scheme soon expanded far beyond this concept to encompass a
complete health care scheme. For a small weekly contribution,
varying from 4d to 6d per week, workers and their families were
entitled to free medical treatment of their choice; a hospital was
provided, and the Medical Fund's Headquarters in Milton Road
housed baths, a doctors' surgery, dentists, chiropodists, and a

A close-up of one of the 'Trip' holiday crowds. In 1905, 24,500 people were transported by the company, around half the population of the town; 22 special trains were run, utilizing 300 extra carriages. (GWR Museum, Swindon)

modern dispensary. By the standards of the day the population of Swindon's railway community were certainly well catered for in health care terms.

A brief look at the local directories of the period confirm the domination of the GWR in Swindon at the time. The 1900 edition of Astill's Guide noted that the growth and success of the town was 'entirely due to the Great Western Railway Company, which selected Swindon as its principal seat on manufactures'. It went on to argue 'how much the existence of its inhabitants and success of its trade depend on the prosperity of the Company'. This prosperity was not entirely universal, since the Works had excess capacity at various periods during the 'Golden Age'; short time was worked in the Carriage and Locomotive Departments on and off from 1895 to 1904 which meant that the staff only worked part of their normal working week. In later years the Carriage Department was particularly hard hit; in 1908, it was on short time all year.

That particular year, in which Churchward's pioneering 4-6-2 *The Great Bear* was built, was not a particularly good one generally, since substantial numbers of men were laid off entirely. What made matters worse was that the company did this in the week before the 'Trip' holiday; there were demonstrations and petitions to no avail, and the *Great Western Railway Magazine* for August 1908 was moved to justify the reduction in staff by arguing that similar actions had been taken in the Ebbw Vale steel works, which should 'give pause to those who seek to promote discontent amongst railwaymen'[25]. This was of course an oblique reference to the increasing influence of trade unions. These lay-offs and short time working showed that not all aspects of the company's 'Golden Age' were necessarily welcomed by everyone, particularly the workforce at Swindon.

Returning to the theme of the railway's all-pervading influence in the town, further evidence can be gleaned from the population statistics. Around 1900 the town's population had reached the 45,000 mark, of which over 12,000 were employed in the Great Western Factory itself. The bustling 'New' Swindon had expanded to the stage where it was coalescing with the 'Old' town. For many years the two communities had been presided over by separate local boards, an arrangement which became more and more unsatisfactory as the town grew. With the turn of the new century, permission for the creation of a single Borough was requested, and this was granted in a charter of incorporation by Queen Victoria in January 1900.

To many, the granting of Borough status forcibly underlined the prosperity and stability brought to the town by the Great Western Railway; it was not coincidental, one might imagine, that the first Mayor of the new Borough was none other than G.J. Churchward himself. To complete the picture, a new Borough Arms was needed; a committee was set up to consider its design, and the Mayor (Churchward) was asked to 'furnish a correct drawing of a modern GWR Locomotive for the use of the Heralds' College'. Perhaps in deference to his Chief, William Dean, a drawing of a 4–2–2 'single' *White Horse*, was chosen. One might imagine that a rather more modern design should have been used, representing progress in the Works; however, it was this design which finally appeared on the arms granted to the Borough in September 1901. The GWR was also represented in the arms by a winged wheel, said to represent travel by railway.

With the reorganization of local government in 1974, the old Swindon Borough was replaced by a new administrative area called Thamesdown; in line with the reduced role of the railway in the town, the arms of the new organization contain no direct reference to the railway — a great shame, bearing in mind the town's rich railway heritage.

PART THREE

THE CORNISH RIVIERA

HAVING spent some time describing two of the most important places on the GWR network, Paddington and Swindon, it is now time to take the reader on a journey out on to the company system, traversing the three routes of greatest significance during the 'Golden Age'.

In the first of our three journeys, we will examine the history and development of the West of England main line from Paddington to Penzance. In contrast to other routes on the network, the fortunes of this line depended largely on tourist and holiday traffic. In the period before the First World War, the Great Western was well aware of this fact and as a result it began to actively publicize and promote both the new improved services it introduced, and the resorts and attractions situated on or near its lines.

The tourist trade was to become an important part of the company's business; the motor car had yet to become popular, and the railways were the only means of transport for many people when considering annual holidays. Thus in this section we will not only spend some time describing the route itself, but we shall also sample some of the Great Western Railway's advertising material produced to publicize the area.

Brunel's Royal Albert Bridge across the Tamar at Saltash provides a spectacular gateway into Cornwall, and we shall concentrate mostly on that county, since it seems that the railway itself spent a fair amount of effort in trying to develop the 'Royal Duchy' as a large-scale holiday area. Until the coming of the railways into the county in the 1850s, Cornwall had been to a large extent geographically isolated; the deep valley of the River Tamar had been a formidable barrier to all but the most determined invader! It was not surprising then to find that in the period we are examining rural parts of the county were still fairly backward, and living conditions were primitive, lacking basic necessities taken for granted by the new generation of town dwellers.

Even after the establishment of excellent rail links to London, few people in such rural areas visited the capital. John Betjeman

*The aptly named 4-4-0
No 3469* Tintagel *draws a
down train off Brunel's Royal
Albert Bridge at Saltash.*
(Alan Parrett Collection)

recounted an apochryphal story about a Cornishman who thought
that the metropolis was completely under glass, since he had never
been further than the Great Western's station at Paddington![1] Artists
such as Turner had begun to popularize the county at the end of the
eighteenth century, but the geographical remoteness already
mentioned kept the number of visitors down. In one of the Great
Western's own publications the difficulties of visiting Cornwall
before the coming of the railway were amply illustrated; in the early
nineteenth century a horse-drawn coach such as the 'Eclipse' or the
'Comet' would be lucky to reach Exeter, some 216 miles from
London, in under 20 hours, and this would only have been achieved
at the cost of 23 changes of horses. To reach Penzance could have
taken twice as long again.[2]

By the 1890s, however, Cornwall began to experience a growth in
the number of visitors from elsewhere in the country, and at the end
of our 'Golden Age', numbers had significantly increased again. In
1906, the importance of the role of the railway in developing the
Duchy was noted by the *Daily Telegraph*, which wrote that there was
'scarcely a place on the coast untouched by the ramifications of
Brunel's famous line[3]. Not all native Cornishmen welcomed these
visitors, who were christened by the locals as 'foreigners'!

ADVERTISING
AND PUBLICITY

BEFORE going on to describe the Great Western's route to the West, and some of the history and events surrounding its development, let us take a closer look at a little of the publicity material issued to attract customers to the 'Cornish Riviera'. In the years before the Great War, the company laid the foundations of its Publicity Department and much advertising material of a high standard was produced, although the department was yet to reach the levels of imagination and consistently good design seen later during the 'twenties and 'thirties.

What was particularly important, though, was that the company took the whole subject of advertising and publicity most seriously. With the appointment of James Inglis as General Manager in

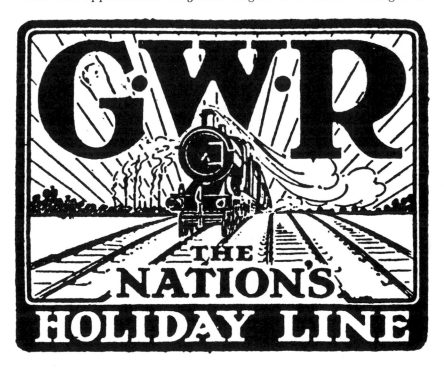

One of the GWR's best-known advertising slogans.

An advertisement for the Great Western's Cornish Riviera *publication. This example dates from 1909.*

January 1904, the GWR embarked on a series of new and innovatory publicity devices which were to reap rich dividends both in terms of increased traffic and enhanced company prestige. By 1910 the Great Western was seen as a leading company in the matter of railway publicity in England. The French magazine *Atlas* wrote about the railway in most glowing terms, and not surprisingly the *Great Western Railway Magazine* reprinted a translation of the magazine's remarks: 'We must say that the internal organisation of the publicity department is evidently quite remarkable. An active and competent staff composes, edits and designs advertisements, posters and booklets according to the most modern methods'[4].

Certainly there was no shortage of ideas for publicity emanating from Paddington. The first of these was a series of travel books published by the company itself. The concept of a railway company publishing anything other than timetables and other booklets related to train services was in itself a new one; in a catalogue of GWR 'Holiday Travel Books' dating from 1909, James Inglis wrote that the travel books issued by the company had been hailed by the press as 'a new departure in a class of literature till now treated as ephemeral'[5].

One of the most unusual pieces of Great Western publicity discovered by the author was an envelope advertising the 'Travel Books' series, which summarized the publications as being 'descriptive of the health and pleasure resorts, and scenes of beauty and interest, served by the Great Western system'[6]. The first in the series produced by the GWR was appropriately titled *The Cornish Riviera* and was described modestly by the company as 'The most popular travel book ever issued by a Railway Company'. The 52-page book was priced at 3d, and as the late R.B. Wilson remarked in his excellent survey of Great Western publicity, *Go Great Western*, at this price the company clearly had not produced this or any of the books which followed for direct profit.

Nevertheless, over 250,000 copies of the first edition of *The Cornish Riviera* were printed, and the indirect effect of such advertising material was extremely important to the company. Like all the other uniform volumes in this series, *The Cornish Riviera* was written by E.M. Broadley, although the author's name does not appear anywhere on the publication. The subtitle of the book referred to Cornwall's 'claims as a winter health and pleasure resort'. Reading through the publication, one soon becomes aware of the approach adopted by the company with regard to its Cornish services; as well as the summer trade, a positive effort was made to attract what we would now call off-season traffic. The geographical location of Cornwall means that it is blessed with relatively mild weather conditions in the winter, and it becomes clear reading this publication and much of the other publicity material issued at the time that this was the aspect of the Duchy which the Great Western was going to emphasize heavily.

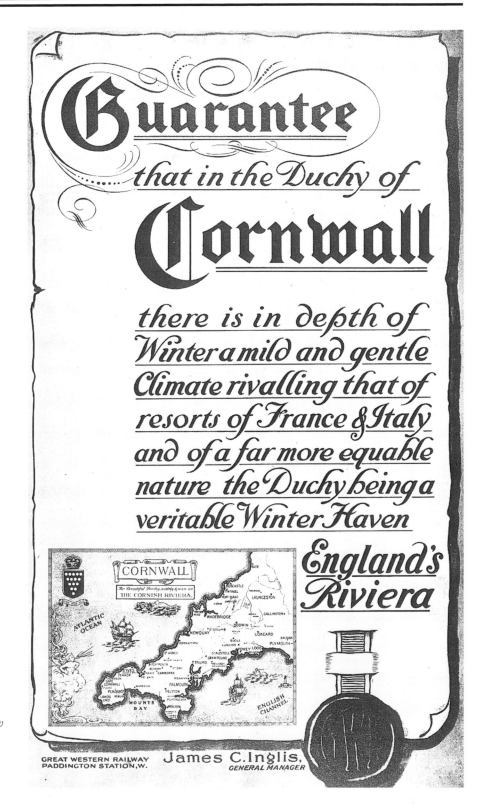

Another imaginative poster of the period. How many of us wish that the British weather could be guaranteed! (GWR Museum, Swindon)

In one of the early sections of *The Cornish Riviera*, the author wrote: 'It is obviously in the best interests of the British householder and taxpayer that the favourable climatic conditions of Cornwall between October and April should be made as widely known as possible'[7]. It might be worth remarking that it was also obviously to the company's interest to make this fact widely known! A considerable amount of space in the book was utilized to justify the county's climatic advantages. On occasions, one feels with hindsight that the company was perhaps stretching the point; however, in the context of some of the advertising 'hype' printed in today's holiday brochures, one wonders whether much has changed in the last 80 years or so!

One particular aspect of the Great Western's promotion of the Cornish Riviera was to compare it with French and Italian resorts; the traveller was promised the 'maximum of amusement at a minimum of expense...for those who elect either for pleasure or health to judge by actual experience the advantages of the Cornish Riviera as compared with its foreign rivals on the shores of the

A poster perfectly illustrating the company's message — why go abroad when the GWR could take you to Cornwall? (GWR Museum, Swindon)

Mediterranean'[8]. In a chapter devoted to Cornwall's climate, the author quoted such venerable authorities as Mr E. Kitto, Superintendent of the Falmouth Observatory, and Doctor Paris, President of the Royal College of Physicians. However, Dr Paris had in fact died in 1846, so how accurate or trustworthy his results were is hard to tell!

Statistics were shown comparing Penzance with Nice and Cannes, between October and April. Penzance had a considerably lower average temperature, 44.55 F compared with 49.8 F for Nice and 50.3 F at Cannes. The author of *The Cornish Riviera* was not convinced, though; he argued that the mean temperature was not representative, and Cornwall had less of a range of temperatures over the year, which was far better than its foreign rivals. One reason for the comparison with foreign resorts may well have been the upsurge in national feelings engendered by the Boer War campaign, touched upon briefly in the first part of the book. A slogan used by the Great Western was 'See Your Own Country First', and a now famous poster was also produced which showed the peninsula of Cornwall compared with a heavily distorted map of Italy, both looking remarkably similar!

The Riviera did, however, have practical advantages, and the Great Western writer noted that 'the blessings of warmth, sunshine and a mild climate may be found during the winter months without crossing the channel or the continent, or incurring the toil and expense of a sojourn in Egypt, a visit to Algiers or even a trip to Nice or San Remo'[9]. A visit to any of these places would have been a long, tiring and expensive business in the years before the First World War, while Cornwall, England's 'Riviera', was, with the fast trains run by the GWR, within eight hours of London.

Yet another medical man, Sir Joseph Fayrer KCSI MD FRS, who had chosen Falmouth as his winter home, was quoted as saying that he lived in Cornwall to escape the 'raw damp cold and fogs of London'[10]. As we have already seen in our look at Paddington, the capital was not such a pleasant place to live, and the GWR was keen to attract those who could afford to 'winter' in the Duchy. Things were obviously no better in the summer, however; in a book published some years earlier, the author J. Arthur Gibbs had written that 'London is becoming miserably hot and dusty; everyone who can get away is rushing off, north, south east and west, some to the seaside, others to pleasant country houses'[11].

This book and other literature issued by the company continued on much the same lines; an article in the *Great Western Railway Magazine* for 1913 entitled 'A Remarkable Tribute to Cornwall's Climate' was no exception, and presumably with some irony it noted that 'there is always something more to be said about Cornwall'[12]. The main topic of the article was the growing of a tropical plant which was normally considered to be hothouse variety, *Furcraea Bedinghausii*, out of doors. Cornwall's climate, it continued, is 'congenial to many exotic plants'. The company lost no opportunity to reiterate its claims for the region; the anonymous writer of an earlier *Great Western Railway Magazine* article had argued that 'English people are world famed for their scepticism, and no doubt many have questioned the GWR Company's claim to have discovered a "Riviera" in the West of England'[13]. The idea would, however, be dispelled by displays of Cornish flowers displayed in the company's London offices which, the writer claimed, were 'living pictures'.

Sceptics there were, even amongst the strongest supporters of the Great Western at the time. The Reverend W.J. Scott, a regular speaker at the GWR Lecture and Debating Society, in 1906 felt that the Cornish Riviera could not be compared with its French counterpart, since the two areas had very different landscapes, the French terrain being much dryer and rougher than the soft and rich landscape of Cornwall. He went on to argue that in 'South Devon and Cornwall you do not get a real frost during one winter in five years, less than you commonly get in the Riviera; but you do not get the same amount of brilliant sunshine'[14].

It is easy with the benefit of hindsight to be rather cynical about the Great Western Railway's sometimes heavy-handed promotion of its 'Cornish Riviera', but the fact remains that its methods did work. Press coverage of the new book on the Riviera produced glowing reviews; *Hearth and Home* called it a 'most alluring guide...those who have never visited the Cornish Littoral will long to start straight away...' *Ladies' Pictorial* went further, claiming the 'unless we are greatly mistaken, Paddington to Penzance is destined...to take the place of Charing Cross to Cannes'; those who read the booklet, it continued, 'are sure to think twice before deciding to give Monte Carlo a preference to Mounts Bay'[15]. Clearly the public were convinced too, since visitor numbers did increase, and as a result these resorts served by the railway developed. To cope with the influx of visitors, a holiday industry evolved, with small hotels, lodging and boarding houses being introduced to serve the needs of the less well off visitors who were increasingly attracted to the Duchy. The Reverend W.J. Scott also had some comments about the lack of such accommodation. 'On the French and Italian Riviera however, there are hotels, good ones and fairly cheap; there may be some British ones, but I have not found them'[16], he complained in 1906.

These words were perhaps prophetic, since in the same year the Great Western took yet another pioneering step in the tourist business when it introduced another new publication of its own, called *Holiday Haunts on The Great Western Railway, Season 1906* [17]. This book would provide a directory of precisely the kind of accommodation already mentioned. In the introduction the company's aims were set out very clearly: 'The object of this little volume is to impart to holiday-makers of all classes – noble and simple, rich and poor, strong and weak — such information as will enable them to secure a maximum of change, rest, pleasure or sport,

The cover of the first edition of Holiday Haunts. *(Great Western Trust)*

'Oh we do like to be beside the seaside' — the Edwardian family on holiday!

at a minimum of expenditure and fatigue'[18]. The book went on to argue that the pace of twentieth-century life was such that rest and relaxation, 'call it by the good old fashioned name of holiday if you like', was a necessity especially if the 'danger of a breakdown was to be avoided'[19].

It was remarked in *Holiday Haunts* that previously holidaymaking had been practically the monopoly of the rich, but at the time of writing was 'well nigh universal'. Certainly more people could afford a holiday than in previous times; the rise of the middle classes who could afford seaside holidays had made possible the expansion of holiday resorts, although it is probably true to say that many working class families could not yet afford to do more than travel to such resorts on short holidays or day trips. *Holiday Haunts* continued to focus a great deal of attention on its claims for the Cornish Riviera, arguing that it had been left to the GWR to prove that in 'the sunny southern coast of Cornwall, England possesses a Riviera which is today defying foreign rivals, and enabling vast numbers of English men and women of all classes to enjoy, during the winter months as well as in summer time'. Furthermore, it argued, 'thousands who have tried it prefer it to far off Monte Carlo or still more distant Madeira'[20].

Holiday Haunts was innovatory in many respects; the main features and places of interest in each county were listed alphabetically, followed by a tabulated list of accommodation offered in each resort. The book also contained advertisements for hotels and boarding houses; 15 pages were devoted to those in Cornwall, and some 22 for Devon. Some estimate of the importance of the Great Western's West of England traffic is gained from the fact that by far the largest numbers of pages were those concerning the counties of Devon and Cornwall. Since the company had published the guide itself, it could, unlike other holiday guides produced in previous years, give space to publicize the developments taking place on the railway generally. Thus in the 1906 edition there were advertisements for the newly opened Westbury and South Wales Direct lines, as well as prominent sections on Fishguard Harbour and the new route to Ireland, which had also opened that year. A section towards the end of the book also gave a list of golf links on or near the Great Western system.

For the first two years of its existence, *Holiday Haunts* cost the princely sum of one penny, being increased to threepence in 1908, when its size was enlarged from the 334 pages of the first issue to a new size of over 580 pages. Each Easter a new edition of the book appeared, and its circulation increased steadily, so that by the outbreak of war in 1914 nearly 100,000 copies were produced annually. Wartime austerity caused the suspension of production in 1916, and it did not appear again until 1921, after which it grew from strength to strength, lasting right up until 1947. To conclude our look at this most typical example of the company's enterprise, here is a further quote from the 1906 edition which summarizes the *raison d'être* for the book from the company's point of view: 'countless English Health and Pleasure resorts, formerly almost unknown, are at the present time household words'.

Apart from these two publications, the Great Western railway found many other ways to promote its service and the resorts on its lines. Another slogan which it promoted in the first decade of the century was 'The Weekend Habit'; a GWR handbill of the period argued that 'the exigencies of modern life make so great a demand on the vitality that the recuperative weekend holiday had become a matter of necessity'[21]. An article in the *Great Western Railway Magazine* for 1909 further remarked that holidays of this type were especially helpful to those indulging in 'hard brain work'. 'Small but regular doses of fresh air, change of scene and invigorating exercise' were, it was reported, being taken 'by nearly every rank of life'. The handbill concluded that 'the tanned face of the tourist as he steps from the train is ample evidence of the vigour and health instilled by the beneficial weekend holiday in England's favourite holiday ground'[22]. It should of course be emphasized that it was improvements to the Great Western's route to the West Country, to be described shortly, which enabled the company to advertise and promote such services.

As well as the more conventional types of advertising such as posters, publications and handbills, the Great Western used other new methods to get its messages across. One such innovation was the use of an 'Advertising Car', a converted motor omnibus which the company sent on promotional tours all over the country. More often than not the vehicle was sent deep into the territory of its rivals, giving out leaflets and handbills advertising its services. The *Great Western Railway Magazine* of 1913 described one such jaunt which took the vehicle on a five-week trip calling at Wolverhampton, the Potteries, Blackburn, Bolton, Leeds, Bradford, Huddersfield, York, Newcastle, Sheffield, Nottingham and Northampton.[23] The 'Advertising Car' also ventured as far north as Scotland in search of potential customers.

Another new medium, the cinema, was also utilized by the GWR early in its history. In 1912 it was reported that the Great Western had put on a successful 'Cinematograph Exhibition' at the Northern Polytechnic Institution, Holloway Road, London. In the show, which the local newspaper, the *Islington Gazette* called 'high class' and a 'cause of edification', films of Devon and Cornwall were preceded by one of a non-stop corridor train leaving Paddington.[24]

One of the Great Western's 'Advertising Cars'. The solid tyres must have made long journeys arduous for driver and passengers. The right-hand poster notes that 'There is a remarkable similarity between Cornwall and Italy'. (National Railway Museum, York)

THE ROUTE TO
THE WEST

IN the dark days before the new spirit of enterprise overtook the Great Western, the old route to the West of England was fairly circuitous, with trains travelling along Brunel's original main line from Paddington to Bristol, before taking the old Bristol & Exeter Railway route to Taunton and Exeter. From here the tracks of the South Devon, Cornwall and West Cornwall Railways were traversed until journey's end at Penzance. With such a tortuous route it was no surprise that the GWR acquired the nickname of the 'Great Way Round'.

The outcome of this arrangement was not only to make travel to Devon and Cornwall a laborious process, but was also to have a deteriorating effect on the efficient running of the large station at Bristol. Observant readers will notice in the course of this book that this great railway centre will only be mentioned in passing; this is not due to a direct omission on the part of the author, but merely a reflection on the areas where the Great Western was concentrating its efforts in the 'Golden Age'. Although there were improvements to the impressive station which the Great Western shared with the Midland Railway in Bristol, major redevelopment of the site was not to take place until the 1930s when Government grants allowed extensive rebuilding of the cramped station surroundings. To a large extent, the story of Bristol station in the 'Golden Age' is one of overcrowding and congestion, for by 1900 it was a very significant railway centre, serving main lines to London, Cardiff, Birmingham and Exeter.

The large and impressive train shed designed by Sir Matthew Digby Wyatt, who, as we have already seen, assisted Brunel with the construction of Paddington, was in many ways inadequate before it was fully finished; the station was simply too small to cope with the level of traffic, both local and long distance, which eventually used it. Plans were made to remodel the track layout in 1914, but were curtailed by the outbreak of war. Writing in 1909, W.J. Scott described the station graphically as a 'great gathering cistern' which was, especially in summer, 'filled to overflowing'[25]. Even the building of a relief line in 1892, which bypassed the station, was only a partial success; it was this line which did, however, help to give some fast timings on 'Ocean Mail' trains, as we shall see later in this part of the book.

To avoid this delay and congestion, the obvious solution was to build a new route to the West of England which bypassed Bristol entirely. What was also needed was a competitive route parallel to that of the London & South Western Railway, which already ran a fast service to Exeter via Salisbury. The idea of a direct line was not in fact new; as early as 1848 there had been some suggestion of a scheme which would use sections of the Wilts, Somerset & Weymouth Railway. The Great Western's new route was to a large extent the linking up of various existing lines, and the upgrading of those routes to main line standard. GWR publicity made much of the introduction of these 'cut-offs', as they became known.

In essence, the new GWR route consisted of three main stages; first the improving of the old 'Berks & Hants' line, second the linking of this stretch with the metals of the old Wilts, Somerset & Weymouth Railway by means of a new line, the Stert and Westbury link, and finally the building of an entirely new railway from Castle Cary to Langport in Somerset, which would connect the new through line with the old Bristol to Exeter main line. In addition, the process was completed by substantial improvements to the Great Western main line in Devon and Cornwall.

Before looking at the modernization of the company's route in the Far West, we will examine in more detail the work done nearer London. The earliest attempts to make drastic improvements to the Great Western's route to the West had taken place in 1882, when Parliamentary assent was given to allow the company to build a new

A sketch map, originally reproduced in The Railway Magazine *for 1906, showing the Great Western's new route to the West.* (The Railway Magazine)

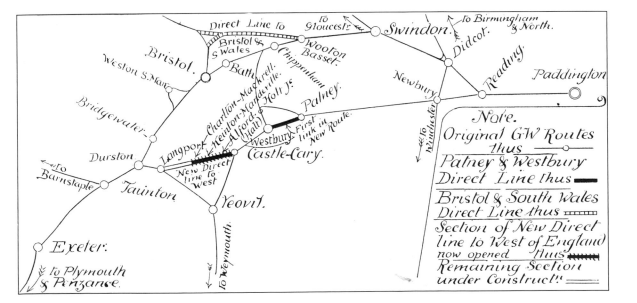

One advantage of the improvements to the Great Western's new route was that through services to Weymouth were much improved; this view shows 4-4-0 No 4115 Marigold passing Weymouth shed around 1912. (Alan Parrett Collection)

line from Castle Cary to Langport, but this had come to nothing, and it was not until the last few years of the nineteenth century that we can observe positive efforts being made by the GWR to improve matters.

In 1897 work began on the widening and modernization of the 'Berks & Hants' line, which dated from 1847, when the Reading to Hungerford section was opened. The 24-mile section from Hungerford to Devizes, known as the 'Berks & Hants Extension' was not completed until November 1862. Built to the broad gauge, the line was only double-tracked from Reading to Hungerford, leaving a steep and tortuous single track section to Devizes. Obviously this was not conducive to main line running, so the 19½ miles of track were doubled, in two contracts; Hungerford to Savernake, and Savernake to Stert. Both portions were carried out by Messrs Paulings & Co of Westminster, and work was finally completed throughout on 29 July 1900. However, the widening of the Berks & Hants necessitated more than a straightforward doubling of the tracks, for the original railway, like many early schemes, had been built as cheaply as possible, so the track had to be raised and lowered at various points, and diversions and new stretches of railway were necessary to enable fast and smooth running to take place.

We have already noted that the line to Devizes was hilly and winding, so it comes as no surprise to find that the Great Western therefore intended to bypass this particular stretch; commencing in 1897, construction began on a new connecting railway joining Stert (later named Patney and Chirton) and Westbury, on the Wilts, Somerset & Weymouth Railway. Like other 'cut-offs', the line was a substantial affair, 14 miles in length, and its completion was delayed by landslips, some quite serious, which were caused by the local geology; greasy water-bearing strata had formed on top of gault or clay, and this was overlain by greensand strata which tended to move. A contemporary observer noted that it seemed at times as if whole hillsides were on the move! Such problems were not difficult from an engineering point of view, as headings could be cut into the sides of cuttings, about six feet square, to act as drains. They did, however, add to both the company's worries and the construction costs.

The link opened for goods traffic in July 1900, and for passenger working in October the same year. Two small stations at Lavington, and Edington and Bratton were opened at the same time. The company's 1902 timetables show that the residents of the small village of Lavington had an 18-minute journey to Westbury where a connection could be made for Bristol, Weymouth or beyond[26]. The old station at Westbury was also considerably altered and rebuilt whilst work on the new route continued. In an account of the new line given to the GWR Lecture and Debating Society in 1907, P.A. Antony remarked that the Stert-Westbury section was 'constructed with a view to fast running — that is, with easy gradients and flat curves'[27].

The third part of the Great Western's new route was the most ambitious, the construction of 32 miles of new line, and the doubling

Lavington station on the Stert–Westbury link just before the First World War; note the wooden platform extension. (Lens of Sutton)

The opening of the Castle Cary 'cut-off', as announced in the 1906 edition of Holiday Haunts. (Great Western Trust)

and reconstruction of 24 miles of old single track. It also involved the rebuilding and extension of eight old stations and the building of seven new ones. The Bill to build a new railway from Castle to Langport was laid before the house in 1898, and a different route to that proposed in the original 1882 scheme was chosen, but some opposition from local people led to a still further modified alignment which required additional Parliamentary powers subsequently granted in 1899.

It was not until 1903 that work actually started on the project; the Great Western obviously eagerly anticipated its completion since the maps reproduced in the 1902 timetables, for example, had the route already marked with a dotted line! The building of the lines involved a variety of different engineering problems; Castle Cary station itself was rebuilt, and the curve at the London end of the station was eased to a radius of 60 chains to allow faster running. After the second station on the line, Charlton Mackrell, the landscape traversed by the railway changed, and the rolling nature of the countryside required the construction of more cuttings and embankments. Considerable expense was incurred outside Somerton, where a 1,054-foot tunnel was driven through hard marl and shale rock.

Whilst this work was being undertaken, steps were made to utilize the old Yeovil Branch line between Langport and Athelney. The railway was widened and improved, with a substantial amount of extra cost being incurred because of the low-lying nature of the land. By this time the Great Western's route had reached the flat area of the Somerset Levels. The landscape was, and still is, one of flat boggy moorland at sea level, crossed by large 'rhines' and artificial ditches. The alluvial soils were often up to 50 feet deep, making the building of substantial foundations difficult. The danger of flooding meant that the Great Western was forced to build its new main line well above the highest recorded flood levels for safety; the possibility of the new line being flooded was a state of affairs which would have been 'a most serious matter'[28]. An embankment was raised between 10 and 25 feet in height and ran for about five miles. This expensive alternative replaced the original alignment of the old branch line which had been almost at sea level.

Two further large bridges over the River Parrett were also required, one a ten-span viaduct where the danger of flooding was the greatest, and the other, a few hundred yards away, a steel girder bridge with a span of over 100 feet. Both these bridges caused the engineers problems since the foundations had to be driven down 50 feet, due to the depth of the peat. The final stage was to link the new line with the old West of England main route; after Athelney, the old branch line joined the Bristol to Exeter main line at Durston. This was retained, but an entirely new deviation line was built for the use of the long-distance express traffic, joining the B&E route at Cogload Junction, about two miles from Taunton.

The whole scheme was finally finished in July 1906, when

Castle Cary station, seen in the 1950s. (Lens of Sutton)

passenger traffic from Paddington to the West of England was switched to the new route. Henceforth much of the Great Western publicity for trains to Devon and Cornwall was advertised as being 'Via Castle Cary'; ironically, few if any of the through express trains run by the company actually stopped there! The Castle Cary route had taken rather longer than anticipated to complete, around nine years, mainly due to engineering difficulties not originally contemplated, and had certainly been expensive to build, contemporary sources estimating its cost at around £1,100,000. The benefits accrued by the new route, however, were soon to outweigh the original high cost of construction. The journey to the West was shortened by 20 miles, and as we shall see in the next section of the book, substantial gains were made by the Traffic Department in shortening journey times. With the switching of almost all daytime express services via Castle Cary, much congestion was also removed from the Bristol area.

Some attention has been paid to these efforts made to improve the West of England route since it is yet another example of the company's policy of enterprise and initiative; considerable sums of money were invested in schemes which would ensure the long-term stability of the Great Western. The company shareholders did not always see this expense as being justified, but it is true to say that the investments made in this period were certainly to reap benefits in later years.

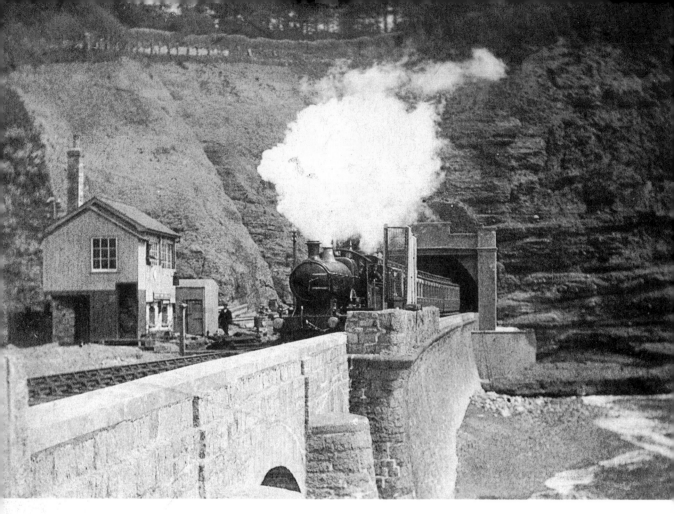

A Great Western 4-4-0 bursts out of Parson's Tunnel between Dawlish and Teignmouth some time after October 1905, when the line was doubled. (GWR Museum, Swindon)

After rejoining the old route of the Bristol & Exeter at Cogload, trains for the West of England continued through Taunton to Exeter. The line was well engineered, although stiff gradients on Wellington Bank and its summit at Whiteball Tunnel prevented extemely fast running. It was only in the section of line West of Exeter that any other major work was done in the 'Golden Age'. The route between Exeter and Plymouth was built as part of the South Devon Railway, and many readers will remember that it was this section of line that was used by Brunel for his 'atmospheric caper' (the story of the introduction and subsequent failure of this novel form of propulsion has been told elsewhere, and need not be described here). What ought to be noted, however, was that as originally built the South Devon Railway was single line, with the exception of two places, at Rattery and between Hemerdon and Plymouth. Doubling was 'taken in hand, piece by piece'[29]; what remained, however, was an awkward section, $1\frac{1}{2}$ miles in length, which was the last section of single track between London and Plymouth.

The stretch of track in question lay along the coast between Dawlish and Teignmouth, and was fraught with difficulties. The Great Western management was, however, extremely anxious to remove this delay to traffic. The widening work involved the modification of no fewer than five tunnels driven through extremely hard red sandstone cliffs. The expense involved meant that there was some deliberation by the company as to the best way of carrying out the work; at one stage a new inland diversionary line was even considered. Such was the magnitude of the work that in 1888 Parliamentary powers were obtained to start the scheme, but it was not proceeded with. In the era before the First World War, however, a more progressive management at Paddington realized that the work would have to be done; as the West of England services improved, even with the introduction of an electric train staff signalling system, delays become more frequent. As the *Great Western Railway Magazine* of 1905 remarked, 'the expeditious working of traffic over a single line is at any time difficult, but when a section intervenes in a main line over which a heavy express train passes, it will be apparent that delays must occur[30].

Renewed Parliamentary powers were obtained in 1900, and work began. The first task was the creation of a massive seawall between Dawlish and Kennaway Tunnel, the by-product of which was a promenade 10 feet wide which is still used by residents and holidaymakers today. The widening of the tunnels was a far more difficult job, since trains were still running at intervals of around 10

On a gloomy winter day, a Churchward 'Saint' brings an express along the newly doubled line near Teignmouth. (GWR Museum, Swindon)

PENZANCE (GWR) STATION AND HARBOUR.

Penzance, the end of the line, as portrayed on an official GWR postcard of the period.

minutes. An experimental 'Shield Arch' was constructed which was erected inside the tunnel over the tracks so that work could proceed above and around the railway without disrupting traffic. The generous loading gauge of Brunel's Broad Gauge helped, but all sorts of other problems still meant that progress was painfully slow; the sea had undermined the cliffs and made seaside retaining walls more difficult to construct. By October 1905, however, it could be reported that 'this month sees the termination of a work unique in character, and important in results'[31]. With its completion, yet another important link in the Great Western's 'Holiday Line' was forged.

We cannot conclude this chronicle of improvement and modernization without mentioning the work actually carried out in Cornwall itself, which has not attracted as much attention as features such as the Castle Cary 'cut-off' scheme. For many travellers, Plymouth was not the primary objective — most holidaymakers were bound for resorts further West. As a result, the Great Western also spent a great deal of money in the early part of the twentieth century upgrading the main line from Plymouth to Penzance itself. In the 1890s the line was single throughout, other than at major stations, and the deep Cornish valleys were spanned by Brunel's impressive yet impractical timber viaducts, dating from the opening out of the line in the 1840s and 1850s.

The rugged nature of the countryside made the realignment of the more difficult stretches of line an expensive process; however, the doubling of the line from Devonport Junction to Penzance was carried out in stages, with the last section, from Saltash to Wearde Sidings, being finally completed in February 1906. Important as this doubling was, a more drastic measure was the building of an entirely new deviation line from Saltash to St Germans. The original section of line it replaced was just over five miles in length, but contained six timber viaducts, five of which needed rebuilding to accommodate double track.

It was decided that a more suitable alternative was to build a new line to the north, away from the sea, which would not require two of the viaducts originally needed, and it was estimated that it would cost little more than the expense of widening the original track and reconstructing the viaducts. More significantly, the new deviation could be laid out with better curves and gradients; instead of the 1 in 75 of the original line, a ruling gradient of around 1 in 200 was planned. This reduction allowed the company to run trains which were up to 25 per cent heavier. Construction began in 1904, with a local contractor, Messrs Relf & Son of Plymouth, undertaking the work. Although only a small line in size, some idea of the magnitude of the project can be gained from the fact that nearly 700,000 cubic tons of rock had to be removed during its construction.

By the end of the period covered by this book, it can be seen that the Great Western had expended considerable amounts of money and effort in constructing a high-speed railway line from the capital to the far West of England. This had involved not only the construction of new fast 'cut-offs' in Wiltshire and Somerset, but also the reconstruction of some of the oldest parts of the Great Western network in Devon and Cornwall. In its own way each of these schemes was important in making the journey to the West easier and quicker for the customer.

PLYMOUTH AND THE OCEAN MAIL TRAFFIC

Churchward 4-4-2 No 189 Talisman brings a mixed train of both clerestory and 'Concertina' coaches into Plymouth North Road station, around 1912. (Alan Parrett Collection)

BEFORE describing the passenger services provided by the GWR on its West of England route, including arguably the best known Great Western express train, the 'Cornish Riviera Limited', we will look at the special arrangements the company made for the rapid transit of both mails and passengers arriving at the port of Plymouth. During the 'Golden Age', these workings proved to be an admirable testing ground for the fast trains for which the Great Western was to become justly famous.

In the years before the Great War, transatlantic liner traffic was itself at a zenith. The British shipbuilding industry was producing 50 per cent of the world's merchant fleet, and the North Atlantic was becoming a major sea route in both directions. Thousands of

Headed notepaper from the Great Western's Ocean Terminal at Plymouth.

emigrants spurred on by the lack of entry restrictions travelled to seek their fortunes in the New World, whilst travelling in great luxury and comfort in the other direction were tourists, businessmen and the rich. To attract the custom of these groups, the shipping companies vied with each other to produce the largest and most comfortable ships they could; not unnaturally, there was also intense competition between the largest ports serving the North Atlantic route.

Plymouth was admirably placed to compete with other Channel ports for this lucrative transatlantic traffic, not only in freight and passengers, but also mail itself; situated at the entrance to the English Channel, the docks were accessible at the stages of the tide, and in most weathers. The position of the port was well marked for navigation purposes by both the Eddystone lighthouse and the South Lizard light, and it was also argued that it tended to attract less fog than some of its competitors further up the Channel. Southampton was nearly 120 miles away, and although the rail journey from there to London took only about two hours, as compared to a four hour journey from Plymouth, a passenger landing at the Devon port still gained around five to six hours due to the shorter sea passage.

The role of the GWR in this story, then, was to provide a rapid train service to whisk the Atlantic traveller from Plymouth to Paddington in as short a time as possible, and during this period the company took positive steps to provide such a train service which would allow the port to maintain its ocean traffic.

As early as 1895 it was recorded that the company was to spend £70,000 on remodelling the passenger and goods stations at Plymouth Millbay and improving access to the dock. Even at this early stage, the company was able to boast that it was in 'a position to run a special vestibule palace car to Paddington in five hours'[32]. This announcement was coupled with the decision of the Hamburg-American Steamship Company to return to the use of Plymouth as its port of call; it calculated that the voyage from New York to Plymouth was six hours shorter than that to Southampton.

By 1905 it was reported that no fewer than 15 major steamship companies had similarly adopted the port. The value of this transatlantic traffic was not lost on the GWR, and in that same year a special booklet, 'Information for Ocean Passengers', was published, which catered specially for this type of customer. Some years later, in 1912, a similar publication issued by the 'Great Western Railway of England' proclaimed that the company was 'the principal of Britain's trunk lines' and 'the requirements of American and Colonial tourists are the subject of special study in all Great Western Services'[33].

The importance of the company's role is perhaps reinforced by the fact that in 1904, 513 ocean liners made a call at Plymouth. Clearly this kind of business could not be ignored, not only in terms of passengers but also the lucrative transit of United States mail. Delays to this kind of traffic were seen as being potentially harmful to the

company's reputation; a circular issued in March 1912 made this clear and reminded staff that much significance was attached to the 'Ocean Mail' trains, and all those concerned were directed to pay special attention to the workings.[34]

It was not until the early 1900s that especially fast times were achieved, and in fact the first fast run was not actually on an 'Ocean Mail' working; it did, however, show what the Great Western was capable of. In March 1902 a special train was run from Paddington to the West of England to carry the newly crowned King Edward VII to Devon for a special visit to the county. The train, hauled by a 4–4–0 'Atbara' Class locomotive *Royal Sovereign*, left the capital at 10.30 am, and ran non-stop to Kingswear, arriving there at 2.53 pm. The 229-mile journey was done at an average speed of 52.62 mph.

Three days later, on 10 March, the monarch was again treated to a rapid non-stop journey, this time from Plymouth to Paddington, arriving in London after a journey of 4 hours $43\frac{1}{2}$ minutes. A further quick non-stop trip was made by distinguished passengers on 14 July 1903, when the Duke and Duchess of Cornwall were whisked from Paddington to Plymouth in 3 hours $53\frac{1}{2}$ minutes, an average speed of 63.4 mph. The locomotive this time was one of G.J. Churchward's latest 4–4–0s, No 3433 *City of Bath*, and it was this class which was destined to put in some very fast runs in the next few years.

Fast though these runs were, the 'Ocean Mail' special traffic would produce even better performances in 1904, which would in due course have an effect in speeding up a good number of the Great Western's express trains. The events of that year were a direct result of a stepping up of rivalry between the Great Western and the London & South Western Railway, which had made a bid to grab some of Plymouth's ocean liner traffic from the GWR. This competition spurred the company to produce a series of high-speed journeys which were to prove the supremacy of the Great Western beyond any doubt.

The *Railway Magazine* for May 1904 went as far as to announce that 'World records broken daily might be the GWR's motto as 1903–4 experiences go'[35]. *The Great Western Railway Magazine* was more circumspect, reprinting the quote and adding, 'whether this be so or not, we venture to think that no such record of speedy journeys has ever been published'[36]. It then went on to list seven extremely fast runs between Plymouth and Paddington, with the slowest train taking 4 hours 18 minutes for the journey. The list culminated with what has now become a world famous run on 9 May 1904. On that day, the SS *Kronprinz Wilhelm* of the North German Lloyd line arrived in Plymouth Sound from New York after a six-day Atlantic crossing. Anchoring at 8 am, over a thousand mail bags were loaded into Great Western tenders, then transferred into five GWR mail vans. The special train, hauled by Churchward 4–4–0 No 3440 *City of Truro* left Plymouth at 9.23 am, and made the 75-mile trip to Bristol in 64 minutes 17 seconds. (At this time, of course, the new 'cut-offs' had not yet been opened, so trains still had to proceed via Bristol.)

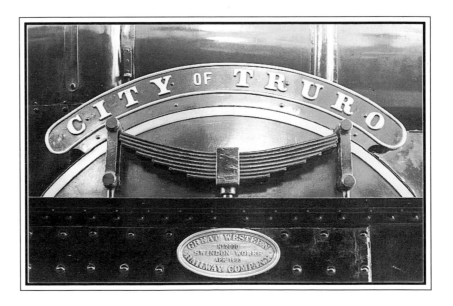

The name and worksplate from the record-breaking City of Truro.

Dean 'single' Duchess of Teck, sister engine to Duke of Connaught which made the record-breaking run in 1904.

At Bristol, a short stop was made to change locomotives, and the 'City' was replaced by a Dean 4-2-2 'Single', No 3065 *Duke of Connaught*. Leaving Bristol at 11.30, it arrived at Paddington at 1.09 pm, the whole trip including the stop at Bristol having taken just 3 hours 46 minutes. This meant that the average speed throughout was $65\frac{1}{2}$ mph, considerably better than anything done previously. Full accounts of this record run were subsequently published in *The Railway Magazine* and the *Engineer* of 1904, since Charles Rous-Marten, a prominent expert of the time, had actually been present on the journey. The management at Paddington, however, forbad him to reveal one vital fact — the top speed achieved by *City of Truro* during its descent of Wellington Bank.

It was not until 1922 that evidence emerged publicly that the locomotive had broken the magical 100 mph barrier, the first steam locomotive to do so; Rous-Marten in fact timed the engine as touching a maximum of 102.3 mph, speeding down the bank. Over the years there has been a great deal of debate as to the accuracy of the timings, but in the author's opinion the *actual* speed attained is academic — what was important was that the GWR had shown it could run trains at a consistently high speed *throughout*. At the time, the company's General Manager, James Inglis, was reluctant to release news of this record-breaking speed for fear of frightening the travelling public, who were unused to such rapidity. What would they have made of today's High Speed Trains?

In fact, the GWR went to great lengths to understate the importance of the run, claiming that 'comment on this record is unnecessary and with such laurels the company may well rest content'[37]. The railway may well have also been reassured by the less impressive efforts of the LSWR, whose best journey time for the 230 miles from London to Plymouth was recorded at 4 hours 18 minutes. Numerous other fast runs were recorded by the GWR in subsequent years, one such being reported in November 1905. The arrival of the American liner SS *St Paul* on the 4th of that month was followed by a fast trip behind a Churchward 'Saint' Class, No 178, covering the 247 miles from Plymouth to Paddington in 250 minutes.

By 1906, the *Great Western Railway Magazine* was arguing that smartly timed runs in relation to the transit of the mails had become so common that it was difficult to pick out special performances. Matters were assisted by the rapid transfer of the mails from ship to shore. On one occasion, 1,700 mail bags were transferred in just 17 minutes, a formidable achievement to say the least!

With the opening of the Castle Cary and Langport line in 1906, the majority of trains were transferred to run on that route. On 13 August that year, revised instructions were issued with regard to

A beautiful period photograph taken at Devonport near Plymouth around 1912. The train is probably a Paddington-Penzance express, since at this time all such trains called at this station. The locomotive is No 3347 Tregothnan, *built in 1900 and fitted with a combined name and numberplate.* (Alan Parrett Collection)

'Ocean Mail' traffic; in the past a van containing mails for Bristol, the Midlands and the North had been slipped at Malago Vale signal box, Bedminster, just outside Bristol, where an engine was kept in readiness to take the slip portion to Temple Meads where the mails could be sorted and transferred[38]. Meanwhile, the main train ran through to London via the avoiding line. Under the new instructions, the coach was slipped at Victory Crossing near Norton Fitzwarren, west of Taunton, and a special instruction noted that an engine should be kept in readiness to take the mails on to Bristol from there.

The tragic train crash at Salisbury on 30 June 1906 effectively ended the rivalry between the two companies; a LSWR boat train running at excessive speed through the station became derailed and ploughed into the rear of a milk train on the down line causing 28 fatalities. Within the confines of the port of Plymouth, though, the archives reveal that in 1907 there was still some tension between the two companies. A dispute arose with the decision of the White Star shipping line to start calling at Plymouth on 30 May of that year. The White Star had obviously made arrangements with the LSWR which discriminated against the GWR in various ways. The ship's crew were reported to have told passengers that the GWR had no special arrangements for ocean traffic, and that the LSWR was the only company to run special trains; furthermore, unlike most other shipping lines, White Star refused to give the Great Western through booking facilities.

The Great Western memo on the subject argued that the GWR was 'treated badly with almost every ship's arrival'. However, the South Western's tactics did not always work to their advantage; on various occasions they were obliged to run special trains with only two or three London passengers. The Great Western also cited, presumably with some satisfaction, that there were one or two cases where the LSWR had to carry a single passenger and his luggage to Waterloo by the special train![39]

In concluding our survey of the ocean traffic dealt with by the company in this period, it is worth mentioning that the port of Plymouth also handled a great deal of freight from the North Atlantic route, which was transhipped and moved to London by train, the rapidity of GWR freight services allowing in 1906, for example, the shipment of Argentinian chilled and frozen meat to Smithfield Market two days quicker than similar loads taken via Southampton.

Finally, to end this chapter on a suitably 'fishy' note, the *Great Western Railway Magazine* recorded a novel 'catch' made by the company in 1910. Whilst emptying its graving dock, the GWR found it to contain thousands of grey mullet. Not unnaturally, the sight of this teeming mass of fish attracted a great deal of public curiosity, and the police were called to prevent the public helping themselves. Needless to say, it was the GWR which reaped the benefit of a harvest of around $4\frac{1}{2}$ tons of fish![40]

THE 'CORNISH
RIVIERA
LIMITED'

THE superlative performances put in by the Great Western in pursuit of its 'Ocean Mail' traffic meant that it was only a matter of time before the results of these runs would be transferred to the running of day-to-day passenger services. Indeed, in the early part of 1904 it was an open secret that the GWR did indeed intend to launch a non-stop service from Paddington to Plymouth; the *Great Western Railway Magazine* for June 1904 carried the announcement that in view of 'the experience gained in the working of Ocean Mail special trains, it has been possible to arrange a revised schedule of times to which Passenger and Mail specials will be worked in future'[41].

Within a month of this statement, the new express had been inaugurated. The as-yet unnamed train was timed to leave Paddington at 10.10 am, and ran the 264 miles non-stop to Plymouth in 265 minutes. Further stops were made only at Truro, Gwinear Road and St Erth, before finally arriving at Penzance at 5.10 pm. This arrival time was some 44 minutes faster than any previous service. In the opposite direction, an up train left Penzance at 10.10 am and, after calling at the same stations (with the addition of Devonport), arrived in the capital at 5.00 pm.

The train was scheduled to run six days a week, and its introduction was, the *Great Western Railway Magazine* boasted, 'received with astonishment in Railway Circles'[42]. This may have been something of an overstatement, however, when one bears in mind the fact that one of the company's other prestige trains, the 'Cornishman' had, since 1 July 1897, done a daily non-stop run of 194 miles from Paddington to Exeter, the longest run without a stop made by any railway in the world. The Great Western's new service boosted this record still further, of course.

Undoubtedly, the company had pulled off an excellent publicity coup; *The Railway Magazine* in its review of Summer Train Services for that year printed the details of both the new train and some of the company's other improved expresses to the West of England and noted: 'Where else shall we find such brilliant timings?'[43].

The new express consisted of seven vehicles — six clerestory-roofed eight-wheeled carriages and a new 68-foot Dining Car — amounting to a 200-ton load, which helped to keep the average speed high. Running by the old route via Bristol, the train was initially hauled by a variety of Great Western motive power; strangely enough, the first down express was hauled as far as Plymouth by the French compound locomotive No 102 *La France* rather than a Churchward or Dean type, before being replaced by the 4–40 No 3448 *Paddington* for the more steeply-graded banks of Devon and Cornwall. In that first week of operation, *La France* was used on four further occasions, on both up and down trains; clearly Churchward was keen to test the mettle of the French engine, as compared with his own designs. Another well-known engine used in that first week was Churchward 4-4-0 No 3433 *City of Bath*.

One key factor in the success of the new trains was the provision of water troughs which enabled locomotives to pick up water without stopping. Ramsbottom's patent troughs were installed at Exminster, cutting out the need for an intermediate stop. The troughs themselves were between 1,700 and 1,800 feet long, and held about 5,500 gallons of water, more than enough to fill the tenders of Great Western engines. Initially the scoop apparatus fitted to locomotive tenders could pick up approximately 1,650 gallons of water at one time, but in 1909 a company memorandum noted that improved scoop equipment would allow 2,000 gallons to be picked up. The same document also showed that it took about three minutes to refill

An official GWR postcard view of the 'Cornish Riviera Express' seen in a similar location to the picture on page 118. The postcard sets issued by the company were eagerly collected by enthusiasts then, as now.

THE "CORNISH RIVIERA" EXPRESS, NEAR DAWLISH.
GREAT WESTERN RAILWAY.

An unidentified 'Bulldog' assists a Churchward 'Saint' into Plymouth North Road, having brought its train from the West. The 'Bulldog' still has a tender fitted with coal rails. (Alan Parrett Collection)

OVERLEAF *Another evocative poster of the period; this example illustrates the point that the company had yet to find a 'house style' for its advertising material. (GWR Museum, Swindon)*

the troughs after the engine had passed.[44]

As has been mentioned, when the new train service was introduced it did not have a distinctive name; *The Railway Magazine* in its coverage of the early runs christened it the '3.T.F.', the 'Three Towns Flyer' — the three towns cited in this rather clumsy title were Plymouth, Stonehouse and Devonport (Stonehouse being a suburb of Plymouth), an odd choice to say the least! The magazine argued that 'such famous trains as those performing...between Paddington and Plymouth are justly entitled to a distinctive appellation'[45]. In its July edition it offered, for the purpose of obtaining a 'suitable cognomen' for the express, a prize of three guineas for the best name. The Great Western's General Manager, James Inglis, quick to see the public relations mileage in such a competition, agreed to judge the entries.

The closing date for the competition was 8 August 1904, and when the result was announced in the September edition of the magazine, it was reported that there had been 1,286 entries; a further 700 suggestions had been sent direct to the company's headquarters at Paddington, but were not considered eligible for the competition itself. The name chosen by Inglis as being most appropriate was the 'Riviera Express', a name suggested by two readers, Mr F. Hynam of Hampstead and Mr J. Shelley of Hackney. In its publicity for the competition, the magazine suggested that the winner's name would become known and handed on to future generations of 'Railway Officers and Railwayacs'[46] as the originator of the train's title. Sadly these two gentlemen did not become the household names perhaps they and the magazine thought.

This may well have been because although Inglis chose the name 'Riviera Express', the train seems always to have been known as the 'Cornish Riviera Limited', or more often in its shorter form, the 'Limited'. Indeed, this title was one of the other suggestions made in the *Railway Magazine* competition; other contenders were 'the 'Cornubian', the 'Riviera Racer', the 'One and All Limited' and the 'Speedwell Express'.

Space on the train was limited; the only exception to this was during the busy summer holidays, when the train could be run in two portions, allowing more passengers to be accommodated. Thus to ensure a seat in these busy periods, booking was imperative, and as a result the GWR introduced a system whereby each seat in the train was numbered. Booking a seat cost the passenger the princely sum of one shilling; this new innovation soon became popular, and over the years the number of reserved seats grew, as the following table shows:

Numbers of registered/booked seats on the 'Limited' expresses[47]

1904	4765	1908	20,217
1905	8379	1909	22,495
1906	9194	1910	25,355
1907	16,959	1911	25,792

[NB Before 1906, the 'Limited' ran in the summer months only.]

The train was also restricted in that no free passes or 'privilege' tickets could be used on it.

The success of the train led to further improvements when the service was re-introduced in the summer of 1905. Three new trains were specially constructed, with space for 232 third class and 36 first class passengers (there was no second class accommodation at all, a portent for the eventual abolition of that class entirely some years later). The new vehicles built at Swindon for the new 'Limited' service set new standards in passenger comfort, although they did attract their fair share of criticism at the time. The carriages were a new Churchward design, known as the 'Dreadnought' type; 70 feet in length, instead of the more common system of having a door for each compartment the new stock had one recessed door in the centre of each coach and a similar door at each end.

The Great Western considered this to be a 'novel' idea and thought that the corridors running on each side of the coach would allow the passenger to have a 'commanding' view of the side of the line.[48] Some passengers, however, complained that the congested nature of the corridors when trains arrived at a station meant that passengers trying to get out had to struggle past those trying to get in! Even the marking of doors with 'Entrance' and 'Exit' did not fully solve the problem, and by 1914 the stock had been replaced with new 'Toplight'-type stock.

Despite the complaints, the train was well fitted out; the first class sections were finished in American walnut, with dark green cloth upholstery in the non-smoking compartments and green morocco leather in the smoking compartment. In the third class, the passenger had to be content with polished oak fittings, with red and black cloth seats for the non-smokers, and red leather seats for the smokers. Class distinction was also reflected in the floor covering, with the first class having thick carpet, but the third 'Kork' matting; the train was fitted with Lucas 'Leitner' electric lighting throughout, the first complete train to be so fitted on the Great Western.

One of the narrow corridors of Churchward's carriages about which the public complained so bitterly!

The interior of a first class Dining Car, seen in 1914. There is much detail to absorb — all the silverware is emblazoned with the company's crest, and the menu is dated 14 February 1914. This picture was probably taken at a less than salubrious location, hence the whitewashed windows! (National Railway Museum, York)

A sumptuous Dining Car was also provided, again well equipped; the first class dining area was finished with sycamore panels, framed in American walnut. The tables, on which all manner of food was served, were inlaid with green morocco leather. The third class accommodation was by no means poor, with mahogany panelling. Thirty-two third and 18 first class seats were provided, with a kitchen between the two areas. A glance at one of the Great Western's timetables for 1908 may assist the reader in gauging the cost of a meal in these elegant surroundings. A five-course 'Table D'Hôte' dinner cost 3s 6d, four courses only 3 shillings; a liqueur coffee to finish the meal cost the passenger a further 3d. In the afternoon, when tea was being served, a pot of tea with cut bread and butter, jam and cake cost 9d, an additional portion of watercress and salad adding another 1 shilling to the bill.

The long non-stop journey made the Restaurant Car a busy place; records surviving for the later part of our 'Golden Age' show that, for the Great Western, providing this service could be particularly profitable too. The Restaurant Car Department kept detailed accounts which show that during the month of July 1912, for example, takings from the No 1 Dining Car of the 'Limited' were £337 for food and provisions, and £67 for wines, spirits and cigars; when compared with the expenditure for the same month, profits of nearly 60 per cent were made.[49] Even in the winter months, large

profits were still being made. The contemporary records show, however, that profits on other trains were much lower; on the 'Ocean Specials' being run from both Plymouth and Fishguard at this time, profits were nearer 30 per cent. Obviously each train had a different clientele and different needs.

The same statistics also show interestingly the expenses incurred by the Restaurant Car Department generally for that year. The highest cost was, not surprisingly, that of staff wages, amounting to over £12,000; board and lodging for staff on overnight or extended duties cost the company another £1,912. Two further expenses which were obviously very necessary were gas, for cooking, which cost £1,639, and laundry which, with the provision of clean napkins, tablecloths, towels and other items, was obviously an essential.

Passengers on the 'Limited' benefited from another new innovation, that of attendants employed to wait on them *en route*. The company reported that the 'ladies' attendant attired in distinctive costume of the type generally affected by nurses is available to look after children while their parents are at lunch, and generally wait on laidies'[50] There was also a gentlemen's attendant, who in addition had the rather less glamorous job of keeping the lavatories clean. The *Great Western Railway Magazine* reported the benefits of having such staff on the train in January 1909, when it cited the safe transit of a four-week-old baby from London to Plymouth. The child was an orphan, and was cared for on the journey by the lady attendant (it should also be noted that the GWR still charged half fare for the poor child!).[51]

On 21 July 1906, the 'Cornish Riviera Limited' began running via the Castle Cary and Langport line already described; with the start of this new regime the departure time of the train from Paddington was also altered, to the time which it retained for the rest of its life, 10.30 am. In 1923 the company was to issue a book about the express entitled *The 10.30 Limited*, immortalizing the departure time which became part of Great Western folklore. The popularity of the service also led to it being run all year round from 1906, and prompted the introduction of a large train with no fewer than three slip coaches. These vehicles were a particular feature of Great Western passenger working, and were fitted with their own independent braking system and an apparatus whereby the guard could release the coupling hook of the slip carriage as it neared its destination, allowing the coach to coast into the station under its own momentum whilst the main section of the train continued on its journey.

In normal working practice a Dining Car and five other coaches formed the Cornish section of the train, with separate coaches being

The 'old order' — an unidentified Dean 'single' on a down train near Teignmouth. (H. Gordon Tidey)

slipped at Westbury for Weymouth, at Taunton for Minehead, Ilfracombe and Barnstaple, and finally at Exeter for Teignmouth, Dawlish and other 'South Coast Watering Places'. When the train was relaunched in July 1906, it started with only two slip portions; the slip coach for Taunton was introduced some months later, in November 1906. Thus, even before the 'Limited' had made its first stop it had slipped at least three carriages, which must have been something of a record! The release of these carriages proportionately lessened the effects of the worsening gradients encountered by the train as it travelled further West, thus allowing the driver to maintain a 'mile a minute' schedule.

The opening of the shorter route reduced the distance between Paddington and Penzance to 226 miles, and the journey time was thus also reduced, to 6 hours 40 minutes. In general, the opening of the 21-mile 'cut-off' had a significant effect on train service times; the journey from Paddington to Taunton was 41 minutes quicker, Exeter some 21 minutes faster, and Weymouth 25 minutes nearer the capital.

In October of the same year a further five minutes was cut off the schedule, and by 1914, with improvements between Plymouth and Penzance complete, the journey was reduced further to 6½ hours.

For the comfort of passengers making this long journey, both rugs and pillows were available for hire at a cost of 6d per article from many of the principal stations on the company's lines. As was the practice in such matters, the Great Western issued a special ticket for

One of the last sections of the line to be doubled was that just outside Penzance itself. Two schoolboys stand grinning at the camera whilst the GWR locomotive hauls its train towards Plymouth.
(Brian Arman Collection)

This view of a Churchward 'Toplight' Saloon could have been taken during our 'Golden Age'; instead, a gloomy day on the Severn Valley Railway in February 1989 creates a period atmosphere.

the purpose. A GWR circular issued in the early years of the century noted that rugs were to be fastened with paper bands, and pillows to be kept in paper bags. Presumably some members of the public appreciated their comfortable GWR rugs so much that they did not return them, since the circular reminded staff to ensure that special steps were to be taken to return rugs and pillows to the issuing station after use![52]

In the summer of 1910, the Great Western introduced another named train to the timetables, known as the 'Devon and Cornwall Special'. This train was advertised to run on every Sunday in August and, apart from one down train, every Saturday in September, with extra trains on the Thursday and Friday of the Bank Holiday weekend. Leaving Paddington at 9.30 am, the down working ran non-stop to Newton Abbot, and called at many of the famous Cornish Riviera resorts including Lostwithiel, Looe, Newquay and Par before terminating at Falmouth at 4.05 pm. An up train left Penzance at 7.55 am, and arrived back in London at 3.42 pm. Like the 'Limited', seats could be booked in advance, and an additional feature was a 'bicycle van'. In order to bring their cycles, passengers paid an additional fare; in 1908, for example, it was 5 shillings for a bicycle and 7s 6d for a tricycle. The new express also had Dining and Tea Cars to provide sustenance for the long journey to and from the West.

In 1912 the company Directors authorized the construction of further stock for the 'Limited'. It was announced that 30 vehicles were to be built to form five new trains; each train would accommodate 352 passengers, and was to consist of 70-foot 'Toplight' carriages (the name of which arose from the distinctive glazed toplights above the windows). Yet again the standard of finish was extremely high; the first class accommodation was constructed in polished walnut and sycamore, and upholstered in green, whilst the third class had polished oak with red and blue 'rep' cloth seating.

Electrically lit, the standard of these vehicles showed the tremendous progress which had been made by the company over some 20 years. Although Great Western coaches had always been well constructed, in the space of two decades steam heating had replaced the antiquated and cumbersome footwarmers, and corridors allowed the free movement of passengers about trains, especially to the new Restaurant Cars, accessible to all classes of travellers. Writing in 1913, a correspondent of the *Great Western Railway Magazine* argued that the Great Western Express train could be likened to a first class hotel, with its 'long and handsomely equipped corridor carriages, its comfortable and well-lighted compartments, its flower-decked dining tables and excellent cuisine.'[53]

To sum up our survey of the Great Western's Riviera route, let us note the thoughts of W.J. Scott, an ardent supporter of the company in the 'Golden Age', who concluded that the 'Cornish Riviera' train, with its non-stop run, was 'the outcome of the spirit of going ahead, of working a railway as well as it can be worked for the benefit of the public, compatible with sound commercial principles'[54].

PART FOUR

THE SOUTH WALES MAIN LINE

THE development of the Great Western's route to Wales in the era before the First World War bears a strong resemblance to much to the company's work described elsewhere in this book, where it was striving hard to overcome problems generated in the Broad Gauge era in order to create a modern and efficient railway. This concept embraced not only the improvement of the railway's facilities in South Wales itself, but also involved the modernization of the lines feeding into the region.

One important difference in this section of our story, however, is that the Great Western did not have everything its own way in South Wales; on the contrary, it was only one of a series of railway concerns competing for traffic in what was probably one of the most densely packed rail networks in Great Britain. Unlike other areas where the GWR dominated, the railways of South Wales remained a collection of largely unconsolidated independent local companies which were fiercely competitive until they were finally absorbed by the Great Western with the creation of the 'Big Four' in 1923.

The reason for this complex and crowded rail network in South Wales was the area's enormous mineral wealth — specifically, the rich coal deposits found in the river valleys of the South Wales mountains. The Taff, Rhymney, Ely, Neath and other valleys echoed to the sound of coal mining and railways, the two partners inextricably linked. Other trades such as iron and steel also made the region one of the most important industrial centres in the country.

By 1900, the rail network in the region could be crudely divided as follows. Along the southern seaboard ran the Great Western's main line from Gloucester and the Severn Tunnel through Newport, Cardiff, and Swansea to south-west Wales. To the east, the London & North Western Railway shared another route with the GWR via Shrewsbury and Hereford to Newport. The LNWR and the Midland Railway also had two other routes into the region, north of the Heads of the Valleys. Contrasting with these trunk routes were a large number of smaller companies such as the Taff Vale and Rhymney Railways linking the valleys with coastal ports.

No 3410 Sydney *stands at Cardiff around 1912, possibly having brought an Ocean Special from Fishguard. Smaller 4-4-0 designs used for the hilly section to the West Wales port were changed at Cardiff for larger Churchward 4-6-0 designs.* (Alan Parrett Collection)

It could be argued that the actions of the Great Western in the 1830s had played an important role in determining the criss-cross nature of the rail network just described. The company strenuously supported the incorporation of the South Wales Railway, which in 1845 received Parliamentary assent to build up a railway from near Gloucester, running along the Severn estuary to Chepstow and Newport, and linking Cardiff, Bridgend, Port Talbot, Neath, Swansea and Llanelly, reaching westwards to Carmarthen, and terminating at Fishguard in Pembrokeshire. Pembroke Dock was also to be linked to the main line by a short branch.

Although ostensibly an independent company, one-fifth of the railway's capital had been provided by the GWR, which also had the power to nominate six Directors. What might have been an ideal arrangement soon deteriorated; the firm objective of the railway as far as the GWR was concerned was to link Paddington with Ireland via a port to be built at Fishguard, which, it was hoped, would be able to compete with the LNWR's Irish Sea crossing from Holyhead. By the end of the 1840s, however, the potato famine in Ireland, and other economic and political difficulties, led to the Fishguard scheme being abandoned. It would be some 50 years before the scheme envisaged by Brunel finally came to fruition.

Slow progress meant that the line from Chepstow to Swansea was not opened until June 1850, with extensions to Carmarthen, Haverfordwest and Neyland (known as New Milford) following in subsequent years.

What had a more lasting influence on the railway network in South Wales generally was the track gauge adopted by the South Wales Railway. Since Isambard Kingdom Brunel was the company's engineer, it naturally followed that the line would be constructed to the broad gauge. Well engineered though the line was, few other companies in the area followed suit, the largest to do so being the Vale of Neath Railway. The growth of the coal trade led to a host of other smaller railways being built to link the mines with the ports, but all of these were of standard gauge construction.

Although transhipment points were provided at all the GWR's major stations, coal producers were unwilling to use them, preferring to ship the coal direct to the ports where it could be distributed to the rest of the country by sea. The broad gauge network thus became rather isolated from the coal trade in general, and the disruption caused is illustrated by the fact that in 1866 over 250 South Wales traders petitioned the GWR against the continuing use of the gauge. The South Wales Railway was finally absorbed by the Great Western in 1863, and the broad gauge had gone by 1872, but by this time it was too late; the company's other competitors had capitalized on its misfortune.

The situation was helped somewhat by the absorption of some of the other companies into the Great Western network. The Vale of Neath, the Monmouthshire Railway and a number of other lines were acquired, allowing the GWR to gain a foothold in the region's rail network and, most importantly, the coal trade. The company's business in this area will be examined later in this part of the book.

THE BRISTOL &
SOUTH WALES
DIRECT RAILWAY

AS has already been intimated, the Great Western in its 'Great Awakening' had not only to improve its position in South Wales, but also needed to radically upgrade its route into the region. This became all the more important with the construction and promotion of the harbour at Fishguard, when the need for a fast direct route from the West Wales port to Paddington became most apparent.

Like the main line to the West of England, the Great Western's South Wales route before improvement was another illustration of the company's nickname, the 'Great Way Round'. Trains from Paddington made their way along Brunel's 'billiard table' line from the capital to Swindon where they then took the steeply graded Cheltenham & Great Western Union Railway from Swindon to Gloucester. From there the traveller took the route of the South Wales Railway, which has already been described, passing through most if not all of the largest and most important ports on the South Wales coast.

This rather circuitous journey was shortened in stages, not least by the opening of the Severn Tunnel in September 1886; the company also took over and modernized the Bristol & South Wales Union Railway which ran from the GWR main line at Bristol Temple Meads, through the northern outskirts of Bristol to Pilning, terminating at New Passage where a steamer hired by the railway ferried passengers to Portskewett on the Welsh side of the Severn. The B & SWUR was absorbed by the Great Western in 1868, and the construction of the Severn Tunnel led to the abandonment of the ferry link and the adaptation and doubling of the route, and completed just before the opening of the tunnel in 1886.[1]

The story of the momentous struggle to complete the Severn Tunnel has been told elsewhere, and strictly speaking occurred some years before the 'Golden Age' period we are chronicling; it goes without saying, however, that the completion of the project was one of the foundation stones of the company's success in the late Victorian and Edwardian era, and that with the shortened journey times that the tunnel could bring, it was clearly one of the most important locations on the Great Western Railway at that time. Considerable problems had been encountered in the construction of the tunnel with the river flooding the workings completely at one stage; to prevent this, a round-the-clock pumping operation was carried out to keep the $4\frac{1}{2}$-mile-long tunnel free of water.

Meticulous records kept for the period before the First World War vividly illustrate the scale of the problem. In 1910 a staggering total of 9,451 million gallons of water were pumped out of the various shafts of the tunnel, using 14 different bucket and plunger pumps. All this equipment was, of course, steam powered, and records show that in the same period exactly 18,633 tons of coal were consumed by the hungry pumping engines at Sudbrook and elsewhere. The weather and season obviously played an important part in determining the amount of water removed; in the summer months it could be some 600-700 million gallons of water per week, and in winter around 800 million gallons. The record daily total for the period was recorded on 15 February 1904 when 34.1 million gallons

Chippenham station in 1899. After the opening of the Severn Tunnel in 1886, many coal trains trundled through here on their way from South Wales to the capital. This rare view of the station with an overall roof was taken by the late Mr Stoker of Chippenham. (Courtesy Mr C. Blade)

The No 1 Pump House at Sudbrook seen in 1989. In the 'Golden Age' it was the home of six massive Cornish beam engines, which were replaced in 1961.

were pumped out of the tunnel in 24 hours.

Added to the expense of pumping, the Great Western also had to pay a considerable amount to keep the tunnel clear of smoke and steam by the use of a great ventilation fan, some 30 feet across. Needless to say, the fan was also steam powered, and consumed over 1,000 tons of coal in 1910, for example. All the same, the 'Big Hole', as it was known to railwaymen, was still not a pleasant place to travel through, particularly on a slow-moving freight train.

A large establishment of men was necessary to operate and maintain this important part of the Great Western network, with enginemen, firemen, boiler cleaners, pumpers, labourers and maintenance staff all contributing to the wage bill of £6,632 5s 2d in 1910. Altogether, the tunnel cost the Great Western nearly £16,000 to run that year, but it was a small price to pay for the benefits accrued by the convenience of the tunnel itself.[2]

We have already encountered several instances of the Great Western's thrifty habits in the course of this book, so the reader will not be surprised to find that the company was not content to see all this water going to waste. Contemporary archives show a proposed scale of quarterly charges for the sale of water to Newport Corporation. Various charges were listed, depending on the amount of water consumed; if the total did not exceed 800 million gallons per quarter, the charge would be one penny per thousand gallons, but if consumption reached 300 million gallons the rate dropped to one halfpenny per thousand gallons! It is not recorded whether the arrangement was actually entered into, although the clerk listing the charges had also helpfully calculated the profits the company might make; at the higher charge the GWR could hope to make £3,209 annual profit after expenses.[3]

In 1909 plans were advanced to build a signal box in the middle of the tunnel, between the two 1 in 100 gradients leading down from the English and Welsh sides. The idea had been tried in the Woodhead Tunnel in the north of England, and presumably the Great Western's Signal Department believed that the box would ease the passage of long trains through the 4-mile 28-chain bore. A company memorandum issued in November 1909 noted, however, the disadvantages of such a scheme; the primary problem was the dense, smoky atmosphere, which would mean signals could be missed, slowing down traffic and being a potential cause of accidents. It was also noted that extra catch points would be necessary to prevent breakaways, but perhaps the strongest argument came from engine drivers who, the memo continued, were confident that they could get from one end of the tunnel to the other in safety.[4]

The two existing signal boxes at either end of the tunnel were linked by a 'tell-tale' wire which, if broken, sounded an alarm — a crude but satisfactory method of communication in an emergency. This company, it seems, did not go ahead with the scheme, but one would imagine that the box would have been a nightmarish location in which to work, situated 30 feet or more under the Severn, and two miles from either portal!

Despite the opening and efficient operation of the Severn Tunnel by the Great Western, traders and industrialists were still far from happy with the arrangements for traffic from the Principality to London. Many people were also less than satisfied that trains for South Wales had to travel via Bath and Bristol which, bearing in mind the delays noted at Bristol in a previous section, was not a particularly rapid route. Such was the discontent that one group of businessmen supported a scheme to build an entirely new railway to London from South Wales, ignoring the Great Western completely.

Running from Cardiff, the proposed line was to cross the Severn on a massive 3,000-yard bridge, somewhere near the site of the present Severn Road Bridge at Aust. The entirely new railway would pass north of the Great Western's line, eventually joining the

Wootton Bassett was the new junction for the 'Badminton Line', as it became known; this postcard view was taken not long after the station was modernized. Closed in the 1960s, the western expansion of Swindon has led to calls for its reinstatement. (GWR Museum, Swindon)

Metropolitan Railway near Great Missenden in Buckinghamshire; yet another major terminus was to have been built in London as a result.

Alarm bells must have been ringing at Paddington, especially when a Bill for the railway was deposited with Parliament in 1895. However, England was spared yet another main line railway when the Great Western settled with the promoters of the scheme, and the Bill was dropped. Subsequently the company announced in the *Great Western Railway Magazine* for October 1895 that notice had been given in Parliament for a Bill to be debated in the next session.[5] This was for a new railway, known as the Bristol & South Wales Direct Railway, 29½ miles in length, leaving the old Bristol to London main line at Wootton Bassett, just west of Swindon.

The new works passed through a considerable number of parishes in Wiltshire and Gloucestershire before joining the Bristol & South Wales Union Railway at Patchway, north of Bristol. As well as the benefits to long-distance through traffic, the magazine concluded that the new line would 'traverse a rich agricultural and grazing district, and place a tract of country now unprovided with railway communication in direct connection with London, Bristol, Newport, Cardiff and other important centres'[6]. The *Bath Chronicle*, reporting the new scheme, rather more pointedly noted that 'the line would be a great convenience in working the heavy goods traffic to South Wales'. Thus, once completed, long coal trains would not have to slowly trundle along Brunel's old main line on their tortuous journey from the coalfields to London.

The completion of the line straddled the Victorian and Edwardian eras. Parliamentary assent was given to the Bristol & South Wales Direct Railway Bill in 1896, and initially the capital was listed as being £800,000, although this total was to rise to over a million pounds as construction continued.[7] As was the case in many railways, a ceremonial cutting of the first sod took place, on 29 November 1897, when the Duchess of Beaufort carried out the task in a field near Old Sodbury.

Thirty-four miles in length, the scheme involved a great deal of heavy civil engineering work, perhaps the most significant item being the excavation of Sodbury Tunnel at the Bristol end of the line. Here the railway cut through the Cotswolds and over 4,000 men were employed to drive seven shafts from ground level to the tunnel base. Headings were then excavated to join up the various shafts; a number of these shafts were retained for ventilation, with the addition of ornamental turrets. A further expense involved the lining of the inside of the 2½-mile tunnel with a staggering 50 million brindle bricks, made both on site and at the local Cattybrook Brickworks.

To the west of the tunnel, a deep cutting had also to be excavated

One of the ventilation towers of Chipping Sodbury tunnel. The Act of Parliament forced the company to built the chimneys with crenellations, giving the effect of a series of small castles across the landscape.

through the hard local Pennant Sandstone; the spoil was not wasted, however, being re-used in embankments elsewhere on the railway. The largest of these was at Somerford, where the embankment was four miles in length, the longest on the line. Not far from Somerford a large depot was set up by the contractors, where many of the construction workers were housed. Presumably the behaviour of the men was not as bad as that of navvies in earlier times, although a mission and reading room were provided for their spiritual and moral benefit!

The line was fully opened to both passenger and goods traffic on 1 July 1903, with seven stations built to Great Western standard designs of the period. The four stations at Brinkworth, Hullavington, Coalpit Heath and Winterbourne had smaller buildings compared with their larger counterparts at Badminton, Little Somerford and Chipping Sodbury. All the larger stations shared the same track layout, consisting of four tracks, with the up and down platforms being served by loops; this allowed non-stop express services to pass unhindered through the station. The buildings were attractively built in red brick, with window sills, plinths and chimneys decorated in contrasting blue brick. The design was completed by the use of a distinctive awning common to all stations.

The line passed through the heart of rich farmland owned by the Duke of Beaufort, and at Badminton station this fact was

Badminton, as seen in the 1906 edition of Holiday Haunts; *the arrangement of platform loop lines can be clearly seen.* (Great Western Trust)

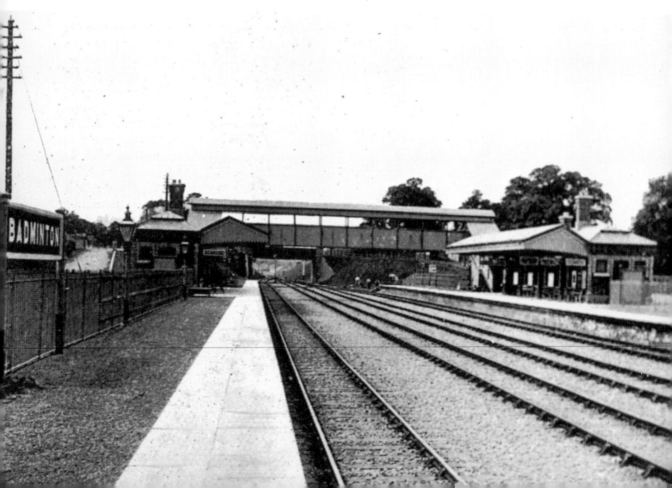

One of the smaller stations, Brinkworth, in British Rail days. (Michael Wyatt Collection)

commemorated by the Duke's coat of arms being set in stone on the up station building. One result of the railway being allowed through the Beaufort estate was that this station was the last to close; objections from the Duke led to Badminton staying open for passenger traffic some seven years longer than other stations on the line, before it too closed in 1968. One final distinctive feature of the station was a cast iron notice, now in the Great Western Society collection at Didcot, which warned locomotive drivers to beware to the foxhounds of the Beaufort Hunt; all efforts were to be made to avoid running them down, and incurring His Lordship's wrath!

From the description given in the last few paragraphs, the reader will have realized that this was a fairly expensive 'shortcut'. However, although it may have been costly to construct, the benefits of the 'Badminton Line', as it became known, soon became apparent; the Company Chairman, Earl Cawdor, reporting the opening of the line at the Great Western halfyearly meeting in February 1904, reminded shareholders that the most important benefits were to be accrued in the working of goods traffic; the expensive earthworks had enabled the line to be laid out with gentle curves and gradients no steeper than 1 in 300, which was then the most severe gradient between Filton and London.[8] All this was a distinct improvement on the steep 1 in 100 inclines at Box and Wootton Bassett on the old line, which had made goods working so difficult.

Additionally, the introduction of more powerful freight locomotives by G.J. Churchward meant that longer trains could be run. In a 1908 booklet issued jointly by Churchward and the Superintendent of the Line, Mr. Morris, maximum loads of engines working goods trains were stipulated.[9] The differences between the old and new routes show themselves particularly in the London-bound direction. With a Churchward '28xx' 2–8–0 locomotive hauling the train, a maximum of 63 loaded coal wagons could be hauled via Bath, as compared to 72 on the South Wales Direct line. An important footnote in the booklet regarding the old Bristol-Swindon route added that banking assistance was necessary on the Box and Wootton Bassett inclines.

As well as the benefits of more efficient freight working, the new direct line also had the very tangible advantage of cutting the distance between Paddington and Newport to 133 miles, which was an improvement of ten miles over the congested route via Bath, and some 25 miles shorter than via Gloucester. Clearly this was a very real step in ridding the Great Western of the 'Great Way Round' tag.

When Parliamentary permission was gained to build the line, agreement was also made with the Midland Railway to provide a connection to its Yate-Stonehouse line, allowing the GWR to have use of the Severn Bridge at Sharpness should the Severn Tunnel be blocked for any reason. In 1910 the important trade from Bristol's Avonmouth Docks was linked to both the Badminton Line and the line to Birmingham and the north by the opening of the Stoke Gifford Direct line, allowing both fast freight and 'Ocean Mail' specials to be run from the port direct to London.

DEVELOPMENT IN SOUTH WALES: 'KING COAL'

IN the early part of the twentieth century, one observer, commenting on the Great Western's policy in South Wales, noted that in building a high-speed link between the capital and the principality, it was noticeable that there was little commercial development of any significance in between. There was some light industrial activity in Reading and Chippenham, but little else. The speaker went on to add wryly that he was glad that the GWR company dividend did not depend on these areas for profit![10]

Certainly, as the Edwardian passenger travelling from Paddington to South Wales emerged from the smoky depths of the Severn Tunnel, it was not until the outskirts of Newport that he would have been aware that he was entering one of the most highly industrialized and prosperous districts in the country. The development of the South Wales coalfield had progressed at a phenomenal rate since the discovery of rich seams of coal in the eighteenth century; by the beginning of the twentieth century the coalfield itself extended from western Monmouthshire across a thousand-square-mile production zone to Carmarthenshire in west Wales.

The coal itself was not of a uniform type or quality; there were distinctly different deposits of bituminous, smokeless, steam and anthracite coal found at various locations over the 100-mile-long production area. It was no wonder that the Great Western was keen to spend money developing its network in South Wales; there were well over 200 collieries in the coalfield, employing over 200,000 men. In 1911 this workforce helped extract over 50 million tons of coal, which was at that time more than 18% per cent of the United Kingdom's output. Well over half of this amount, nearly 31 million tons, was exported from South Wales docks, and thus had to be transported from pit to port.

As we have already noted, the Great Western itself did not have a dominating influence in South Wales; its main line ran firmly across the southern shore of the area, but in many places traffic was handled by small independent companies like the Taff Vale and Rhymney Railways. The company itself was forced to admit that it was not in a

An advertisement from Holiday Haunts *showing where luncheon and tea baskets could be obtained. A number of stations on the South Wales main line are included.* (Great Western Trust)

LUNCHEON & TEA BASKETS

EN ROUTE.

For the convenience of Passengers, Baskets containing HOT or COLD LUNCHEONS, or TEA, can be obtained at the Refreshment Rooms, at the following Stations, on notice being given to the Guard. The notice should, as far as possible, be given at a preceding stopping Station:—

Bath	Neath	Shrewsbury
Birmingham (Snow Hill)	Newport	Swindon
Bristol (Temple Meads)	*Newton Abbot	Taunton
Cardiff	Oxford	*Tenby
Chester	Paddington	Trowbridge
Exeter (St. David's)	Plymouth (Millbay)	*Truro
Gloucester	Plymouth (North Road)	Westbury (Wilts.)
Hereford	*Pontypool Road	Wolverhampton
*Leamington	Reading	Worcester (Shrub Hill)

* Hot Luncheons are not supplied at these Stations.

Hot Luncheon, 2/6—Steak or Chop, with Vegetables, Bread, Cheese and Butter. Wines, &c., extra.

Cold Luncheon, 2/6—Chicken, with Ham or Tongue; or Cold Meat, Bread, Cheese and Butter. Wines, &c., extra.

Tea Baskets.—Pot of Tea or Coffee, Bread and Butter, Cake or Bun. Basket for One Person, 1/-; Two Persons, 1/6.

N.B.—Orders for Hot Luncheons should be given to the Guard at least an hour before required.

Although strictly speaking just outside the 'Golden Age' period, this poster nevertheless graphically illustrates the problems which the sheer numbers of coal wagons in South Wales brought. (GWR Museum Collection)

£7 10s. REWARD

MISSING

NINE 8-TON

COAL WAGONS

Owners' Plate Numbers	-	33311	33315	33316
Paint Numbers	-	246	248	252
Owners' Plate Numbers	-	33322	36411	33327
Paint Numbers	-	701	702	706
Owners' Plate Numbers	-	33332	33336	33326
Paint Numbers	-	707	708	709

These Wagons were Marked **J. M. Haime, Cardiff**

The above Wagons are the Property of the NORTH CENTRAL WAGON COMPANY, ROTHERHAM.

Any person giving information to the said Company, or to B. WATSON, 55, Adam Street, Cardiff, so that the said North Central Wagon Co. may recover the above Wagons, will be paid the Reward of Ten Shillings for each Wagon found.

E. BALL, Secretary, North Central Wagon Company, Rotherham.

ALSO SIX 8-TON

COAL WAGONS

Owners' Plate Numbers	-	27367	27371	27375
Paint Numbers	-	63	132	133
Owners' Plate Numbers	-	27376	27377	27378
Paint Numbers	-	134	98	86

These Wagons were Marked **J. M. Haime, Cardiff**

The above Wagons are the Property of the SCOTTISH WAGON COMPANY, EDINBURGH. Any person giving information to the said Company, or to B. Watson, 55, Adam Street, Cardiff, so that the said Scottish Wagon Company may recover the above Wagons, will be paid the Reward of Ten Shillings for each Wagon found.

H. H. HORSFIELD, Secretary, Scottish Wagon Company, St. Andrew Place, Edinburgh.

February 10th, 1888.   WOOD & SON.

position of overall pre-eminence; speaking in 1912, W.S. Parnell argued that although the Great Western had 'played an important role in the development of the South Wales coalfield, we cannot say that we were the pioneers'. Where the company had taken over or absorbed smaller railways in the period before the First World War, its position was better; thus it had the principal share of bituminous and steam coal from the Monmouthshire valleys, the Aberdare, Merthyr, Llynvi and Ogmore and Gilfach districts, as well as the Ely valley. As far as the anthracite and semi-anthracite coals were concerned, the company had influence in the Neath, Llanelly and Amman, and Gwendraeth valleys.

West of Newport and Abergavenny, the Great Western's mileage of running lines amounted to approximately 700, divided almost equally between single and double or quadruple lines. With the addition of relief lines, sidings and other goods facilities, that total almost doubled. Despite therefore having over 1,000 miles of track in South Wales, some statistics might help put the company's operation in the coalfield into perspective. In 1910 the Great Western carried over $18\frac{1}{2}$ million tons of coal over its system, of which $15\frac{3}{4}$ million tons was mined in South Wales.[11] This figure should, however, be compared with the amount carried by the Taff Vale Railway in the same year. This very much smaller operation carried over 18 million tons of coal to the docks for export.

Similarly, although the Great Western had running powers and access to the majority of ports and docks in the South Wales area, it did not have a dominating influence in any one major location.

Many of the smaller independent railway companies had themselves started as dock concerns, and in many cases the Great Western shared facilities with other railways. At Cardiff, for example, the docks were host to the Great Western, Taff Vale, Rhymney, Barry, Cardiff and London & North Western Railway companies!

Although perhaps not in such a strong position as it could have been, the Great Western was nevertheless ruthlessly determined to maintain the traffic it had. In 1905 the Barry Railway deposited a Bill before Parliament proposing a number of lines which would give it access to the Sirhowy Valley, a Great Western stronghold. At the Parliamentary hearing, powerful allies of the company gave evidence on its behalf and, after several days, the Bill was thrown out.

In a company publication of 1907, approximately 340 collieries were listed as being on lines operated by the Great Western Railway, with the vast majority being situated in South Wales.[12] The railway did, of course, also serve collieries in North Wales, Shropshire, South Staffordshire and Worcestershire, as well as the smaller Somerset coalfield, including five pits in Bristol itself. As well as listing collieries in both the eastern and western valleys of Monmouthshire, and those further west, the book does underline the point already made by including a further substantial list of mines on

Alexandra Docks, Newport. This postcard view clearly shows the way in which coal was tipped directly from rail wagons into the ship.

Alexandra Dock, Newport.

A Train of 25 G.W.R. 20-Ton Coal Wagons. Length 612 feet. Capacity 500 Tons.

A Train of 50 Mixed Wagons (12 and 10 tons, and under). Length 1,009 feet. Capacity 500 Tons.

A comparison of the new and old methods of carrying coal. (Great Western Railway Magazine)

the lines of other companies such as the Brecon & Merthyr, Neath & Brecon, Rhymney, Burry Port & Gwendreath Valley and Lllanelly & Mynnyd Mawr Railways.

The GWR spent a substantial amount of time and effort in ensuring the efficient operation of its coal traffic in South Wales. Since many collieries were situated in narrow valleys, siding space was usually at a premium. Once coal was mined, graded, weighed and loaded into rail wagons, the company had to shift it quickly from the mine to the nearest port or marshalling yard for transport elsewhere. If not, sidings and yards at collieries could easily become clogged, with the consequent effect of causing work at the mine to cease.

As the reader can imagine, in a busy mining district the variations in day-to-day traffic must have been phenomenal; differing rates of demand for and production of coal made timetabling a problematical proposition. In an attempt to coordinate what was an extremely complex operation, the company introduced a 'Train Control System' in the Monmouthshire section. In the area of both the eastern and western valleys, including collieries and other industrial concerns in the Blaenavon, Abersycan, Ebbw Vale, Aberbeeg and Risca districts, traffic could vary significantly from one month to another; in a lecture to the GWR Lecture and Debating Society in 1911, E.S. Hadley quoted an instance when traffic had increased by over 92,000 tons in one week.[13] It was new technology, in the form of telephones, which allowed this Great Western innovation to be successful; controllers in Newport kept in close touch with railway depots, colliery owners and dock authorities, allowing coal to be moved at the right time, and making far better use of both the lines themselves, since there was less congestion, and the motive power. For the Company Accountant, always keen to see economy practised, this was a useful innovation!

What is perhaps also important in this discussion of coal traffic is to point out that in the 'Golden Age' far more importance was being attached to freight traffic in general. Some idea of the change in attitude of the company may be gauged by first noting the comments of Henry Lambert, General Manager in 1895. At the International Railway Congress held in London in June and July of that year, he reported that after examining data given to him by 20 of the largest railways in Britain, the most economical working of goods trains was obtained at the slowest speeds, 10 mph for coal or mineral trains, 16 mph for other goods, and 23 mph for perishable traffic.[14]

This statement is perhaps typical of Great Western and other railway company attitudes of the time; however, the new spirit of

A GWR cast iron notice typifying the era before continuous braking. At the point marked by the sign, the guard would have to pin down wagon brakes before descending an incline.

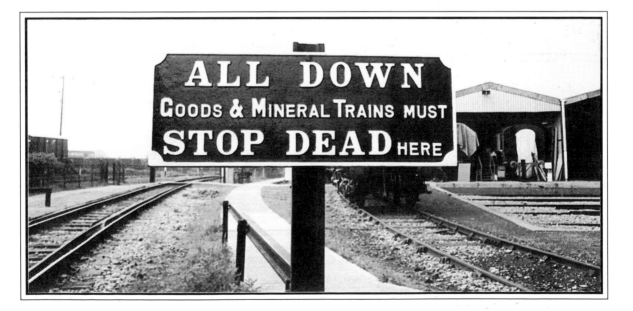

Another 'period piece', a '2301' 'Dean Goods' locomotive, seen at Cardiff around 1912. Before the introduction of Churchward's standard classes, these engines were the mainstay of the company's goods and coal traffic. This example is in sparkling condition — note the reflection of the spectacle plate on the boiler. (Alan Parrett Collection)

enterprise flowing through the GWR meant that it would change. There were, though, formidable obstacles to be overcome, one of the biggest being that a large number of wagons used by the railway companies in South Wales to transport coal were old and their axle boxes were lubricated by grease which had a tendency to overheat at faster speeds, so that every 40 miles or so stops had to be made for examination.

The use of continuously braked 'fitted' trains was at first rare; most wagons still possessed the old-fashioned lever brakes which had to be manually pinned down by the guard when gradients of any ferocity were reached. Since many of the wagons used by the GWR were actually owned by the collieries themselves, the company found great difficulty in persuading the mine owners to buy new rolling-stock, a problem which persisted well after the First World War.

The introduction of larger and more modern freight locomotives assisted in increasing economies. Larger trains could be run, and as a result the mileage actually run by freight trains decreased steadily in the 'Golden Age'. In 1905, Board of Trade figures for the Great Western revealed that the company's goods trains had run 155,200,000 miles in the previous year, a decrease of 4.2 per cent over the year before.[15] In the period before the Great War, these figures continued to decrease, as the company's goods operation became more efficient.

This is not the place to provide the reader with a detailed account of the improved locomotives introduced by both Dean and Churchward in the period before 1914; more specialized books on this subject are listed in the Bibliography. However, one or two general points can be made; over the period the smaller, mainly 0-6-0 types such as the '2301' 'Dean Goods' engines were replaced by larger, more powerful locomotives. By the First World War, much of the traffic handled by the Great Western in the valleys was tackled by Churchward '3100' 2-6-2 tank locomotives, which were supplemented by the more powerful '4200' 2-8-0 tanks. Commenting on their introduction in 1912, The *Great Western Railway Magazine* noted that the locomotives had been put into service in the Llanelly and Swansea district where traffic was most congested.[16] The article went on to conclude that 'gratifying results' had followed their introduction since they were capable of taking double the load of the ordinary 0-6-0 type previously in service.

The use of the 2-8-0 wheel arrangement for a tank locomotive was fairly unusual, but the class proved to be very useful for short-distance work in the valleys of South Wales to the extent that some 40 examples had been built by 1914.

Considerable attention was paid not only to the tractive effort of such engines, but also their braking power; when taking coal trains from the collieries to the docks, locomotives were for a large part of their journey running downhill, thus good brakes were a must! Returning to the collieries, the trains were somewhat less heavy, consisting principally of empty wagons.

It is difficult to describe the locomotives of the '4200' Class as beautiful, but the sheer power and sense of purpose evident in their design is most apparent. (GWR Museum, Swindon)

FROM THE
CRUMLIN VALLEY COLLIERIES Ltd.,
HAFODYRYNYS, Near PONTYPOOL.

FIBROUS RAINPROOF PAPER LABEL, HUGHES, PONTYPOOL.

TO THE

Great Western Railway
LOCO. DEPT.

Truck Number *559*   Weight *9 : 15*

The GWR also shipped coal to its own locomotive depots; this 1914 label was consigned to Worcester shed. (GWR Museum, Swindon)

A postcard view of one of Churchward's masterpieces, the '28xx' 2-8-0. No 2851 is seen at an unidentified location.

Attempts were also made during the period to speed up freight working. Elsewhere on the system, fast vacuum-braked good trains carrying perishable produce were introduced, and much importance was attached to the rapid transport of coal from South Wales to London and other parts of the Great Western system. In the period between 1900 and 1908, freight train mileage dropped by 14 per cent but trains loads increased by 35 per cent; this was due in no small way to the introduction of larger improved freight engines.

William Dean had begun the process with experimental 4-6-0 tender locomotive No 36, nicknamed the 'Crocodile'. Fitted with 4 ft 7½ in driving wheels and outside frames, this rather ungainly-looking engine was introduced in 1896 and, despite proving its success in hauling large coal trains from south Wales to Swindon via the Severn Tunnel, was scrapped in 1905.

Three years after the introduction of the 'Crocodile', another heavy goods prototype was outshopped from Swindon; this too was a 4-6-0 with outside frames and 4 ft 7½ in wheels, but it was fitted with a domeless boiler and a Belpaire firebox. Whereas No 36 was ungainly, the 'Kruger' design (named after the South African General in the Boer War campaign) was plain ugly; the effect was compounded by a strange sandbox, in the form of a saddle, resting on the top of the boiler near the front of the engine. Another of these engines was turned out by Swindon in 1901 and was promptly nicknamed 'Mrs Kruger' by the Swindon workforce. Two years later eight further locomotives were built for use on the South Wales coal

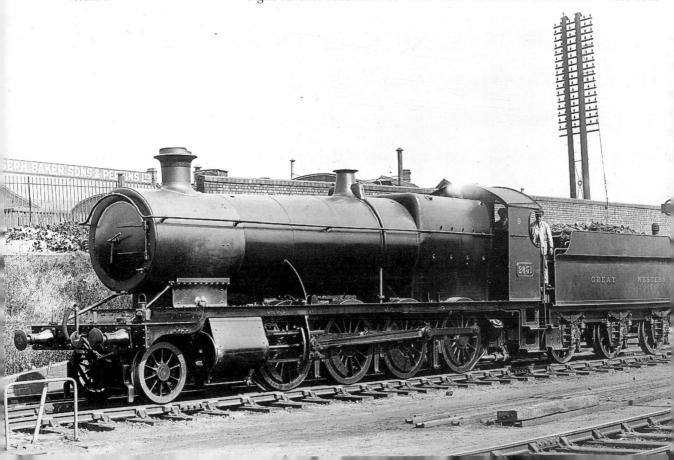

A 100-wagon train assembled at Acton to test another example of the '28xx' Class in 1913. (Swindon Reference Library)

THE MIDDAY
IN DON TO OLD OAK
DS, COMPOSED OF
WAGONS OF
AL, WAS CALLED
NG TOM" RAN
TIL THE START
WORLD WAR II.
H "2800" CLASS
ENGINE.

trains, but they were never popular with Great Western footplatemen.

Unlike the first 'Kruger', No 2601, the remaining engines in the class were built as 2-6-0s, and it was this wheel arrangement which was used for a rather more successful design turned out of Swindon in 1900 and 1901. These were known as 'Aberdares' and, unlike the largely experimental locomotives just described, were based on more successful Dean designs, namely the 'Atbara' and 'Badminton' types. One can perhaps detect more of the influence of Churchward in this type than in the 'Krugers'. The name of the class betrayed the area in which the locomotives were to do much good work, and an initial batch of 20 was built in 1901 with the total eventually rising to 80 in all.

In 1903 a further development of the Great Western heavy freight locomotive emerged from Swindon, with the construction of the prototype 2-8-0 No 97, later renumbered 2800. This two-cylinder Churchward design had the standard 4 ft 7½ in driving wheels, and its success led to the construction of 55 further examples of the class before the First World War. The design proved so successful that

The company's station at Newport, seen in 1913; also seen is a superb selection of enamel advertising signs. (National Railway Museum, York)

with only a few changes, the Great Western was still building engines of this type in 1941!

For many years this class was principally used on coal traffic, and numerous examples were allocated to the sheds at Severn Tunnel Junction, Pontypool Road, and Aberdare and Llanelly. To balance return workings to Wales, further engines were kept at Old Oak Common, Bristol and Oxley. Their power and reliability was appreciated by company officials and enginemen alike, and they were capable of hauling enormous trains by the standards of the day. By 1907 the *Great Western Railway Magazine* was able to report that a considerable number of these engines were in service, and that on one test, a train of 120 wagons was hauled from Swindon to Acton at an average speed of over 30 mph. A further more testing duty for one engine was to haul 24 wagons and a brake van up the Gowerton Incline near Swansea; the 385-ton load was hauled up the $2\frac{1}{2}$-mile

1 in 50 gradient at an average speed of 12.5 mph, which the magazine regarded as 'a highly creditable performance'[17].

In a statement sent to Mr J.B. Grant, the Parliamentary Engineer, in May 1907, G.J. Churchward stated that engines of the 2–8–0 type were capable of hauling trains 20 per cent heavier than those of the 2–6–0 'Aberdare' and 'Kruger' designs.[18] Despite the improved motive power, goods train working could still be slow; on busy lines, long freight trains were often shunted into lay-by sidings so as not to obstruct the passage of express services, and many long-distance coal trains were run during the hours of darkness. An additional factor was that the long trains made possible by these new more powerful locomotives could often not be fitted into the siding space available; thus much wasted time was spent in marshalling and remarshalling trains in traffic.

Whilst it did not come to dominate totally in South Wales until after the Grouping in the 1920s, the Great Western made strenuous efforts to help attract other business to the area; this was particularly true in Newport, and in an article written in 1906, H. Aldridge argued that the continued development of the town was largely due to the company — 'Trade follows Rail'[19]. With a population of 100,000 at the beginning of the twentieth century, Newport, as well as being close to the coalfields of the Monmouthshire valleys, was also host to other heavy engineering concerns, including steel, tinplate, tubemaking and copper smelting works, as well as shipbuilding yards and sawmills.

Various attempts were made by the company to attract firms from other parts of the country to relocate in the area; one such advertisement appeared in the publication on collieries served by the GWR referred to earlier. The company boasted that adjoining its system there were 'in various localities considerable areas of land admirably suited for the erection of works, factories, warehouses and other industrial undertakings'. The most obvious way that the Great Western could benefit from such relocation was to 'enter into arrangements for sidings or connections to be made with the railway'[20]. This it did all over South Wales, and indeed elsewhere on the network, and the private sidings proved a good source of income.

Bearing in mind the kind of depressing landscape created by the heavy industry just described, it was not surprising that the Great Western encouraged its staff to try to maintain stations in these areas in the best order possible. One incentive was a competition for the best-kept station garden, and each year over 400 stations competed. Although many prizes were won each year by staff in the more picturesque parts of the system such as Somerset, Devon and Cornwall, stations in the industrialized South Wales coalfield were also often prize winners. In 1908, for example, a special £5 prize was won by Pontllanfraith station in Ebbw Vale. A circular issued in 1913 by the company noted that 'it is particularly desired to impress on members of staff in mining or manufacturing districts the desirability of establishing and maintaining gardens, which, if properly attended to would not fail to be a distinct improvement...contrasting with, and the more appreciated because of the unattractive surroundings which are often a feature of such districts'[21].

THE LABOUR PROBLEM

IN South Wales, the proximity of both coal mining and railways gave the area a background of industrial and political strife throughout the period we are examining, so it is perhaps right that we should choose this particular point in the book to briefly examine relations between the Great Western and its workforce generally.

In the period 1895-1914, great social and political changes took place, and particularly after the death of Queen Victoria the old order was threatened. One reason for the widespread unrest and increased trade union activity in the years before the First World War was that in real terms the value of wages of groups like railwaymen, engineering and building workers actually fell in relation to prices. Also importantly, relations between employee and employer which had existed in the Victorian era began to change quite rapidly; it is probably true to say that in the 'Golden Age' the relationship between the public and the workforce was better than that between the railway companies and their staff.

In very general terms, the Great Western's attitude to its staff was one of autocracy tempered by paternalism; we have already seen some aspects of this in our survey of Swindon in the years before the Great War. However, as time went on the workforce was less inclined to accept company directives without question. Two major issues dominated industrial relations at this time, namely staff hours and conditions of work, and trade union recognition; both were eventually to lead to serious industrial unrest culminating in a strike in 1911.

A job on the Great Western in the period we are describing was not without its advantages; by the standards of the day wages were reasonable, particularly when compared to those of agricultural labourers, for example. One other advantage of railway work was job security; by and large, providing a man was reliable and honest he was guaranteed a job for life. Life on the railway was hard, however, particularly for certain groups; one particular grievance was that of the long hours worked by some workers, especially guards.

A typical track maintenance gang of the period. Despite job security, life on the railway was hard work for many, and it seems to be etched into the faces of those in this picture. (National Railway Museum, York)

In 1899 a deputation of goods guards had travelled to Paddington to meet Earl Cawdor, the Company Chairman, in support of a call to the company for shorter hours and other changed conditions of service. On this occasion the workforce was indeed fortunate, for the Board agreed to reduce the standard hours of duty for guards from 66 hours to 60 hours per week. The deputation did not, however, leave without being lectured by the Chairman that 'The Company's Goods Guards enjoyed many advantages, and there were always many who were anxious to fill such posts'[22].

Much debate continued over the long hours worked, and there was widespread public concern after various accidents in other parts of the country. Some years earlier, a Board of Trade Inspector had noted that 'the hours of work of men responsible for the safe working of trains are habitually excessive'. One stronger comment was that 'Railway lines are worked with insufficient staff, with systematic overwork indistinguishable from white slavery'[23]. This may have been exaggerating the point somewhat, but in 1906 the company was forced to comment further on the issue, arguing that it was difficult to equate the hours of duty of railway servants to the daily variations in traffic which could be caused by abnormal weather, additional business, or delay. It further added that the size of the Great Western system made the maintenance of 'clock-like working…a task of difficulty and magnitude'[24]. Whilst these were reasonable points, many critics of the company argued that many instances of excessive hours being worked by men were caused by the company's refusal to employ relief staff to cover for just such eventualities as bad weather or delays. Indeed, in 1908 the Great Western acknowledged that such a system was a costly proposition.

Some concern was also felt over the safety of railway servants. Certain groups of railwaymen seemed to be more at risk, particularly those involved in shunting and rolling-stock movement. In 1911 it was calculated that the chances of a Great Western employee being killed whilst in the company's service were 1 in 93,994 train miles. Over the period 1906 to 1911, 174 Great Western employees were

An interesting letter thanking a locoman for averting a potential disaster on the South Wales main line.

> **Great Western Railway.**
> *Locomotive & Carriage Department.*
> *Engineer's Office.*
> Swindon, 19th Dec 1901
> WILTS
>
> LETTER OF COMMENDATION.
>
> *Accident on Pyle Bank*
> *30th September 1901*
>
> This case was enquired into by the Directors on the 13th ultimo and they desired that their commendation should *together with a gratuity of a guinea* be conveyed to you, for your prompt and judicious action on the 30th September last when, shortly after passing Pyle Sand Siding, your train (the 5.50 am Goods ex Gloucester to Landore) parted, & the tail end got foul of the Up line, whereupon you took steps to warn the Engineman of an approaching Up train of the obstruction
>
> Engineman W. Cooke,
> Gloucester

A page from the 'Safety Movement' booklet.

killed whilst on duty, and 2,502 were seriously injured. The GWR was concerned about these figures, and set about improving them by launching a 'Safety First' campaign, in which each employee was given a booklet showing dangerous practices, coupled with articles in the *Great Western Railway Magazine* on the same subject. It was calculated that around 5 per cent of accidents were caused by faulty equipment, and that large numbers of accidents were caused by human error. Lecturing at Paddington in 1912, H.D. Anderson argued that 'a large proportion of the personal injury cases now occurring might be avoided by the excerise of greater care, and the stricter observance of regulations framed in the interest of safety'[25].

Perhaps the most important labour relations issue in this period was the rights of trade unions to represent the workforce on just the sort of matters described in the last few paragraphs. The Great Western, along with other railway companies, resolutely refused to deal directly with trade unions, although workers were allowed to be members of a union.

This had not always been the case, though; in 1865 the 'Railway Working Mens Provident Benefit Society', an early union started by Great Western Railway guards, had been crushed by the wholesale dismissal of its leading members. The first real railway union was ASRS (the Association of Railway Servants) which was set up in 1871. A typical example of railway company attitudes to trade unions was shown in 1892, when a report was compiled by Mr Richard Channing MP for the 'Select Committee of the House of Commons on Railway Servants (Hours of Labour)'. In Sir George Finlay's opinion, 'you might as well have a trade union or amalgamated society in the army, where discipline had to be kept at a very high standard, as have it on railways'[26]. Amazingly some employees were actually dismissed for giving evidence to the committee, but when word of this became public, the Directors of the companies concerned (not the Great Western as far as the author can ascertain) were summoned to the House of Commons and severely admonished.

Railway employers generally felt themselves to be in a strong position, particularly after the events of the 'Taff Vale Case' in 1900, when the sacking of a signalman in Aberdare had led to a fortnight-long strike by other employees of the Taff Vale Railway. The ASRS, who had supported the strike, was sued by the company for damages. The Taff Vale won the case, and the Union was forced to pay £23,000 damages. To the railway companies, this ruling was seen as a tremendous victory, although in the long term it had more serious consequences, since it caused many unions to ally themselves more closely to the fledgling Socialist movement, which was gaining strength at this time. Matters were compounded by the 'Labour Representation Committee', which was formed in the same year as the 'Taff Vale Case'. This grouping was a coalition of the Independent Labour Party, the Fabian Society and the Social

Democratic Federation, and, joining together with trade unions, eventually became the Labour Party in 1906.

Events came to a head with the 'All Grades' movement in 1906 and 1907, by which attempts were made by the unions to reduce the deep-rooted idea of railwaymen's grade snobbishness; demands were made for a standard eight-hour day for railwaymen engaged in 'the manipulation of traffic', and a maximum ten-hour day for all railway workers, excluding, for some reason, platelayers. The Great Western, in a later publication, noted in 1906 that there had been considerable unrest among 'certain classes' of railwaymen; despite the demands already mentioned, what was really at the heart of the discontent was the problem of union recognition. At the National Conference of the ASRS in November of that year, a new programme of action was put forward.

The programme was forwarded to the railway companies by Richard Bell, the Union's Secretary, with the request that the companies should meet a deputation. In common with all other companies, the Great Western refused to meet with the trade unions. In the *Great Western Railway Magazine* for September 1907, the company made its position clear. In coming to its decision 'after very careful consideration', it had been influenced by the fact that the ASRS had stated that it had no wish to interfere in the management of the railway; in this, the GWR noted, 'practice did not accord with theory'[27].

The famous 'Taff Vale cheque', which was written to pay damages to the TVR after the 1900 rail strike. (NUR)

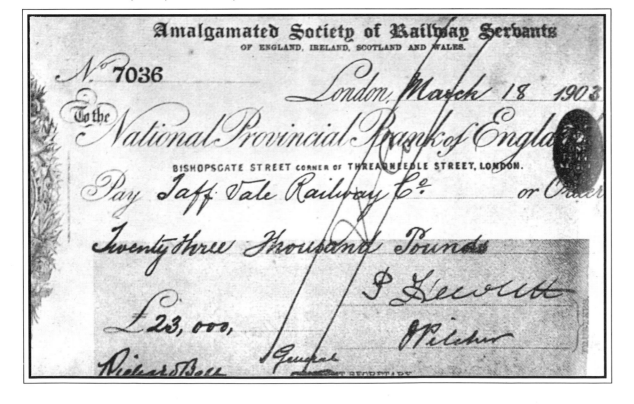

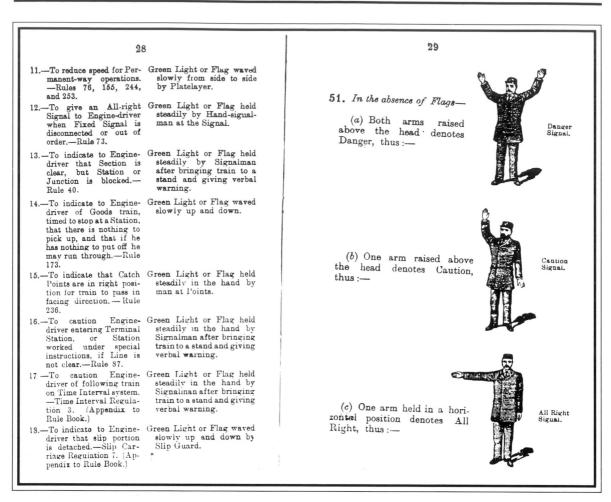

28

11.—To reduce speed for Permanent-way operations.—Rules 76, 155, 244, and 253. | Green Light or Flag waved slowly from side to side by Platelayer.

12.—To give an All-right Signal to Engine-driver when Fixed Signal is disconnected or out of order.—Rule 73. | Green Light or Flag held steadily by Hand-signalman at the Signal.

13.—To indicate to Engine-driver that Section is clear, but Station or Junction is blocked.—Rule 40. | Green Light or Flag held steadily by Signalman after bringing train to a stand and giving verbal warning.

14.—To indicate to Engine-driver of Goods train, timed to stop at a Station, that there is nothing to pick up, and that if he has nothing to put off he may run through.—Rule 173. | Green Light or Flag waved slowly up and down.

15.—To indicate that Catch Points are in right position for train to pass in facing direction. — Rule 236. | Green Light or Flag held steadily in the hand by man at Points.

16.—To caution Engine-driver entering Terminal Station, or Station worked under special instructions. if Line is not clear.—Rule 87. | Green Light or Flag held steadily in the hand by Signalman after bringing train to a stand and giving verbal warning.

17 —To caution Engine-driver of following train on Time Interval system.—Time Interval Regulation 3. (Appendix to Rule Book.) | Green Light or Flag held steadily in the hand by Signalman after bringing train to a stand and giving verbal warning.

18.—To indicate to Engine-driver that slip portion is detached.—Slip Carriage Regulation 7. (Appendix to Rule Book.) | Green Light or Flag waved slowly up and down by Slip Guard.

29

51. *In the absence of Flags—*

(a) Both arms raised above the head denotes Danger, thus :—

Danger Signal.

(b) One arm raised above the head denotes Caution, thus :—

Caution Signal.

(c) One arm held in a horizontal position denotes All Right, thus :—

All Right Signal.

Pages from the 1905 Rules and Regulations.

The feeling that the unions would interfere in the smooth running of the railway was further amplified a month later, when the company again felt it necessary to comment on the labour problem. It was argued that the company's men 'know perfectly well that the fullest consideration is always extended to each and every representation they make to the Directors'[28]. With the general rejection of the union's programme, agitation continued, and in November 1907 strike action was threatened. This threat was taken seriously by the Board of Trade and its President, Lloyd George, who intervened to avoid a national railway strike.

Representatives of both unions and employers met the Government separately, and out of these talks emerged what became known as the Conciliation and Arbitration Schemes; if railway workers were unhappy with conditions of service or wage levels, and could not obtain satisfaction from the management, they could then go to an independent Conciliation Board. This process was not without its problems; furthermore, the whole question of union recognition had not been resolved. By 1911 discontent had again grown to a high level, with great dissatisfaction with arbitrators' awards; needless to say, the railway companies were not going out of their way to help employees bring their grievances before the Conciliation Boards.

On 15 August 1911, a joint letter was sent to the railway employers by the four main unions in which they pointed out the seriousness of the situation, arguing the dissatisfaction existing was 'not limited to one railway or section of men, but common to all for whom we speak'. The resolution of the unions was to offer the railway companies 24 hours to negotiate a new settlement; the main reason given for the threat of industrial action was that the employers had failed 'to observe the letter and spirit of the Conciliation and Arbitration Scheme of 1907'[29]. No satisfactory answer was received, and as a result a General Strike was called the next day. Tempers flared, the strike coming as it did in the wake of disputes by other groups such as dockers and mineworkers, and Winston Churchill called out the troops in some areas; Prime Minister Asquith, however, argued for less drastic measures, and on 19 August a meeting was held between management and unions, the first time the two sides had ever met across a table. Subsequently an agreement was reached allowing the strike to be called off after two days, on 19 August.

Police escort supplies of food near Paddington during the August 1911 railway strike. (NUR)

Industrial action had been patchy as a whole. On the GWR network it was estimated by management that only about 40 per cent of the workforce had actually gone on strike. There was, however, maximum disruption since it was the busy summer period, and the Great Western calculated that it had lost around £100,000 as a result of the strike and the extra expense it had entailed.

A Royal Commission under the chairmanship of Sir David Harrel KCB CCVO ('impersonating impartiality,' as one Fabian Society publication put it!) was convened to investigate the working of the 1907 scheme. The Commission reported on 18 October, and recommended an amended Arbitration Scheme, and the speeding up of the whole process. After some further discussion, the whole Conciliation and Arbitration Scheme was patched up, and it continued in use until 1913, when further negotiations began. The outbreak of war in 1914 led to the deferring of any more discussion, and a 'Truce Agreement' postponed debate until after the end of hostilities.

The 1911 agreement did lead to wage increases for many men; in December of that year, earnings for a typical week increased from 25s 9d to 26s 8¼d. The power wielded by the Boards was much the same as it had been, although it was allowed to deal with conditions of employment as well as wages and hours. Questions of discipline and management, however, were not included within the remit of the Conciliation Boards, a significant exclusion.

The events described in the last few pages are in stark contrast to the company's own publicity of the period; the Great Western was certainly making great strides in many directions, but even the traditionally conservative and loyal GWR workforce was less than happy. The problems chronicled in this chapter were only a reflection of the more general unrest felt countrywide in the years before the First World War.

The era after the death of Queen Victoria was characterized by social unrest generally; the contrast between the wealth and influence of the aristocracy and the poverty and hardship suffered by many working class people could no longer be ignored. The rise of the Labour movement, which gave working class people a voice, shook the very foundations of the establishment. Lloyd George's 'People's Budget' of 1909, which taxed rich landowners in order to provide finance for social reform, was even more radical, and its rejection by the House of Lords prompted a constitutional crisis; the ensuing General Election called in January 1910 left the Liberals without an overall majority. The rise in the popularity of the Labour movement was reflected in the fact that by 1910 there were 40 Labour MPs in Parliament.

Great Western Railway services were further disrupted in 1912, with the calling of a National Miner's Strike in March of that year. This was not the first time that the company's traffic had been affected; in April 1898 a similar dispute had cost the Great Western

The empty platforms at Paddington suggest that this postcard view may have been taken either during the 1911 railway strike, or during the 1912 colliers' dispute. (Brian Arman Collection)

around £138,000, and had led to wage cuts and compulsory holidays for staff while the strike was in action. The 1912 dispute started on 1 March, and within three days the company had issued a handbill describing a substantially reduced passenger service, which was intended to effect economies in the use of coal. More reductions were to follow. Interestingly, the first pamphlet was detailed 'Alterations' to the service; by 15 March the GWR was referring to 'Suspensions of Service' and further 'Restrictions'.

As the strike worsened, more services were withdrawn, including all special and excursion traffic with the exceptions of workmen's, ocean passengers', military, naval and 'Shipwrecked Mariners' tickets. A further circular issued on 12 March noted that the company could not undertake to run any theatrical or football specials until the dispute was settled.[30]

Goods and mineral mileage was also considerably reduced, obviously due to the reduced output of works and factories. In fact, over the whole strike the total mileage saved by the Great Western amounted to 1,818,175. An indication of the progressive nature of the dispute can be gained from statistics which show that in the first week of the strike services were down by 21.2 per cent, rising to a high point of 55.1 per cent in the week ending 30 March 1912.[31]

This reduction of traffic led to staff being laid off; length of service determined who in the main was to lose work, although a Conciliation Board was set up between the company and representatives of the men which attempted to share the work available fairly between the men working in a particular district. This arrangement was the choice of the men themselves, although the company did guarantee to reinstate those laid off as soon as circumstances improved.

As the reader can imagine, the South Wales area was particularly hard hit, since it contained a large number of coal mines; services between Newport and Pontypridd, Llantrisant, Penygraig and Tonypandy were suspended completely, whilst on the Newport-Ebbw Vale line, for example, the service was restricted to four trains each way, with no Sunday trains at all. By 10 April the company could announce the partial restoration of passenger train services, but it was not until 22 May 1912 that the Great Western could state that the ordinary train service as detailed in the Penny Timetable of February 1912 was back in operation signalling the end of yet another tumultuous episode in a period of considerable unrest as well as progress for the Great Western Railway.

FISHGUARD

VARIOUS projects of significance have already been described showing the Great Western Railway's spirit of enterprise in the 'Golden Age'; and if anything really exemplifies this policy, it is the building and promotion of the port of Fishguard.

At the beginning of this section it was noted that Fishguard was always intended by Brunel to be the terminus of the South Wales Railway. The great engineer saw the location as a suitable place to build a harbour serving Ireland. However, financial problems, and the potato famine in Ireland, prevented the construction of the line as far as Fishguard, the Great Western eventually getting access to the Irish traffic through a port at Neyland, renamed New Milford by the company.

Steamer services run by the GWR itself commenced in 1872, when the company purchased four vessels from Captain Jackson of New Milford, who had run services to Waterford since 1856. Three new ships were also purchased to replace the *Great Western*, *South of Ireland*, *Malakoff* and *Vulture*, which were by this time rather old.[32] The new vessels, *Milford*, *Limerick* and *Waterford*, cost over £40,000 each, and made the crossing to Ireland in between $7\frac{1}{2}$ and $8\frac{1}{2}$ hours. Before the opening of the Severn Tunnel and the Badminton line, the journey from Paddington to Waterford took 17 hours, not a journey for those with a weak disposition!

The service run from New Milford proved adequate for some years, but in time its disadvantages became more apparent; facilitites at the port were by no means lavish, and were not suited to expansion. The main disadvantage was perhaps its geographical position, situated in Milford Haven which meant that any passage to Ireland was likely to be a fairly long one in comparison to a port on the west coast of Pembrokeshire. The new route from Fishguard would be some 55 sea miles shorter than the old one.

One further disadvantage suffered by Irish travellers using the Great Western's steamers from New Milford was that although facilities on the ships improved by the turn of the century, it was still necessary to carry passengers, cargo and cattle in the one vessel. One

A general view of the harbour at Fishguard. On the left can be seen the sheer rock face, and, beyond the GWR ships at anchor, the breakwater.

correspondent noted that discomfort to passengers had been reduced to a minimum 'by the up-to-date methods of ventilation in the holds of steamers'. For the more sensitive passenger, though, this still would not have been an entirely pleasant experience, especially in hot weather!

Despite the copious amounts of publicity issued by the Great Western with regard to the Fishguard scheme, one aspect of the whole project which the company chose to quietly ignore in later years was the fact that in many ways it had been forced into the whole scheme by the activities of rival companies. In the latter part of 1897, the Great Western Directors became somewhat alarmed by the activities of the small but grand plans of the North Pembrokeshire & Fishguard Railway Company, and its counterpart, the Fishguard & Rosslare Railways and Harbours Company.[33]

Both these enterprises were controlled by one individual, a Birmingham solicitor by the name of Joseph Rowlands. He had acquired a major interest in what were a series of small lines in the Prescelly mountains of south Pembrokeshire. The first was the 8½-mile Narberth & Maenclochog Railway, opened in 1876 linking Rosebush, near Maenclochog, with Clynderwen. The second, the North Pembrokeshire & Fishguard Railway, originally formed in 1878, had a complicated and financially perilous development, and until Rowlands took over the running of the company in 1892 it had made little progress in its plan to build a line from Rosebush to Fishguard itself.

In 1893, however, Rowlands obtained Parliamentary permission to build a harbour at Fishguard, and to link it to the North Pembrokeshire Railway by a short stretch of line. The following year this project was absorbed by a new venture, the Fishguard & Rosslare Railways and Harbours Company. At this point Rowlands approached the Great Western in the hope that the company would acquire the whole project, except for the Irish port facilities, but Henry Lambert, the company's General Manager at the time, only agreed to Rowlands' use of the company's traffic facilities.

Having failed to interest the Great Western, Rowlands then tried to connect his scheme with the London & North Western Railway by means of a new line to Abergwili, north of Carmarthen, which, despite GWR objections, was given Parliamentary assent in 1895. Even more ambitious proposals planned to extend this line to Swansea and beyond. Although this Bill was rejected by Parliament, and despite the fact that Rowlands did not have the capital to complete either scheme, alarm bells were again beginning to ring at Paddington; even if Rowlands did not have the capital to bring about such a project, there was a very real danger that one of the Great Western's rivals, especially the LNWR, did.

Therefore it is interesting to note that the whole Fishguard project was, like the South Wales Direct Line, partly motivated by the company's fear that a rival could poach valuable revenue from it; it is not enough, however, to cite this as a reason for the considerable effort and expense which was to follow. By 1897 the spirit of enterprise, already mentioned at some length in this book, was beginning to take hold; the Great Western management was well aware of the benefits of a shorter steamer route to Ireland, and the disadvantages of the present packet station facilities at New Milford. As a result, the company acquired the North Pembrokeshire & Fishguard Railway in February 1898, and some 14 months later signed an agreement with the Great Southern & Western Railway of Ireland, by which both parties agreed to complete harbours on both sides of the Irish Sea and to develop suitable lines linking these ports to their respective rail networks. The whole enterprise now came under the Fishguard & Rosslare Railways and Harbour Company, and was jointly financed by both undertakings.

The construction of both the harbour and station facilities at Fishguard are worth describing in detail, since they vividly illustrate the lengths to which the Great Western would go in provision of services in its 'Golden Age'. The engineering difficulties encountered in the project would have been enough to put off many less determined companies; although the port had been surveyed by the Admiralty as early as 1790 with a view to constructing a harbour there, the practical difficulties envisaged meant that only a small pier had been constructed in the end.

The location did have superb natural advantages which made it an ideal location for a harbour; two headlands, Pen Anglas and Dinas Head, formed the natural entrance to a bay sheltered on three sides by mountains. Excellent anchorage was provided on a rockless sea bed, and there was little in the way of tidal currents. One other particular advantage was that the area was relatively fog-free, unlike Plymouth and Southampton. The company boasted in 1906 that there had not been any fog interfering with the working of the harbour for more than three years.

However there were still the formidable problems to be overcome, despite these natural advantages. At the point planned for the harbour, the sea washed up against the edge of a sheer mountainside, with not even a footpath available along the shore. As a result of the terrain, both the station and harbour facilities were created on land literally blasted out of the mountainside. In fact, when construction began, the rail link from Letterston to Fishguard had not yet been completed, which meant that machinery and plant had to be manhandled overland and lowered over the cliffs to the point where work was to begin. It was said that in the early stages of work the Great Western did actually employ mountaineers who were lowered down the sheer rock faces to plant the first explosive charges!

Blasting went on for some years, as millions of tons of rock were extracted; one imagines that the residents of the formerly tranquil resort of Fishguard and Goodwick were less than happy with the

A general view of the station showing the facilities, including the cattle pens, in the foreground.

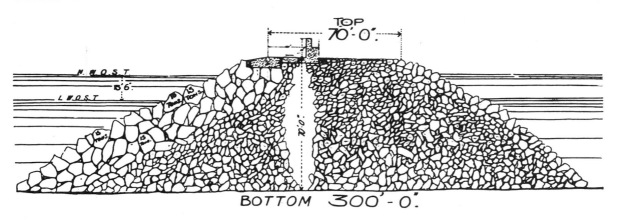

TOP
70'-0'.

N. H. O. S. T.

L. H. O. S. T.

70'-0'.

BOTTOM 300'-0'.

A cross-section of the breakwater, from a sketch originally reproduced in the proceedings of the GWR London Debating Society.

situation. During the first year, 'rock powder' was used, being replaced by an explosive called 'Tonite' in later years. Some idea of the force of the explosions is gained by the fact that they could be clearly heard in Newcastle Emlyn, some considerable distance away.[34]

In true Great Western fashion, none of the rock blasted from the cliffs was wasted, providing much of the material for the breakwater. As well as the blasting already mentioned, Ingersoll pneumatic drills were at work almost continually either drilling deep holes for explosive charges, or excavating tunnels into which even larger charges could be placed! After each blast, steam excavators and cranes moved the waste rock into railway wagons where it was either taken to the breakwater or to the crusher, where it could be made into ballast to be used all over the Great Western network. This device also made enough sand and chippings for the making of concrete to be used in the quay wall, and elsewhere on the site.

The largest blocks, weighing from 5 to 15 tons each, were used to construct the long breakwater, which extended out from the western shore; it was made 'by simply throwing the rocks pell-mell on top of one another and allowing them to settle'[35]. The top of this mound was capped with a concrete parapet rising 20 feet above high water, to prevent waves breaking over the whole structure. The breakwater grew at a rate of about 10 feet a week, until its full length of 2,000 feet was reached; the final touch was a lighthouse beacon at its seaward end.

The quay provided at Fishguard was over 1,000 feet in length, big enough to allow three large steamers to come alongside at once. The quay wall itself was constructed of large concrete blocks made on site varying in size from 6 to 10 tons; a staggering 4,900 were needed to build the quay wall, which was nearly 20 feet thick at its base. Built into the quay wall below passenger level was a useful innovation, a gallery for cattle, which enabled them to be unloaded from ships out of sight of passengers. A subway brought them out onto the platform, where a pen over 650 feet long was provided. The Irish cattle trade was of great significance to the GWR, and it suffered a severe blow in

OVERLEAF *Although this is a well-known photograph, it is worth repeating for the glorious detail it shows. The embarkation of the passengers for Ireland is closely watched by St David's captain on the bridge. (National Railway Museum, York)*

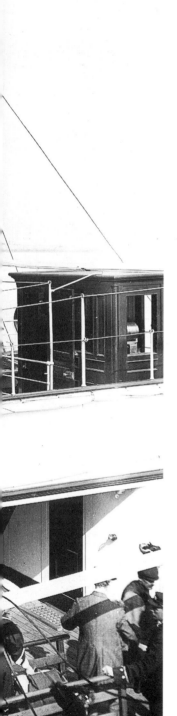

1912, when a severe outbreak of foot and mouth disease led to the suspension of the trade for some 11 months. The port only reopened in June 1913 after extensive alterations to the cattle pens; from that time onwards, Irish cattle had the benefit of both roofed and electrically lit accommodation.

On the quay, passenger platforms of over 800 feet in length were built, connected by subways and electric traversers. The station was well equipped, with ample waiting and refreshment rooms. Two goods platforms of a similar length were situated next to the passenger facilities; to assist with the unloading of goods, nine modern 30 cwt electrically-powered cranes were provided, with a more powerful 21-ton crane for larger cargo or the coaling of ships. Behind the station a large array of sidings were provided, amounting to about six miles of track in total. Electricity for the entire harbour and station was provided by a generating station built specially for the purpose.

To service this impressive establishment well over 100 staff were needed, excluding those employed in the Marine Department. Before the station opened it was estimated that apart from the Stationmaster and his normal staff of clerks, porters, shunters and inspectors, between 25 and 30 coaling men would be needed to refuel the company's steamers. Because of the fluctuating nature of the traffic, it was also calculated that around 50 porters would be employed on a casual basis, to assist with the unloading of cargo or cattle, and the cleaning out of cattle pens and wagons. Staff of this kind were to be paid by the day, which was considered to be ten hours by the GWR management of the day.[36]

Needless to say, all these staff needed somewhere to live, and concern was voiced early in 1906 that there would not be enough suitable accommodation available for the entire complement of staff when the new harbour was completed. Fifty-seven houses of differing sizes were therefore built for the staff varying in cost from £148 10s to £175. Most were described as being of a picturesque appearance, and had two or three bedrooms, a living room with a cooking range, and a scullery.[37]

Accommodation of another sort was provided by the company at its Fishguard Bay Hotel; the Great Western purchased an existing hotel close to the harbour, originally named the Wyncliffe, which had, an advertising leaflet proclaimed, 'every modern convenience', including electric light and lifts to every floor. It was, the leaflet continued, an excellent place to stay *en route* to or from Ireland, or for a winter or summer holiday. In another 1908 company publication it was argued that the 'pine-sheltered' hotel was well situated for lovers of wildlife: 'seals and wildfowl abound, and occasionally a rare specimen of the almost extinct wild goat may be seen'![38]

When the harbour opened for business in August 1906, the Great Western switched its Irish traffic from the New Milford-Waterford route to the new Fishguard-Rosslare passage. At the same time it also

A postcard view of the Fishguard Bay Hotel, possibly taken after the Great War.

transferred the entire Marine Department staff to the new port. With the opening of the new sea route the Great Western took the opportunity to acquire three new vessels for the Irish traffic. The SS *St George* was built by Cammell Laird at Birkenhead, and was launched on 13 January 1906, whilst the SS *St David* and the SS *St Patrick* were built in the Clydebank shipyards of John Brown & Co. Both the *St David* and the *St Patrick* were delivered to Fishguard some weeks after the harbour officially opened, at the end of August 1906; both had a carrying capacity of 1,398 passengers whilst the *St George*, which was not delivered until 4 September, was capable of carrying 1,432 passengers.

In the September 1906 issue of the *Great Western Railway Magazine*, a correspondent wrote that it was 'entirely satisfactory to say that the new turbine steamers are the subject of unqualified admiration on the part of passengers who have used them'[39]. Two years after Fishguard opened for business, a fourth vessel, the SS *St Andrew*, was added to the fleet. In the first summer season of 1906 both day and night services were inaugurated, leaving Paddington at 8.45 am and 8.45 pm. The sea passage itself took just under three hours.

Less than six months after the opening of the harbour, the company also completed a new stretch of line from Clarbeston Road, on the old Milford Haven railway, bypassing the steeply graded Letterston branch. About a mile of this project utilized the old workings of the original Brunel scheme of 1845, a rather ironic coincidence in the circumstances. The junction of the new line, 26 chains west of Clarbeston Road, was laid for fast running, with 30-foot switches, only the third location on the GWR system to feature such points at the time. When the railway opened on 17 December 1906, no stations had been constructed; the *Great Western Railway Magazine* correspondent thought, however, that the local population would 'agitate for a motor service and halts'[40].

In the years just before the First World War, the Great Western completed another 'short cut' which enabled it to speed up both Fishguard services and coal trains. The improvements in this case were in the Swansea area, and were known as the 'Swansea District Lines'. The whole area had been something of a bottleneck, containing as it did one of the highest concentrations of coal traffic on the whole railway; heavy coal trains were the order of the day, but problems were exacerbated by ferocious gradients, especially on the line between Gowerton and Gockett, where loaded trains were worked up a gradient of 1 in 50 for 2½ miles, and between Gockett and Landore where the same trains had to negotiate a 1 in 52 incline in the opposite direction.

The new relief lines were brought into operation on 14 July 1913, leaving the old SWR main line at Skewen near Neath and running to the north of the congested Swansea area, rejoining the Fishguard trunk route south of Pontardulais. In common with other 'cut-off' lines built by the Great Western in this period, the construction of the Swansea District Lines must have involved the company in considerable expenditure; in the 11 miles of line there were three tunnels, the largest being Llangyfelach, nearly 2,000 feet long, as well as two considerable viaducts. It was estimated that in the course of construction, some 350,000 cubic tons of earthwork had been dealt with by the two contractors involved in the project.

The SS St Patrick *with another GWR ship in the background, possibly the SS* Great Western.

As well as relieving congestion, it was also hoped that the new line would allow access to as yet unworked coal seams in valleys to the north of Swansea, which were 'awaiting the miner's pick and drill'[41]. A further important use for the line was as an alternative route for expresses from Fishguard; to this end, the cut-off was laid with the company's standard heavy type of rail.

Returning to our survey of Fishguard itself, it is worth noting that in typical fashion the Great Western did not waste much time in starting to promote and advertise its new port and sea route. In the same month as the harbour opened, the company published a book entitled *Southern Ireland: Its Lakes and Landscapes*. As well as describing the history and topography of Southern Ireland in some detail, considerable space was dedicated not surprisingly to the new port and sea route. The opening to the Great Western's new service would, the author argued, 'mark an epoch in the history of travel in Southern Ireland'[42].

Traffic using the new quicker sea route did increase, helped no doubt by the fast comfortable trains run to connect with the company's turbine steamers; the *Great Western Railway Magazine* for October 1910 reported that traffic in 1909 was 12 per cent up on that of 1907.[43] As it did in numerous issues, it reported some of the more famous or privileged passengers it had carried. On this occasion it noted the use of the service by the Duchess of St Albans, the Earl of Shaftesbury, and 'Princess Marie-Louise of Schleswig-Holstein'.

Traffic of all types flowed in both directions; up and down day and night services were inaugurated after the opening in 1906, with the boat trains allowed $5\frac{1}{2}$ hours for the 261-mile journey to Paddington. In September and October 1907, the Great Western ran a number of day excursions from Paddington to Killarney, including a record

A cartoon from the Western Mail *for 28 August 1906, titled 'Drawn Nearer Together'. It is perhaps significant that the GWR is portrayed as a devil!*
(Courtesy Western Mail)

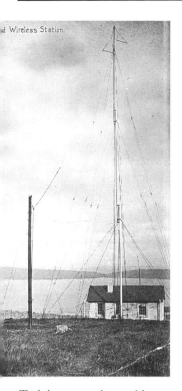

To help communicate with inward-bound transatlantic liners, the company set up a wireless station on the headland overlooking the harbour. Fitted with Marconi equipment, yet another unusual occupation was created on the GWR — that of wireless operator!

non-stop 5-hour run from the capital to Fishguard. The night services were no doubt improved by the introduction of new 70-foot sleeping cars brought into use in 1907; fitted with six-wheeled bogies and a double-layer floor filled with sawdust for quietness, they reached new heights of passenger comfort. The Great Western boasted that 'no expense has been spared...in producing a sleeping car which should easily satisfy the most exacting of passengers'[44]. In May 1907, W.J. Scott sang their praises, and added that 'such a night faring is well worth 7 shillings and sixpence'[45].

Some years later, the company ran special services of a different nature; in September 1913 it was reported that the GWR had assisted in the transportation of 3,000 pilgrims from the south of Ireland to Lourdes. After travelling by GWR steamer, the company laid on special corridor trains with Resturant Cars which ran direct to Folkestone and the ferry to France. The Great Western also claimed credit for improving economic conditions in Ireland with the establishment of its route; much agricultural produce was carried and the *Great Western Railway Magazine* argued in 1909, 'trade has increased by no small extent'[46].

In its publicity material released soon after the opening of the Fishguard facilities, it soon becomes clear that to use a rather apt nautical cliché, the Great Western was after 'bigger fish' than just cross-Channel Irish travellers; the company was re-enacting the aims of Brunel some 60 years earlier, in trying to attract transatlantic traffic. The 1906 publication already mentioned noted that Fishguard would play an important part in increasing the volume of traffic between England and Ireland, but also would 'in all human probability...become a port of call for Ocean Liners, to which it offers many manifest advantages'[47].

As has already been noted in the chapter on Plymouth, the Great Western management was most anxious to develop the transatlantic traffic. The period before the First World War was something of a 'Golden Age' for the great ocean liners too, with each company vying to produce the fastest and most luxurious ships. The Great Western had obviously already attempted to tap some of this traffic through its facilities at Plymouth, but at Fishguard the company saw the opportunity to develop its own purpose-built Ocean Terminal. The harbour also had considerable geographical advantages, since the sea passage between New York and Fishguard was some 50 nautical miles shorter than that to Plymouth, and over 100 miles nearer than Liverpool.

The first major shipping company to use the Great Western facilities at Fishguard was in fact not running transatlantic services as such; when the first Booth Line ship, the SS *Lanfranc*, called at the harbour on 2 April 1908, it was on a service linking England, Spain, Portugal and South America; later other ships of the same line called. A special non-stop train was run to Paddington after the passengers had disembarked, and the process was repeated when the SS *Antony* called at the port later in the month. The *Great Western Railway Magazine* for May of that year anticipated that 'in the near future it will be no uncommon thing for large liners to call at Fishguard'[48].

It was not until August 1909, though, that the Great Western finally managed to engineer the event which put Fishguard firmly on the map as a port of call for large ocean liners. The GWR management arranged with the Cunard Line to allow its magnificent flagship, the RMS *Mauretania*, to call at Fishguard; this was indeed a publicity coup for the company, since the great liner was the holder of the 'Blue Riband' and along with her sister ship, the *Lusitania*, was probably the best-known ship of the period until the advent of the *Olympic* and *Titanic* in 1911.

Great efforts were made to ensure that nothing went wrong when the great liner arrived; for some days before the arrival of the ship, most of the GWR 'top brass' from Paddington were in attendance at the harbour and, as a final measure, the Company Chairman Viscount Churchill joined the *Mauretania* at Queenstown, Ireland, for the final leg of the voyage.

When the ship was sighted from the headland above Fishguard, three small Great Western tenders were sent out to meet it; this

A GWR tender, the Sir Francis Drake, *alongside* RMS Mauretania, *enabling passengers to be ferried to the harbour to board their trains.* (National Railway Museum, York)

operation was necessary since the *Mauretania*, at over 30,000 tons, was too large to dock in the harbour itself. Once the ship had dropped anchor at 1.17 pm, the first tender offloaded the American Mails, which were then taken straight to a waiting special train for Paddington. These out of the way, the passengers and their luggage were then ferried to the quayside; after Customs checks, they boarded two special trains for the capital.

For the steeply graded section as far as Cardiff the trains were double-headed, hauled by GWR 4–4–0s Nos 3402 *Halifax*, 4108 *Gardenia*, 4111 *Anemone* and 4116 *Mignonette*. At Cardiff both teams were replaced by the more powerful Churchward 'Star' Class 6–0s Nos 4021 *King Edward* and 4022 *King William*. To ensure that a rapid journey would be accomplished, a Locomotive Inspector rode with each train, and specific instructions were issued to staff along the line. It was noted that 'it is of supreme importance that an ABSOLUTELY clear road is to be kept for each of the special trains'[49]. One imagines that this instruction must have been adhered to since both trains arrived at Paddington ahead of schedule; the first left Fishguard at 2.53 pm, arriving in London at just before 7.30, whilst the second left the Welsh port at 3.05, and arrived 27 minutes after the first train. The *Daily Telegraph* praised the running of the trains, noting that 'there was not a single jolt from start to finish'[50]. Both trains were running with a Restaurant Car allowing an 'excellent dinner' to be served *en route*. The *Daily News* added that there were 'enthusiastic scenes' at the London terminus, and that 'there were cheers as the train drew alongside the platform, nearly a quarter of an hour before it was expected'[51].

All in all, the whole event was a huge success for the company; the landing and the subsequent train journey attracted a large amount of publicity which the company, never slow in blowing its own trumpet, published in the form of a lavishly illustrated leaflet entitled 'Cuttings from the Press...Inauguration of the New Shortest & Quickest Route New York to London'. The *Mauretania* had of course assisted the company by making a record crossing of the Atlantic, but the success of the Great Western's end of the operation, particularly its rapid non-stop run in just over $4\frac{1}{2}$ hours, led to hopes that Fishguard would take over from many of the other established ports as a translantic destination.

The *New York Tribune* noted in April 1910 that Fishguard was 'threatening the supremacy of older ports', and that 'Times change, even in England, and the mania for speed has affected so thoroughly British a thing as the old established chain of harbours'[52]. Although describing Fishguard as a 'delightful old-fashioned sort of place', it reported that with its high-speed rail link to London, the saving in time over Liverpool had often been up to 24 hours.

The management at Paddington was further heartened in March 1910 when Cunard announced that it was dropping the Irish port of Queenstown as an eastbound port of call in favour of Fishguard. The

The postcard photographer has positioned his camera outside the GWR railings, but has captured the sight of No 4111 Anemone *and No 4116* Mignonette *hauling one of the special trains run on 30 August 1909. A sizeable proportion of the local schoolboy population appears to be on the footbridge.* (Brian Arman Collection)

New York Times reported that by using the Great Western Railway, passengers arriving at Fishguard in the early afternoon could dine on the way to London, and still have enough time to comfortably catch the 9 pm Boat Train for the Continent. Irish feeling was not surprisingly incensed at this decision, which as we shall see in due course would have an important effect on the long-term future of Fishguard.

Meanwhile, further prestige was brought to the harbour by the announcement of yet another shipping line's decision to use it as an Ocean Terminal; in September 1910, the Blue Funnel line of Alfred Holt & Co announced its intention to use the harbour as a port of call for its new passenger service between England and Australia. Three liners, the *Aeneas*, the *Ascanius* and the *Anchises*, each over 10,000 tons, were to work the service, which commenced in November of that year. To mark the occasion, the Great Western published its own publicity booklet, 'Fishguard: Ocean Port of Call & Departure Point for Australia'. This 32-page pamphlet called the inauguration of the Blue Funnel service 'a decision of great consequence to travellers', and concluded that Holt Line passengers would gain that 'satisfaction which the new port has already afforded to multitudes of Ocean passengers from the United States and elsewhere'[53].

There is also some evidence that in 1911 the Great Western was considering the possibility of luring the new White Star liners *Olympic* and *Titanic*, then under construction, to call at Fishguard; but a letter from the Great Western Goods Depot at Liverpool reveals that the decision had already been taken to run the White Star transatlantic service from Southampton.

With increased liner traffic at Fishguard, it became obvious that the facilities at the harbour would have to be upgraded in order not only to sustain the business of the shipping lines already using the port, but also to attract further trade. One of the main disadvantages of the harbour was the fact that the larger ships had to anchor offshore, and mail and passengers had to be disembarked by GWR tender. This operation was fine in good weather, but in heavy seas vessels were forced to go elsewhere; one such example was reported by the *Morning Post* in January 1911, when the *Lusitania* was unable to land her passengers and mail at the harbour due to a strong northerly wind, proceeding to Liverpool instead.[54] Some months later, the *New York Herald* noted that the Cunarder's sister ship, the *Mauretania*, had encountered similar difficulties in a north-easterly gale off Fishguard; the 500 passengers had again disembarked at Liverpool as a result.[55]

Such occurrences lost the Great Western both valuable revenue and prestige, so a programme of improvements was proposed. The *Great Western Railway Magazine* for September 1910 argued that the ultimate aim of improvements at the harbour was to 'do away with the chore of using tenders'[56]. The plans included an entirely new breakwater extending in a north-easterly direction from the Goodwick Sands, a new Ocean Quay, and a considerable amount of dredging to allow ships of at least a 38-foot draft to use the docking facilities. New rail connections of some length were also necessary to link up the new breakwater.

Work began on some of these improvements but there is evidence that the Great Western management was becoming somewhat more circumspect about the expending of large sums of capital on projects such as these; the Board commissioned Sir William Matthews, an eminent harbour engineer, to report on the possible development of the harbour. Accompanied by the General Manager, he visited the site in February 1912, and by June of the same year it was reported that the company had reconsidered its plans for the port. Large gangs of workmen engaged on the new breakwater and an associated cutting were discharged. The *Morning Post* noted, however, that the company had no intentions of abandoning either its deep dredging of the harbour, or its long-term plans for the use of the port by Atlantic traffic.[57]

The cause of the Great Western's abandonment of the more expensive parts of the extensions to Fishguard may in some part be due to pressure on the Board by shareholders. After a decade or more of enterprise and investment in the the GWR network, it appears that some investors in the company were less than happy with this continuing drive for expansion. A further possibility is that although Fishguard was attracting a fair number of ocean liners, it still had not attracted sufficient to really justify the kind of expenditure originally envisaged for the harbour.

Despite the curtailment of the more ambitious aspects of the GWR's plans for the port, it nevertheless pressed on with obtaining Parliamentary powers to make further improvements. When the Fishguard & Rosslare Railways and Harbour Bill was debated, it became clear that the company was facing formidable opposition, particularly from the Irish Nationalist members. The diversion of traffic away from Queenstown had caused a great deal of anger in Ireland; a deputation of politicians and civic dignitaries had even gone to the extent of visiting the Postmaster-General and the President of the United States to air their grievances.

When the Bill came to a vote, it was defeated by 133 votes to 95, mainly by a coalition of Irish and Labour members. Strangely, the Members of Parliament for West Wales also did not vote for the Great Western scheme, which seems to suggest that pressure was put them not to support it for fear of exacerbating the already tense political situation in Ireland. The *Great Western Railway Magazine* implicitly acknowledged that bigger issues were involved when it reflected that the scheme was rejected because of 'real or fancied grievances arising out of what may have happened in the past in Ireland'[58].

Thus the company decided to postpone indefinitely the works proposed for Fishguard, arguing that 'the traffic could be adequately handled with the harbour works as at present carried out'[59]. The outbreak of war 12 months later, further political disturbance in Ireland and the subsequent concentration of much transatlantic traffic at Southampton after the conflict, brought an end to the Great Western's dream of the West Wales port becoming a bustling Ocean Terminal; even today, Fishguard is a sad shadow of a port for which the company had such high hopes.

PART FIVE

SUBURBIA AND BEYOND: THE BIRMINGHAM ROUTE

IN the last section of this book we will look at one of the final developments in the modernization of the Great Western network in its 'Golden Age'. In many respects, the completion of the new 2-hour route to Birmingham, and the rebuilding of the fine station there were the closing pages of the story of company enterprise that we have been considering.

The background to the Great Western's efforts to complete its route network by shortening the route to Birmingham and the North is very similar to that described in other parts of this book. In the years before 1895 particularly, the company was lethargic in providing any quick services to the West Midlands. Some idea of the problems faced by the traveller in the dark days before the turn of the century can be seen in the fact that journey times actually got longer after the abolition of Brunel's Broad Gauge; before the conversion, the $129\frac{1}{2}$-mile trip from Paddington to Birmingham took 2 hours 50 minutes. In the 1870s, however, the GWR had slowed the service to between 3 hours 20 minutes and 4 hours! It made no effort to compete with its main rival for the West Midlands traffic, the London & North Western Railway, and as a result almost lost out entirely.

The key to a route to the Midlands was the crossing of the County of Buckinghamshire, which even up to the turn of the century was a largely agricultural area. The county was first crossed by railway in the 1830s when the London & Birmingham, later to become part of the LNWR, ran up through the Chilterns via Watford and Tring. Throughout the latter part of the nineteenth century various speculative schemes were put forward, but none came to fruition.

In 1895, however, the Great Western was shaken to its very foundations by a new proposal, supported by the LNWR, the Midland and the Manchester, Sheffield & Lincolnshire Railways (the latter was later to become the Great Central). All supported the idea of a 'London & South Wales Railway'. This scheme, already touched on in an earlier chapter, was a serious threat to the Great Western, being an attempt to steal away the South Wales coal traffic which, as we have already seen, was a lucrative source of income to the Great Western; after the trauma of the abolition of the broad gauge, the company needed every penny it could get.

The new main line would have run eastwards along the upper Thames valley to Oxford, then to Bledlow where it would divide, with a line north to Missenden and another south to Beaconsfield and thus, eventually, the capital. As Stanley Jenkins noted, this was clearly a 'darkest hour' for the Great Western[1]; matters were resolved, however, when the company was able to forestall the building of this new main line by careful negotiations, especially with the Manchester, Sheffield & Lincolnshire Railway, to whom concessions were offered.

The reader may remember from the previous section that the unrest amongst coal owners and other business groups in South Wales was also eased somewhat by the building of the Bristol & South Wales Direct Railway as a result of these 'London & South Wales' proposals. Not surprisingly, the Great Western's own company history, written in 1927 by E.T. McDermot, makes little mention of the 'London & South Wales' episode, although it now seems that it may well have been one of the key factors in fully wakening the Great Western from its late-nineteenth-century lethargy. The involvement of the GWR with the MS&LR, after 1897 known as the Great Central Railway, was to have important consequences in the story of the new line to Birmingham and the north, as the reader will now discover.

A map of the new Great Western/Great Central joint line, as reproduced in the 1906 Holiday Haunts. *(Great Western Trust)*

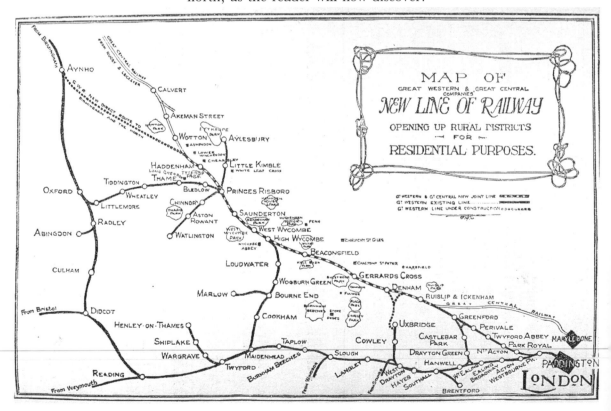

THE NEW BIRMINGHAM ROUTE

THE joint railway built and run by the GWR and CGR was the last main line to be built in Britain, and formed part of the last of the 'cut-offs' promoted by the Great Western to end its reputation as the 'Great Way Round'. In 1897 the company obtained Parliamentary powers to build the Acton & High Wycombe Railway, which was partly to replace the original branch line to Wycombe from Maidenhead, opened in 1857. Built originally to the broad gauge, this cheaply constructed single-track line was converted to standard gauge in 1870, but was never really suitable for traffic of any real consequence.

The plans for the new railway were also in response to a rival scheme by the Metropolitan Railway, which was expanding out into the western hinterlands of London at this time. The Great Western scheme was chosen in preference to that of the Metropolitan, which, Parliament decreed, would terminate at Uxbridge.

With the Great Western having secured powers to build the Acton-Wycombe line, the Great Central Railway now became involved. The two companies were already cooperating closely in the construction of an 8-mile line north of Banbury, which was to link both systems. The whole arrangement was something in the way of a 'pay-off' for the assistance which the Great Central's predecessor, the MS&LR, had given in the crisis of 1895; this certainly seems to be the case when one notes that the Great Western undertook to lend the Great Central the capital to complete the project, and also had Parliamentary powers to finish the line should the GCR be unable to. The actions of the Great Western were not totally philanthropic, however, since the completion of the route between Banbury and Culworth Junction would also open a lucrative new source of traffic between the north and south and west of England.

The Great Central Railway was in the process of completing its main trunk line from the North to London; under the leadership of its Chairman, Sir Edward Watkin, the company had made great strides in improving both its lines and services, and was hoping to gain access to the capital by sharing the tracks of the Metropolitan

Evidence of the new partnership between the two companies can be seen on this memorandum, which has an added rubber stamp for the Joint Committee.

Evidence of the new partnership between the two companies can be seen on this memorandum, which has an added rubber stamp for the Joint Committee.

Railway's Aylesbury branch. This idea was greatly assisted by the fact that Sir Edward also happened to be the Chairman of the Metropolitan!

The use of some 40 miles of track between Quainton Road and Neasden was at first sight a good idea. It would save the Great Central the expense of constructing yet another main line into London with all the costs of heavy tunnelling and earthworks involved in cutting through the Chiltern Hills. However, having arranged the agreement between the two companies, Watkin was forced to retire, and without his charismatic personality to hold things together the partners soon began to squabble. Matters deteriorated to the extent that at the end of July 1898, the Metropolitan prevented Great Central coal trains from traversing their lines to gain access to the GCR's own terminus at Marylebone.

This proved to be the last straw for the Great Central, which then resolved to work with the Great Western. There were also practical reasons for finding an alternative to the Metropolitan route, since it had steep gradients and would in all probability have been too congested to cope with the kind of future traffic envisaged by the GCR. The Acton & Wycombe Railway, just authorized by Parliament, seemed a better proposition even though it would be $4\frac{1}{2}$ miles longer to Marylebone, via a connecting line from Northolt Junction.

Matters were formalized in August 1899 with the setting up of the Great Western & Great Central Joint Committee, which was to link both systems 'with lines old and new'. Parliamentary powers were obtained to construct jointly a new line between Northolt and High Wycombe (the existing line between Acton and Northolt remained Great Western property). The Act also specified that the $8\frac{1}{2}$ miles of the old Wycombe Railway between High Wycombe and Princes Risborough was to be purchased from the Great Western by the joint undertaking, then doubled and modernized. Finally, the Committee was to construct a further 15-mile joint railway from Princes Risborough to Grendon Underwood, where a junction with the southern extension of the Great Central's main line was to be built.

Some months after the passing of the Parliamentary Act, a 'Commemoration Dinner' was held at the Guild Hall in High Wycombe. The Chairman of the Great Central, Alexander Henderson MP, believed that the interests of the two companies were so tied together that it would be impossible for the new line to be good for one and not the other. He said that the GWR and the GCR had 'put their horses together' and, he added, had put High Wycombe in a position that he believed in its 'most sanguine days it never dreamed of'[2]. As the *Great Western Railway Magazine* noted in 1904 that with the setting up of the Great Western & Great Central Joint Committee, the scope and character of the Acton and Wycombe line was transformed completely; in the event, it enabled the Great Western to extend far further, and create a much more ambitious project — the direct line to Birmingham[3]. The accompanying map may help the reader to note the different locations mentioned.

In practical terms, the building of the Acton to Wycombe section, the doubling of the existing Wycombe branch between Wycombe and Princes Risborough, and construction of the first $3\frac{3}{4}$ miles of the railway from there to Grendon Underwood was supervized by the Great Western itself, with the remainder left to Great Central engineers; this may account for the fact that although supposedly a joint railway it was to a large extent pure Great Western!

It was estimated that the new joint venture would cost around $£1\frac{1}{4}$ million, with 38 miles of new railway in all. A great deal of preparatory work was necessary, the *Great Western Railway Magazine* for October 1899 reporting that over £150,000 had already been spent on the purchasing of land alone.[4] The first section to be commenced was that linking Acton and Northolt, with the work done by the well-known contractor J.T. Firbank, who had already done considerable work for the Great Central on its southern extension to London. The first contract involved 23 bridges, two viaducts, and stations at Greenford and Park Royal; four smaller halts were also provided at North Acton, Twyford Abbey, Perivale and Castle Bar Park.

For the purpose of high-speed running, gradients were kept down to a maximum of 1 in 225, and apart from the junction with the GWR main line at Acton, the line was free from sharp curves. With an eye to the future, the railway was laid out with enough space for four tracks, perhaps anticipating additional suburban traffic; initially, however, only two lines were actually constructed. Work moved apace on this section, and the company's General Manager,

This photograph of Greenford
has been reproduced before, but
is worth repeating since it not
only shows the substantial
nature of the station facilities,
perched on the embankment,
but also highlights how
undeveloped this area was at
the time. (Lens of Sutton)

J.L. Wilkinson, speaking at the Dinner mentioned earlier, noted that London-bound travellers could not fail to notice 'the army of men at work there, and engines dashing about, and removing hills of soil and material just eastward of Acton'. The junction at Acton would, he added, see the 'interchange of large amounts of traffic the Companies knew would spring up from the line'[5].

By 1901 the Joint Committee was in a position to recommend that tenders be invited for the construction of the next section of line between Northolt and Wycombe, and the improvement of the existing stretch of line between Wycombe and Princes Risborough. James Inglis submitted a report to the Committee in March of that year in which it was estimated that, exclusive of land and works for a locomotive depot, the Northolt-Wycombe stretch would cost £616,341. Between Northolt and Ickenham four lines were to be laid and, as with the first contract, beyond Ickenham overbridges and foundations for bridges were to be built to allow the future provision of four tracks.

The report also showed the high cost of improving and modernizing the original section of the Wycombe branch itself, which was estimated at the considerable sum of £259,230.[6] Contemporary records also show that a fair number of meetings were held between the two railways to determine the spread of cost between them on the joint line. One such meeting took place in April

1901 at Princes Risborough where, apart from more weighty matters, the maintenance of clocks was discussed. It was decided that a charge of 3s 6d per annum should be made for each brass time piece, and 5s per annum for each Booking Hall clock. Water was also pumped to joint stations by the Great Western, who charged the joint organization 10s per tap per year.[7]

Further evidence of the Great Western's almost legendary zeal for economy comes in a letter written some years earlier, on 26 July 1899, just before the GW&GC Committee came into being, which noted that after 1 August the line from the east of High Wycombe to the west side of Princes Risborough was vested in the joint organization. Station masters were thus warned to make a very careful inventory of stores and stationery, so that the Joint Committee could be properly debited. This process was even to extend to the reading of gas meters at each station![8]

The doubling and development works between Princes Risborough and Wycombe were quite substantial. On the old line the ruling gradient was 1 in 88, whereas the new railway was engineered to the more reasonable figure of 1 in 164, which enabled longer and heavier trains to be run. In line with the engineering of the entirely new sections of the Acton & Wycombe Railway, improvements to the curves also took place; at one point near Saunderton the up and down lines were separated in order to facilitate better gradients and curves. Considerable money was spent in building completely new stations at both High Wycombe and Princes Risborough, the latter becoming an important junction, with branches to Oxford, Watlington and Aylesbury all connecting with the new line at this point.

Before the completion of the project, the two companies agreed that the northern end of the joint line should be at Ashendon instead of Grendon Underwood Junction, so the Great Central completed the remaining 6 miles of the connecting line itself. The new joint line opened for goods traffic between Northolt and Grendon Underwood on 20 November 1905; the Great Central began a regular service of mineral and goods trains on that date, but the Great Western did not initially run any regular goods service either through or local, although it did provide special trains where necessary.[9]

It was not until the beginning of April 1906 that the Great Western inaugurated its passenger services over the Acton-Wycombe line, reportedly amidst 'great local enthusiasm'. The Directors of both concerns were invited to luncheon at High Wycombe by the local Chamber of Commerce, with special trains being run from both Marylebone and Paddington for the purpose. The effectiveness of the new railway was proved by the Earl of Carrington, who chaired the luncheon; he left early, catching a train to London to arrive well in time for proceedings in Parliament.[10]

Mr Alfred Baldwin MP, the company Chairman, speaking on behalf of the Great Western, said that both companies 'felt that their

Another distinctive feature of the joint line was the boundary markers used to delineate the extent of railway property; this example has been preserved by the Great Western Society at Didcot.

prosperity depended upon that of the districts they served'[11]. The businessmen of the district had reason to be pleased; apart from the modern stations and facilities provided, the new railway was also more direct, being 6 miles shorter to the capital than by the old route via Maidenhead.

From April, the GWR also began running local and through goods train on the joint line, from this point all goods trains from London to the North being diverted onto the new route. Once open, both the Great Western and the Great Central had two local goods trains working both directions over the line, certainly a testimony to the volume of goods traffic moved by rail in the period. Under the agreement between the two concerns, Banbury was to be the junction at which traffic was to be exchanged. There were some exceptions to this — consignments of hay, for example, from Thame or Watlington bound for Marylebone were exchanged at Princes Risborough or High Wycombe.[12]

Important though the completion of this link was, the Great Western was well aware that further work was necessary if it was to eliminate the final cause of its reputation as the 'Great Way Round'. With the opening of the Acton & Wycombe Railway, trains for Birmingham and the North still had to run via Oxford; although the route was 8 miles shorter than via Didcot, it could be the source of delays in busy periods. The line west of Princes Risborough was also not seen as being suitable for high-speed express trains.

Plans were thus advanced for a final 'cut-off' to be built. The Ashendon and Aynho line was authorized some months after the inauguration of the joint railway in August 1905, and ran from a junction at Ashendon, where the GW&GC line ended, to another junction with the Oxford to Birmingham line at Aynho.

In a similar fashion to the other 'cut-offs', the new railway was engineered to be as flat and straight as possible, ensuring the highest speeds; the ruling gradient in this case was 1 in 193. By the middle of the decade, the company was perhaps more aware of the environmental problems caused by the building of new trunk railways, and its effects on communities nearby; the *Great Western Railway Magazine* reported that 'In a highly-civilized country any new line must naturally, as far as possible, avoid interference with important properties or interests'[13].

Just over 9 miles north of Princes Risborough, the new deviation line left the Great Western & Great Central line by means of a 'flying' junction, the up line passing over the Great Central line to Grendon Underwood by means of a girder bridge; a similar arrangement at the other end of the line ensured that fast through trains were not slowed at junctions. In common with the other 'cut-off' lines discussed earlier, the Ashendon and Aynho route was not a cheap option. A series of fairly major engineering difficulties had to be overcome, including a 192-yard tunnel and various large cuttings; one 2 miles in length and 50 feet deep near Ardley ran through solid

Brill and Ludgershall station on the new Aynho 'cut-off'. The newness of the structures suggests that the picture was taken not long after opening in 1910. Note the similarity with stations on the Badminton Line. (Lens of Sutton)

rock which had to be blasted before removal. Clearly the company thought the expense worthwhile, however; in an article on the new line in the *Great Western Railway Magazine* for July 1910, F.C. Warren argued that the company would 'reap a full reward commensurate with its bid for enhanced favour from the travelling public in shortening the time occupied in transit'[14].

A fair proportion of the 3 million cubic tons of clay and rock excavated by the company in the construction of the line must have been used in the building of a particularly enormous embankment which extended for almost 7 miles. This structure was pierced only by a dozen or so underbridges, with Bicester station actually being built on the embankment itself. The stations on the line, at Bicester, Brill and Ludgershall, Blackthorn, Ardley and Aynho Park, were constructed to the standard pattern used elsewhere on the system, as as well as having admirable passenger facilities, were also well provided with 'ample siding room for the various descriptions of agricultural traffic'[15]. Coal, roadstone, timber and livestock were also catered for, with 'lock-ups' at the smaller stations, and a larger standard goods shed at Bicester. In the event, it is probably true to say that the spacious goods facilities provided by the Great Western were never matched by the local traffic which used them!

The new railway opened for goods trains on 4 April 1910, and at the beginning of June the Company Directors made a special tour of inspection. The train, which left Paddington at 10.22 on the morning of 7 June, arrived at Birmingham at 12.50 where lunch was served at the Grand Hotel.[16] The new route was opened for passenger traffic some months later, on 1 July 1910. From this time the GWR was able to timetable 2-hour Birmingham expresses. Shortly before the departure of the first of these trains, a well-wisher threw a horseshoe onto the footplate of the engine hauling the train; on hearing of the incident, G.J. Churchward arranged for the shoe to be mounted and fixed in the cab of the locomotive, 'Saint' Class No 2902 *Lady of the Lake*. The engine itself was scrapped in the 1950s, and the present whereabouts of the souvenir of that day are unknown.[17]

The Directors of the company had every reason to be proud of the achievements and improvements brought about by both the Acton and Wycombe and the Bicester cut-off lines; they gave the Great Western a new route to Birmingham, Wolverhampton, Shrewsbury, Chester and Birkenhead, which was $18\frac{1}{2}$ miles shorter than the old route via Didcot, and $2\frac{1}{2}$ miles shorter than any other rival company's line. The shortening of the journey to Birmingham to 2 hours made consequent improvements to destinations both north and west of there; the copious advertising in the 1910 timetables made much of these improved timings. Birkenhead was brought within 4 hours 37 minutes of Paddington; by comparison, in 1902

A 'Two-Hour' Birmingham express hauled by De Glehn compound No 102 La France *near Park Royal around 1913.*

As has been remarked earlier in this volume, some of the company's attempts at advertising seem a little heavy-handed to our modern eyes; this handbill illustrates this point, although it does get the message across! (Great Western Trust)

the same journey took well over 5 hours. Services to Cambrian Coast resorts like Aberystwyth and Barmouth were also improved; with the opening of the new route, it took 6 hours 25 minutes to reach Aberystwyth. For the final part of the journey the Great Western used the Cambrian Railways route over the hills of mid-Wales.

One particularly speculative map in the new timetable, entitled 'GWR New Route via Bicester to the Continent', showed the Great Western's connections via Folkestone and Queensborough to the Continent; the hardy traveller could, using the new route, travel as far as Brussels, Paris, Cologne, Berlin and Hamburg!

Rather nearer home, the timetables revealed that five down and seven up expresses were run each day, with an additional 'Breakfast Car' train to and from Birmingham each Monday, for the benefit of the business community. The *Great Western Railway Magazine* for July 1910 added that the needs of the districts through which the trains were to run had not been ignored by the company; one express in both the morning and afternoon stopped at High Wycombe, whilst carriages were slipped at Leamington for Stratford, and at Knowle for the 'convenience of the suburban residents in the district of Birmingham returning home from town after business'[18].

One particular type of traffic which benefited directly from the opening of the new line was theatrical traffic. The Great Western carried a great deal of this kind of trade; in the Edwardian era particularly, drama and music hall were immensely popular with the public, and theatre companies with their props and equipment were ferried about the country by train. Special rates were charged on luggage for groups of this kind, and a new kind of goods vehicle known by its telegraphic code as a 'Monster' was introduced to carry the more bulky items of scenery. Special efforts were made to cater for particular performances by theatre companies; one example of this occurred in April 1913, when the St James Theatre Company of London, including Sir George Alexander and Miss Irene Vanbrugh, gave a matinée performance of the play *Open Windows* at the Prince of Wales Theatre, Birmingham. The company travelled to the city by one of the Great Western's 'Two-Hour' expresses, returning to the capital in enough time to do their usual performance that evening.[19]

As well as transporting theatrical companies around the country, the Great Western also responded to the interest in drama by running special excursion trains; one such example of this came in 1913, when it made special arrangements for a Shakespeare Festival at Stratford. Under the direction of F.R. Benson, amongst the variety of works performed by a distinguished cast were *Richard II, Troilus and Cressida, The Taming of the Shrew* and *Henry IV Part 2*. On Thursday and Saturday, the Great Western ran Cheap Day Excursions up the 'New Line' departing from Paddington at 9.10 am and arriving at Stratford at 11.20. The trains also called at Ruislip, Denham, Gerrards Cross and Beaconsfield. Similar tickets for these matinée performances were also available at various London suburban stations, as well as Paddington, including Clapham, Battersea, Hayes and Edgware Road. The cost of this day out to the theatre was 7 shillings![20]

The new direct route to Birmingham competed directly with the London & North Western Railway's line from Euston, and there seems to be some evidence that the Great Western was slightly reticent about this. In August 1910, the Company Chairman, Viscount Churchill, was at pains to point out that 'care had been taken not to clash with the times of London and North Western trains'[21]. Some five years earlier, Alfred Baldwin MP, in noting the importance of the Ashendon & Aynho Railway, said that 'the construction of new lines must not be regarded as an aggressive policy against other companies'[22]. The Great Western Board, he continued, were 'most anxious to be on amicable terms with their neighbours' but 'claimed the right to peacefully develop the line'. There was no doubt, however, that the opening of the new route led to keener competion with the LNWR, since its line ran in much the same direction as that of the Great Western and, through branch or main line junctions, served much the same area. The locomotive trials of 1910, when Great Western and North Western engines were matched, probably added to the rivalry, especially since G.J. Churchward's engine *Polar Star* easily outclassed its LNWR counterpart, 'Experiment' Class 4–6–0 *Worcestershire*.

Apart from putting the GWR on a more even footing with its direct rivals, the completion of the 'New Line', as it was always called by Great Western railwaymen, also marked the end of major developments on the Great Western in its 'Golden Age'; apart from the completion of the Swansea District lines mentioned in the previous section, and improvements to Paddington station, no further work of consequence was completed before the outbreak of the First World War. The process of modernization begun in the 1890s by Lord Cawdor and his General Manager Joseph Wilkinson was essentially complete, with all the major towns on the network linked by fast direct lines. As the company's historian, E.T. McDermot, concluded, 'the old stigma of the "Great Way Round" had been wiped out forever'[23].

SUBURBIA: RAIL AND ROAD MOTORS

IN the main, much of the development described in this book has concerned the Great Western's attempts to improve its major trunk routes. In this chapter we will discover some of the work done by the company in trying to attract trade to the less important routes, particularly suburban traffic around the various large urban developments on the network. There is not space here to document events on the various rural branch lines operated by the GWR during this period, but in the course of the narrative some points relating to their operation will be mentioned.

By the end of the 'Golden Age', the process of urban growth which had begun in the nineteenth century showed little sign of slowing; the 1901 census showed that 25 million people lived in towns, with over $4\frac{1}{2}$ million living in London. The overcrowding and poor quality of life suffered by large numbers of the urban population meant that those who were able to do so attempted to move to the outskirts of cities and beyond. Although the advent of rail transport helped in the development of suburbs, Jack Simmons has rightly pointed out that suburbs were not created by railways alone; in fact, they existed long before railways were even thought of [24]. What rail travel did do, however, was to enable larger numbers of people to escape from the grime and despair of urban life.

The traditional image of the commuter has always been that of the white-collar worker travelling each day from his home in the suburbs to an office in the city; in general terms, however, three fairly distinct general groups can be discerned when looking at the 'Golden Age' period. The first group were those with a fairly substantial income, which enabled them to move further out into the countryside; this group included businessmen who perhaps travelled to town once a week to conduct their business. Also included in this category were those who had retreated to the suburbs on retirement. On the Great Western network, the kind of area occupied by this class of traveller extended along the Thames valley to Reading, and north-westwards into Buckinghamshire on the new Acton & Wycombe Railway. As Jack Simmons has pointed out, in many cases suburban development of this kind 'shaded away into the country village'[25].

The second group of people were those whose work determined that they could not move so far; this included white-collar workers who needed to be close to their City jobs. At this time, a house in the inner suburbs of London could be bought for around £850, and furnished for another £150. The services run by the Great Western to Ealing, Acton and Westbourne Park fall into this category.

The third group of daily travellers in and out of cities had their own particular tickets issued; these were 'Workmen'. The idea of fares for this particular group was promoted by many who realized that the dispersal of population from the overcrowded slums of city and town centres would reduce some of the problems already apparent in the urban centres. From the late 1860s demand for reduced fares grew louder, culminating in the ratification of the Cheap Trains Act in 1883. The Bill exempted railway companies from paying duty on all fares at a penny a mile or less, but more significantly gave both the Board of Trade and the Railway Commissioners the power to force railways to run such trains. With this legislation in place, the number of Workmen's Tickets issued dramatically increased, with up to 25,000 tickets being issued daily at one time.

What actually constituted a 'Workman' seems to have caused the Great Western and many other railway companies some difficulty. In the report of the Select Committee on Workmen's Trains of 1905, it was argued that such diverse occupations as shop and warehouse assistants, barmaids, charwomen, corn-samplers, commissionaires, costermongers, lift-boys, postmen, pageboys and sign writers had been included in this category. The Great Western sent out one of its photographers to Slough to prove the point, arguing that this kind of traffic was losing them legitimate revenue.

A GWR 'County' tank, hauling a motley selection of carriages, somewhere in the London area. Although this design was introduced in 1905 for short-haul suburban passenger work, they were short-lived, the 2-6-2 design being preferred to the 4-4-2 wheel arrangement of the 'County'.

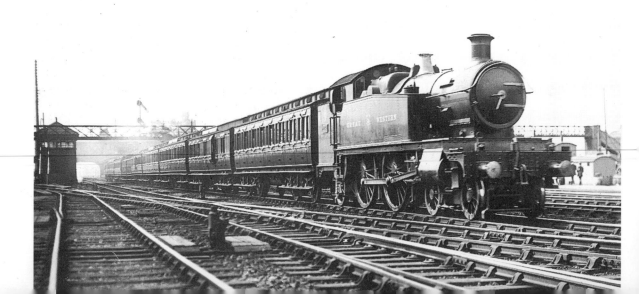

It is worth pointing out at the outset of this discussion that the Great Western did not run a suburban service similar to that operated by many other companies running trains into London; it did not have the same kind of intensive inner-city suburban schedules as those operated by the Great Eastern out of Liverpool Street station, for example. T.B. Peacock, in his book on Great Western commuter services, notes that the trains run by the GWR were characterized by their 'continual variety, initiative and experiment'[26]. In truth, many of the company's services extended far further than the inner suburbs. Speaking in 1911 with regard to the extent of GWR suburban services, W.J. Scott argued that in his opinion High Wycombe and Reading could legitimately be considered as being 'suburban', not least by the measure of the number of season ticket holders using the stations.[27]

The reader will appreciate that there is not space in a book of this kind to give a detailed enumeration of the kind of commuter services run by the company in its 'Golden Age'; several authors have already done an admirable job of describing this traffic in some depth. However, the company's operations can be briefly summarized as follows. In the first instance, a large number of passengers came from what could be defined as 'outer suburban' locations, encompassing towns like Slough, Windsor, Maidenhead and Taplow. In 1911 Slough was 23 minutes from Paddington, and Maidenhead 31 minutes. Slough had six non-stop trains to London, whilst Maidenhead had five.

This photograph shows a good example of the long-distance suburban trains run by the GWR in the 'Golden Age'. The up Reading train is hauled by 2–4–2 tank No 3607, and the maroon livery of the rolling-stock dates the picture around 1912. (Real Photographs)

The Great Western made some effort during our period to cultivate this longer-distance suburban traffic, especially with the opening of the new direct route to Birmingham. Reference has already been made to the substantial nature of station facilities on both the Acton & Wycombe Railway and the Bicester cut-off; clearly the company was keen to cultivate season ticket trade from these places. A GWR handbill issued in 1913 lists prices of both daily and three-monthly season tickets; from Denham, a 3rd class ordinary day return was 10d, whilst a three-monthly season ticket was 17s. From Wycombe, the daily fare was 3s 6d, and the quarterly season £4 8s.[28]

In a 1909 publication, *Rural London*, the company argued that the purpose of the volume was to call to 'the attention of the public the manifold advantages as a great residential centre of the district known as the western Borderlands of the Metropolis'[29]. The book gave descriptions of the largely undeveloped Chalfont Country and Thames Valley which were 'all to be found within a few miles of that pleasant, busy, fog-ridden, smoke-begrimed London one loves so loyally and abuses so lustily'[30]. Although largely a topographical and historical description of the Berkshire and Buckinghamshire countryside, even to the most casual reader the promotion of the area as a place from which commuting was easy on the Great Western's services is most clear.

A rather more crude attempt to stimulate growth came with the publication in 1912 of *Homes For All : London's Western Borderlands*. The object of this publication, the company argued, was to 'call attention to the manifold residential advantages offered to city workers within the part of the country enclosed by drawing a triangle on a map with London and Newbury at the base, and Banbury as the apex'. Certainly the book covered a wide area; chapters described the West London suburbs, including Acton, Ealing, Southall,

Uxbridge, Staines and Slough, and the Upper Thames including Taplow, Maidenhead, Henley and Burnham. The country covered by the new direct line to Birmingham as far as Bicester and Aylesbury was also described, as well as the more distant Kennet and Lambourn valleys. There were, the Great Western argued, 'a diversity of delightful districts which are less than half an hour's journey from the metropolitan terminus of the GWR'[31].

The publication noted that at various points along the company's lines, 'garden suburbs are in the course of development where convenient and healthy country homes can be obtained within the possibility of the most moderate incomes'. The book, which was published and updated at regular intervals, contained advertisements for both new housing developments and individual properties; in the January 1912 edition, a house on the Elm Park estate at North Acton was advertised at £375 leasehold!

The Great Western was also not afraid to play on the class-consciousness and snobbery of the period; in its description of Gerrards Cross, for example, on the Acton & Wycombe Railway, after some eloquent prose noting that its elevated position gave it a 'bracing' climate, it went on to state that 'there are practically no terraced houses in the place'. This presumably implied that there was little working class housing in the area!

How much influence publications such as these had is difficult to judge. What is obvious yet again is that the Great Western showed considerable enterprise in trying hard to attract business to its lines.

A fine action shot of Churchward 2–6–2 No 4408 as it speeds through a London suburban station. (GWR Museum, Swindon)

In concluding the January 1912 *Homes for All*, the company was, however, clear about its objectives; if having read the volume, the reader was induced to reside at 'one of these delightful places where he — and those dependent upon him — can breath the purest of air and revel in scenery of no ordinary beauty, "Homes for All" will have achieved its object'.

The company's operation of commuter trains nearer the capital was not without its critics; W.J. Scott argued that the Great Western's inner suburban services were 'not wholly effective', since trains ran at irregular intervals making the overall effect generally very patchy.[32] The congestion around the outskirts of Paddington already alluded to in the first part of this book did not help matters either, slowing the passage of trains into and out of the station. Scott went on to point out that the company was losing out 'especially where — as at Ealing Broadway — there are effective competitors'.

Competition there certainly was, with the commuter having the choice of underground railways, trams, and the new motor car and omnibus. As we have already observed on more than one occasion, competition or threat from one source or another was often a spur to the Great Western to introduce an innovation, and this case was no exception; trams were a particular threat to railways, since to the commuter they were a more convenient method of transport, with a more frequent service and more stopping points. The Great

Ealing Broadway station, shared with the Central London Railway, on a particularly gloomy day in the years before the Great War. One of the company's new parcels lorries can be seen on the station forecourt. (National Railway Museum, York)

Western's solution to this threat was to introduce what they termed 'Motor Services'; these took two forms, the railmotor, which was a steam-powered railcar, and the road motor, which was a motor bus vehicle.

The introduction of both these new methods of travel came in 1903. At the half-yearly meeting of the company in August of that year, the Chairman, Earl Cawdor, noted that the shareholders had probably all 'heard a great deal about motor-cars'[33]. Referring to the dangers of road competition, he noted various ways in which the Great Western was to combat this new threat. The first was that the company would be 'putting on a motor-car service, a combined car which can carry 52 passengers, and run on rails of our own line'[34]. The reader should note that in these early days there appears to have been some confusion of terminology; the terms 'railmotor' and 'road motor' soon evolved to cope with these new-fangled innovations!

During that August meeting, the Chairman announced that the idea of a railmotor was to be tried in October of that year, running between Chalford and Stonehouse on the Swindon to Gloucester line. The new trains were to stop at existing stations, but with the sanction of the Board of Trade would also pause at level crossings and roads coming up to the line. The idea was to try and emulate the flexibility of trams, which picked up and put down passengers at much more frequent intervals than conventional trains. As the

A rare view of the pioneering railmotor service in the Stroud valley. Car No 32 prepares to leave Chalford, whilst a trailer car is parked in the station bay siding. (GWR Museum, Swindon)

reader will discover, the Great Western attempted to adapt much tram practice into the running of its rail motors. It is thought that the idea of creating these minor stops between stations came from continental railway practice. What sprang up was a series of 'Haltes', relatively low-cost stations which in country districts may only have consisted of a low short platform, a lamp, and a station nameboard. Passengers gained access to the railmotor by a set of retractable steps.

The majority of halts (the 'e' was dropped in 1905) were more typical of the Great Western philosophy of building to last; the platforms were substantial timber decking lit by oil lamps, and often in evidence were characteristic corrugated iron shelters nicknamed 'pagodas' from their vaguely oriental shape. Halts were unstaffed, with passengers purchasing their tickets on the railmotor itself.

When he announced the introduction of the Stroud valley service, Earl Cawdor argued that 'I do not put it higher than an experiment, but I think it is an experiment of a useful nature'[35]. If he and the Great Western management were sceptical, then a report in the company's magazine two months later must have pleased them; it noted that on the opening day of the service, 2,500 passengers were carried, and that the hourly service in each direction was a great success.[36] In the next few years the Great Western adopted the railmotor and halt with great enthusiasm; by 1913 it was reported that there were over 160 halts on all types of line, both main, suburban and rural branch.

As well as its introduction with regard to suburban traffic, the railmotor also enabled less well used country lines to be more economically used; the *Great Western Railway Magazine* reported in 1913 that 'residents in sparsely populated districts are enjoying travelling facilities long before an ordinary train service could be justified'[37].

The Great Western's emulation of tram practice was also apparent in the construction of the railmotors. Although there were a substantial number of variations according to the type of work for which the motor was built, the basic designs were very similar. Power was provided by a small steam locomotive unit inside the carriage, fitted with 3 ft 6½ in driving wheels and Walschaerts valve gear. The boiler, pressed to 160 lb, was supplied with water from a 450-gallon tank slung underneath the coach, and controls were provided in each cab, allowing the unit to be driven from either end.

Inside, the similarity with tram design was most striking; many were fitted with both longtitudinal and cross seats, made from woven wire covered with plaited rattan cane. The actual structure of the body was pure Swindon, however, with the framing constructed of teak, and Baltic and Canadian oak; the upper part of the outside was

A preserved 'Pagoda' shelter at the Great Western Society's Didcot Halt.

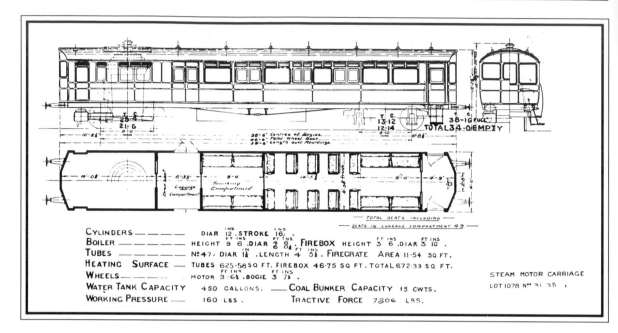

CYLINDERS ————— DIAR 12 .STROKE 16, .
BOILER ———————— HEIGHT 9 6 .DIAR 4 6 . FIREBOX HEIGHT 3 6 .DIAR 3 10 .
TUBES ——————— N° 47, DIAR 1¾ .LENGTH 4 5¼ . FIREGRATE AREA 11·54 SQ FT.
HEATING SURFACE — TUBES 625·58 SQ FT. FIREBOX 46·75 SQ FT. TOTAL 672·33 SQ FT.
WHEELS ———————— MOTOR 3 6½ .BOGIE 3 7½ .
WATER TANK CAPACITY   450 GALLONS. —— COAL BUNKER CAPACITY 15 CWTS.
WORKING PRESSURE ——   160 LBS .   TRACTIVE FORCE 7306 LBS.

STEAM MOTOR CARRIAGE
LOT 1078 N°° 31, 35 ,

A drawing of a GWR steam railmotor. Various different designs were turned out for both suburban and branch use. (GWR Museum, Swindon)

panelled with Honduras mahogony, the lower part with matchboarding. Eight large windows were fitted with spring blinds, and running down the whole length of the passenger compartment were two brass rails to which leather handloops were fixed for the use of passengers, a feature which was certainly in common with trams.[38]

One further similarity with the tram car was the fact that on the railmotor tickets were issued to travellers by a conductor; the tickets themselves were often not the more conventional Edmondson type, but were of the 'bell punch' type. Even keen to earn extra revenue, the company sold the space on the backs of these tickets for advertising purposes; on the inauguration of a railmotor service on the Halesowen branch, the Divisional Superintendent at Birmingham wrote to local staff urging them to find a suitable advertiser for such tickets. In this instance, the charge was to be 30s per 10,000 tickets![39]

The conductor was also responsible for ensuring that the passengers got on and off in safety, particularly where they had to use the moveable steps to a low platform. One problem which became apparent was that since many halts were small, insubstantial affairs, it was easy for a passenger to miss a stop. Thus, the company noted, 'conductors in charge of single cars must announce the names of stations and halts in a clear and distinct voice'[40]. More generally, conductors were instructed that 'in dealing with passengers, and in general intercourse with the public, employees must be uniformly polite and courteous'[41]. Company records of the period note that enginemen on railmotor duties were paid 5s 6d per day on branch line work, whilst his fireman was paid 3s per day. A 6d per day supplement was to be paid if the motor ran on the main line. The

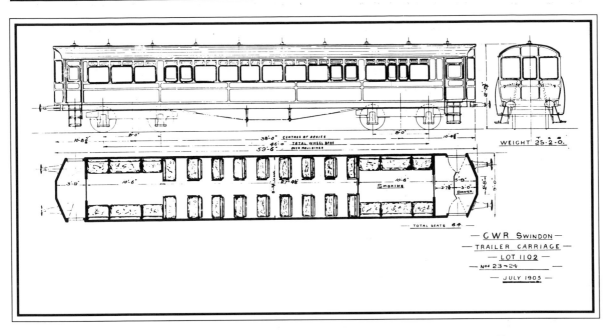

— GWR Swindon —
—TRAILER CARRIAGE —
— LOT 1102 —
— Nos 23~24 —
— JULY 1905 —

Trailer cars for railmotor services were very similar in design to their powered counterparts; some were converted into autocoaches at a later date. (GWR Museum, Swindon)

GWR railmotor 'bell punch' ticket.

conductor was paid between 18s and 21s per week.[42]

One final instruction to the staff was that a copy of the current company timetable should be hung in 'a conspicuous position' in each railmotor, and receptacles should be fixed in each vehicle for the company's smaller publications, which should always be well supplied.

The wooden construction of the vehicle and the rattan seats led to the banning of smoking for obvious reasons. Cleanliness was also essential if the motors were to keep up with their competitors, and a handbill issued by the Great Western when a new service was introduced between Stourbridge Junction and Stourbridge Town in January 1905 clearly illustrates this; as well as being well cleaned daily at the Locomotive Depot at Stourbridge, the Stationmaster was instructed to arrange for them to be swept out and 'kept thoroughly clean during the day'[43].

The success of the steam railmotor led to the company experimenting with a diesel railcar in 1912. Trials of an experimental vehicle built by the British Thompson Houston Company were conducted on the Windsor and Brentford branches; the vehicle weighed 14 tons and could carry 44 passengers. The *Great Western Railway Magazine* reported that the railcar might be of use on lines which had 'hitherto not presented the likelihood of paying loads'[44]. The widespread use of diesel traction was not, however, to be adopted by the company until the 1930s.

The success of the railmotor experiment exceeded all the company's expectations, and year by year more and more services of this kind were introduced. In 1914, statistics issued by the General Manager's Office at Paddington showed that the Great Western had a fleet of 94 vehicles, giving a total of 5,277 available seats[45]; it should also be mentioned that on busy services trailer cars, which looked very similar to the railmotors, could be coupled to the motor itself.

The introduction of these railmotors brought various advantages. The vehicles were relatively cheap to run and, in conjunction with the halts, the services they ran were easily accessible to the public. One further feature was that very frequent and convenient services were run, which could be interlaced with, and connected to, main line trains. As T.B. Peacock observed, in suburban areas a completely new form of transport was created, with an intensive new service created on existing lines. One such venture was the service run by the company on the Great Western & Great Central Joint Line; the stations on the line, as we have already noted, were substantial affairs, and the running of normal locomotive-hauled trains made them uneconomic except at peak periods. The introduction of railmotors helped stimulate the residential growth the company wanted, assisted by the running of a frequent service at a fraction of the cost of a normal train. Similar trains were run on the outskirts of many large towns and cities on the Great Western network, including Bristol, Birmingham and Plymouth.

In the same year that railmotors were first used the GWR introduced a yet more radical innovation. This was the inauguration of a motor omnibus service between Helston and the Lizard, in Cornwall, and like the railmotors the idea was initially an experiment, with only five vehicles being purchased in the first instance. The main factor which prompted the company to add motor buses to its fleet was that independent concerns were already running feeder services along roads linking Great Western stations with remoter areas and, as the Company Chairman noted, it was better 'that this means of convenience be in our own hands than in the hands of others'[46]. This new venture, and that of the railmotors, were, he added, 'experiments in the right direction to keep us up to date'. This statement, the *Great Western Railway Magazine* reported, was followed by applause, so it seems that the shareholders felt that the company was moving in the right direction.

The motor industry had itself made great strides in our 'Golden Age' period. Britain had slipped behind some of its continental rivals until the 'Red Flag' Act was finally repealed in 1896 (this was the law which had necessitated a man running in front of any motor vehicle with a flag to warn other road users). Following its repeal, a distinction was made between traction engines and lighter vehicles, and the Local Government Board set a speed limit for motor vehicles of 12 mph. In 1899 the first death due to a petrol-driven vehicle was recorded in England and by 1903 the increasing sophistication of motor vehicles led to the speed limit being increased to 20 mph. As well as cars becoming faster, safer and more reliable, their sheer numbers increased rapidly. In the same year that the 20 mph limit was introduced, vehicle registration was also brought into effect,

One of the company's road motors in a rural setting in the years before the First World War. (National Railway Museum, York)

which required the motorist to pay £1 to register his vehicle, display numberplates, and also pay 2 guineas to license the car. In the first year that this system was in force, some 23,000 vehicles were registered, and within six years the total had risen to over 100,000.

The increasing sophistication of motor cars had a consequent effect on the design of the motor bus; also significant in 1903 was the passing of the 'Heavy Motor-Car Act', which allowed the use on public roads of vehicles up to 5 tons in weight. These developments sounded the death knell for the horse bus, which had already been badly affected by the introduction of the tram. By 1908, over 1,000 motor buses were at work in London, and the last regular horse bus service was withdrawn in August 1914, as a consequence of the requisitioning of horses for the war. With all these new developments taking place, the Great Western was keen not to be left behind, and within a short space of time it had embraced the 'road motor' with almost as much enthusiasm as its rail-borne companion.

The Helston-Lizard venture was introduced in place of a proposed light railway scheme, which was not proceeded with. Initially, two 16 hp Milnes-Daimler vehicles, each capable of carrying 22 passengers, were put into service, with three trips run in each direction. Stops were made at Ruan Major for Cadwith, Penhale for Mullion, Carry Cross Lane and Lenarth for Gunwalloe. The scheme was a great success, and since the Great Western was the first railway company to run its own motor bus service, it attracted a great deal of press and public attention, including a cartoon in *Punch* magazine.

Despite the success of the Helston-Lizard experiment, it ran into trouble less than a year after its introduction when the Local Authority, Helston Rural District Council, objected to providing for the steam-rollering of roads within the district; this rolling, the *Great Western Railway Magazine* reported, was needed to 'consolidate the metalling'[47]. It was later revealed that the Council's contribution was only likely to be £10 per year, but the incident reveals that in these early days not everyone welcomed the coming of the internal combustion engine with open arms! The company experienced similar problems in 1905 when it attempted to inaugurate a road motor service between Moretonhampstead and Chagford in Devon; the local County Council refused to contribute towards the cost of improving the road, and as a result the scheme was postponed until the spring of the following year.[48]

The success of the initial Cornish experiment, Local Councils apart, led to the Great Western purchasing 25 more vehicles, and this complement was added to year by year. In 1910 W. Bailey listed the various different locations from which GWR road motor services ran, and included in the list were places as diverse as Wrexham, Abergavenny, Stourbridge, Redruth, Carmarthen and St Austell.

The introduction of motor services led to the employment of a new type of railway driver; staff were recruited from outside the company, and it was noted in 1910 that these new recruits were not used to the idea of 'Railway Discipline', or had a 'too-exalted idea of the status of a motor department'[49]. In typical fashion, the company had soon issued a Rule Book for the use of both motor drivers and conductors; the driver, it instructed, 'should practise working the brakes, and learn to estimate distances'. It was also important that 'great care must be exercised in descending hills'. One assumes that the passengers were not made aware of these reassuring instructions![50]

The conductor's duties included obtaining fares for all passengers, luggage, parcels and goods carried; to ensure that the car kept to its advertised schedule; to ensure that the vehicle was kept clean; and 'to tell the driver if the car is giving off an objectionable smoke'. Conductors were also expected to bring with them on every journey 'bell-punch, tickets, pouches, small change', and to ensure that the vehicle also had lamps, numberplates, destination boards, seat aprons, dusters, handbrushes and two lengths of stout cord, presumably used to secure luggage.

Perhaps anticipating other 'road-hogs', staff were warned that 'strict propriety of conduct, absolute avoidance of profane or indecent language…is required'. Furthermore, the book warned,

The title page of the Great Western's rule book for motor staff. (GWR Museum, Swindon)

'Employees should not enter into an altercation with anyone, no matter what provocation may be received'. Except for major work which was carried out at the headquarters of the Road Motor Department at Slough, the driver was responsible for the general upkeep of the vehicle itself. By and large the vehicles purchased by the Great Western appear to have been fairly reliable, and by 1910 many had run between 60,000 and 70,000 miles. In August of that year the Company Accountant noted that the newer vehicles were more economical, and thought that some of the older motors could be safely scrapped and used as a source of spares.[51]

Petrol for road motors came from the storehouse of the Great Western empire, Swindon. It was supplied in truck-loads of 390 gallons, contained in 5-gallon drums packed in wooden cases. It was said that drivers were paid a bonus of a penny a mile for every gallon of petrol saved over the standard 4 miles per gallon consumption.

As well as running motor services from its stations to outlying areas, the company also used its vehicles for pleasure trips. One such circular tour already mentioned was that showing the sights of London, described in Part One, but the Great Western also ran trips in more scenic areas. One such ran from Cheltenham into the Cotswolds, visiting Cranham Woods, Painswick and Stroud. Through tickets from various locations could be purchased, allowing passengers to connect with rail services; the handbill issued for the purpose noted that space on the excursion 'was strictly limited', and passengers were to give three days notice that they wished to travel.[52] Road motors could also be hired for special trips by the public, at a cost of 2s per mile. Golfers were also catered for in some places; from October 1909, the golfer was able to telephone for a GWR omnibus to take him from Slough station to the golf course at Stoke Poges.

Although successful in attracting this extra business, the company's philosophy with regard to this new kind of business was clear; its primary function was 'to act as feeders to the railway', as a Great Western correspondent wrote in 1910.[53] This statement was illustrated by statistics from several of the most successful routes used by the company; on the Helston-Lizard service, in one month, over 73 per cent of the passengers carried were GWR rail travellers. In the same month, a similar figure was produced by the Moretonhampstead-Chagford route.

The GWR management was probably heartened by the reasonable amount of profit made by the road motor service; for obvious reasons, profits were always higher in the second half of the year, including the busy summer period. In the half year ending December 1908, for example, the surplus of receipts over expenses was £4,163, as opposed to only £123 for the first half of that year. In a 1910 memorandum, however, the Company Accountant, in typical fashion, voiced concern over the amount of capital tied up in the whole operation, at that time being over £90,000, although he did conclude the memo by noting that the prime importance of the road motor service was its contributive value to the railway as a whole, which was a strong justification for its retention.[54] In a further attempt to increase profits, there is some evidence that the Great Western considered the use of trailers hauled behind road motors; a note made in 1910 shows, however, that the Local Government Regulations prohibited any passenger-carrying vehicle from towing a trailer.

The period before the Great War was to prove a high point in the company's operation of motor bus services but by the 1930s competition from other sources led to the gradual reduction of its own services.

BIRMINGHAM
SNOW HILL AND
BEYOND

THE final 'destination' in our survey of the Great Western system in its 'Golden Age' was at the end of the 'New Line' described earlier in this section. The redevelopment of Birmingham's Snow Hill station was one of the final events in the chronicle of enterprise and development we have examined so far.

The Great Western had originally gained access to Birmingham by the absorption of the Birmingham & Oxford Junction Railway in August 1848, although the line to Birmingham was not actually opened until 1 October 1852. The inaugural train hauled by Daniel Gooch's broad gauge single *Lord of the Isles* suffered an unfortunate accident near Aynho when it collided with the back of a goods train. There were no serious casualties, but the planned trip to Birmingham was curtailed at Leamington.

The terminus of the Great Western's broad gauge line at Birmingham did not actually acquire the name Snow Hill until 1858, presumably to prevent any confusion with other competitors' stations. The wooden structure erected at Birmingham was intended to be temporary, but like many other buildings on the GWR, including the original Paddington station, Birmingham's temporary station lasted for almost 20 years. Then a new, more permanent structure replaced the wooden building, which incidentally the Great Western did not scrap; it was dismantled and removed to Didcot where it was re-used as a carriage shed.

Impressive though the new station was when it opened in 1871, by the turn of the century, like many of the other lines and features described already, it was becoming far too cramped and restricted for the levels of traffic using it. As early as 1854, a mixed gauge line had been built linking Birmingham with Wolverhampton, and thus through trains from Paddington to the North also used the station. A further factor was the increasing volume of suburban traffic using the terminal; by the turn of the century Birmingham was a thriving commercial and industrial city, and, like London, many of its workers lived outside the centre of town. A 1903 handbill lists arrangements for Birmingham suburban services; between Snow

Birmingham Snow Hill station before rebuilding. Despite the crack in the glass negative, this picture still reveals a wealth of detail, and shows how gloomy it must have been under the station canopy. (National Railway Museum, York)

Hill and Handsworth, Workmen's Tickets were valid between 5.40 am and 7.10 am., and cost 2½d daily, or 1s 3d weekly.[55] Eventually, a new smaller station at Moor Street, opened in 1903, took over from Snow Hill as Birmingham's main suburban terminus.

The plans held by the Great Western for the upgrading of its main line to the North meant that the bottleneck at Snow Hill had to be overcome. The authors of an article in *The Engineer* in September 1912 pointed out that 'contemporaneously with the provision of new station accommodation there has been effected considerable improvement in the lines and travelling facilities between London and Birmingham'[56]. The advent of the 'Two-Hour' expresses meant that the poor station facilities an offer at the latter place could be tolerated no longer. The Stationmaster, Mr H. Herring, appointed in 1897, noted that 'as fast as one train passes out of Snow Hill, there is another and yet another in its wake waiting the opportunity of squeezing into the station'[57]. In 1900, congestion had become so much of a problem that stock was not stored within the confines of the station, but was cleaned and marshalled at Bordesley Junction and Smallheath, 2 miles away.

Matters were made worse by the overall roof which, despite the removal of its end panels, made the station a very dark and smoky place. Clearly, with the altered circumstances of increased traffic and the growing importance of the city, it was imperative that the company have a large prestigious station as the end of its new route.

The reconstruction of Snow Hill was not an easy task, especially bearing in mind the severe physical difficulties which had to be overcome. The 1871 station had been built into the side of a hill, and was surrounded on three sides by considerable residential and commercial development on Snow Hill itself, and Livery Street to

One of a series of posters issued to promote the two-hour route to Birmingham. Note the less than realistic portrayal of GWR locomotives and rolling-stock! (National Railway Museum, York)

One of Birmingham's suburban stations, Small Heath, around 1900. (National Railway Museum, York)

the west. This meant that lateral expansion, to widen the cramped station layout, was almost impossible without an inordinate amount of expense on the company's part in purchasing surrounding properties. To make matters worse, on the south side of the station was yet another obstacle, a 596-yard tunnel by which the railway passed beneath the central part of the city, the mouth of which abutted directly on the end of the station, and which was constructed on a 1 in 47 gradient. Originally the tunnel had been an open cutting, but it was covered over in 1874, and above it were erected some of the most important commercial premises in Birmingham. This meant that any expansion had to be in a northerly direction, since the excavation and widening of the tunnel would be a laborious and expensive task.

In 1905 moves were made to begin the modernization project. Speaking to the GWR Board, the company's New Works Engineer, Mr Walter Y. Armstrong, succinctly described how expansion could be carried out in the restricted space available. He argued that 'If we retain the former hotel as administration offices, then build on three levels, cellars for the storage of foodstuffs, the track bed level along with the station buildings surmounted by a glazed semi-open roof, coupled with this extend the platforms in a northerly direction for some distance, I firmly believe we can accommodate the trains required'[58]. The Directors, realizing the problems inherent at the existing station, gave permission for the project to begin in 1905, although work did not begin in earnest until September 1906.

The work undertaken was of an extremely ambitious nature, since the new station was to be almost twice the size of the original, and all rebuilding work had to be done whilst the existing station was still open for business. One advantage was the closing of the old Great Western Hotel, which had been built in 1863 almost directly over the mouth of the Snow Hill tunnel. By the turn of the century, business in the hotel had been steadily falling off, mainly since its central location, next to a noisy, smoky railway station, was hardly attractive to the clientele! Once the decision to close the premises had been taken, it was almost immediately taken over by the company as office accommodation for the station staff, allowing a modicum of normality in operations while the station itself was being redeveloped.

Since operations continued within the area of the station, a protective shield was erected under the old overall roof whilst it was being demolished; the resident engineer, Mr C.E. Shackle, writing in 1913, reported that 'no inconvenience was caused to traffic beyond occupation of the middle road during lifting operations'[59]. The new layout at Snow Hill consisted of two enormous island platforms, which extended for some distance northwards. Both the main up and down platforms were over 1,110 feet long, so with the addition of a scissors crossover it was possible to accommodate two trains at each. Both relief platforms were of similar length. The platform surfaces were made with 'Victorite' paving slabs, treated with carborundum to make them less slippery.

Both island platforms also had two-road bays, giving four extra platform faces. The down bay was fitted with an electric sector plate, an ingenious device which allowed the locomotive of a train which had just arrived to be traversed to an unoccupied track, without complicated trackwork, thus saving space in the tight confines of the station. Controlled by the signalman at the North signal cabin, this useful item, manufactured by Ransome and Rapier, was taken out of use in the 'thirties when the high cost of maintenance led to its replacement by a more suitable arrangement. The buildings on the platforms were of a pleasing brick design, with a plinth of blue engineering brick and chocolate-coloured facing bricks above.

Perhaps the most impressive aspect of the rebuilding work was the construction of a new overall roof; it covered two-thirds of the station, excluding the bays, and was around 500 feet long, extending from a bridge over Great Charles Street up to the steps of the footbridge. The main part of the roof was of the 'ridge and furrow' type, and was carried on girders running at right angles to the railway lines. Although much work could be done on site, the fact that trains and passengers were using the site almost continuously day and night, meant that the contractors employed on the project, E.C. & J. Keay, had to come up with an ingenious arrangement to enable the main roof girders to be raised some 28 feet above the platforms and to be riveted to the supporting columns, which were spaced at intervals of around 35 feet. What the contractors devised was a moveable erecting stage, which was strong enough to support both a 7-ton capacity travelling crane, used to lift material up to roof level, and the actual weight of the roof girders themselves, which could be upwards of 15 tons each. The stage also had to provide some measure of protection to the travelling public underneath![60]

Once the requisite rivets had fixed each roof truss in place, the whole arrangement was winched along to the position of the next girder; the erecting stage could move 36 feet at one time, which took a dozen men hauling at a winch around 2 hours to achieve. Nearly 6,000 tons of iron and steel were used in the roof, which came to be known as the 'Crystal Palace' of the Great Western. By 1911 the main section was complete, and the erecting stage, having reached the southern end of the station, was dismantled.

A spacious new Booking Hall was completed at the southern end of the station in 1912, and there was provision for access by both horse and motor vehicles from Livery Street. The hall was covered by a graceful arched roof, and the walls were faced with white 'carrara' terra-cotta tiles. Seven ticket windows were provided, each fitted with the most up-to-date 'Regina' ticket-issuing machines, although the station had possessed, since late 1906 an automatic ticket-issuing machine (others had been introduced at Lawrence Hill, in Bristol, and at Bordesley and Plymouth). Presumably these were popular with the public, since the *Great Western Railway Magazine* for December of that year reported that up to October, 651,400 tickets had been issued by that means.

Parcels traffic was dealt with below platform level. Glazed bricks were used to a great extent, and C.E. Shackle wrote that the general effect of the latter was 'the combining of utility where light is not good, with a pleasing appearance'[61]. Both Parcels Offices were large and commodious, and three lifts were used to transport goods from floor to floor. Like all Great Western stations of the period, Snow Hill also had 'Cloakrooms' where luggage could be stored; reading GWR timetables one is confronted with an amazing selection of items which could be stored for only 4d per day; these included 'Bath Chairs, Bicycles, Hawkers' Hand Carts, Street Pianos and Scissor Grinders' Machines'.

The old Great Western Hotel was also refurbished, and although most of the building was retained as office accommodation, new Refreshment Rooms were opened to complement the new station. Seating 200 people, the Rooms were 'the most handsome and elaborately fitted'; the counters were made of Austrian 'fumed oak', topped by red rouge marble. The kitchens were underneath, and food and dirty dishes were transported up and down by a double food lift. The *Great Western Railway Magazine* of April 1909 described the Rooms as 'artistically furnished', and concluded that 'as a fitting sequence to the dining rooms, from a masculine point of view attention may be directed to the large and comfortable lounge'. The

The Station concourse at Snow Hill in 1913, with a wonderful selection of road vehicles on display. The two 'Excursion' ticket windows are at the left-hand end of the seven. (National Railway Museum, York)

Rooms, it further noted, were also available for 'balls, cinderellas, concerts, at homes and dinner parties'[62].

One final aspect of the new station layout was its signalling arrangements; a Siemens all-electric system was utilized, which did away with the large amounts of point rodding needed in complex track layouts; in the confined location of the new station this was quite an advantage. Two signal boxes were built; the North box had 224 levers, whilst its counterpart, the South box, was slightly smaller, with only 96 levers. By today's standards, the method of powering this 140-volt system was very cumbersome; two storage batteries, each of 71 cells, were used one at a time, each lasting between 24 and 30 hours before being recharged by a generator. In June 1912 a similar 64-lever box was put in at Hockley North, with lack of space again being the cause of the adoption of electric power.

Two of the seven windows in the Booking Hall were reserved for excursion traffic. Many such trains were run for sporting or social events, and in the years between 1895 and 1911 the numbers of passengers carried by the GWR on special excursions increased from 1,298,406 to 2,261,023. Mileages run by trains of this type increased as a consequence, from 566,235 miles in 1895 to 911,932 miles in 1911.[63] During the 'Golden Age', spectator sports also became a mass affair, their nature changing dramatically from annual events to more organized league programmes which attracted crowds from all over the country. In the period before the First World War, football in particular became a powerful force, with matches drawing enormous crowds; on one average Saturday in 1908, 32 cup-ties were

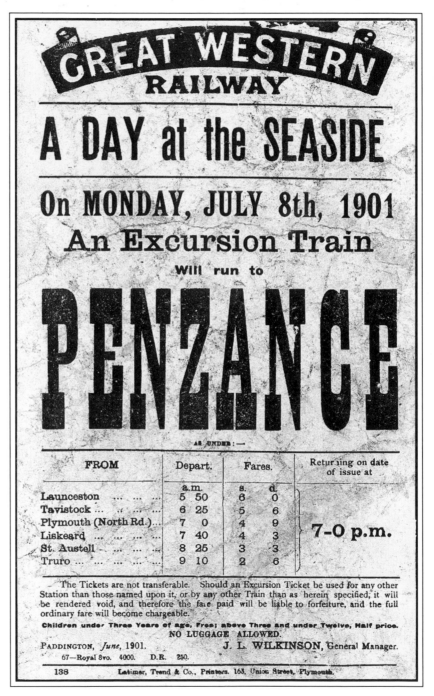

An early excursion poster, from Cornwall, promoting a trip to the seaside. (GWR Museum, Swindon)

watched in all by 450,000 people. It was also around this time that transfer fees were introduced; at the end of the 1904–5 season, one Middlesbrough player was transferred for the record sum of £1,000!

The railway companies of the period vied to run the best excursions to allow football supporters to see their favourite team, and the Great Western was no exception. In 1913 it ran no fewer than 30 trains to London from various parts of the system for the Final of the FA Cup at Crystal Palace. Twelve of the trains were run from the West Midlands area, and carried the Aston Villa team and their supporters, who mainly occupied specially reserved saloon carriages. Unlike some so-called football supporters of our own era, the followers of teams had a rather different attitude to the game, and many saved all year for the cost of the outing, refreshments, a sight-seeing tour round the capital, and a reserved ticket for the match.

Although football attracted large crowds, another sport which was becoming almost a national obsession was horse racing. This sport had always attracted large crowds over the whole class spectrum, and the Great Western, and indeed other railway companies, once again did their best to run as many excursions and special trains as they could in order to extract as much business as possible from these events. One only has to look at excursion handbills of the period to realize how many small racecourses there were, let alone the more

Newbury racecourse with, in the background, the Great Western's own specially-built station for race-goers. (National Railway Museum, York)

famous locations like Ascot, Goodwood and Newmarket. Horse racing had, of course, been popularized by King Edward VII, who was an avid race-goer and owned numerous horses of his own. The Great Western went one step further than just running excursions to racecourses; at Newbury, one of the best-known courses within its own network, it actually built and operated a station specifically for race-goers.

Both the specific types of excursion traffic already mentioned and many others to various sporting events allowed the urban population to travel out of the city to other locations; likewise excursions were also used to transport people from smaller towns and rural areas into the cities in order to take advantage of the many entertainments available in town. This included Music Halls, theatres, fairs and shops. As a result, the many and varied attractions of the late Victorian and Edwardian city were brought within the reach of less accessible parts of the country, a valuable contribution to the development of society generally.

To a large extent, Birmingham was also an important mid-point in the Great Western's operation between its northern sections and the rest of the network; this is therefore a relevant point at which to describe some of the cross-country routes and services operated by the Great Western during its 'Golden Age'. As early as 1906 the company had realized that passengers might wish to travel on journeys which did not necessarily correspond to the main trunk routes that it was so busy improving; in the *Great Western Railway Magazine* it was noted that 'nowadays business requirements and the pursuit of pleasure frequently necessitate what are known as cross-country journeys, for which the railways must provide'[64].

The article in question reported that a new service had been inaugurated linking Cardiff, Newport, Leicester, Nottingham, Sheffield, York and Newcastle. Using the lines of several companies, the hardy passenger leaving Cardiff at 10.10 am did not arrive in Newcastle until 6.40 pm! Needless to say, a Dining Car was provided, serving a table d'hôte luncheon and afternoon tea *en route*.

The increase in this north-south cross-country traffic led to the company taking further steps to speed the journey. One of the main problems in operating this kind of traffic was the rather circuitous route which the Great Western had between Bristol and Birmingham. In the earliest days of the railway's history it had failed to anticipate the need for such a line, and it had fallen to the standard gauge Bristol & Gloucester Railway (later absorbed by the Midland Railway) to build it. Thus in 1908, Great Western services between Bristol and Birmingham used firstly their own lines from Bristol to Westerleigh, where a junction had been opened onto the Midland route to the North; at Gloucester, trains used the avoiding line, then the GWR's Cheltenham to Honeybourne line, continuing to Birmingham via Stratford and Bearley.

As Rex Christiansen has observed, the Cheltenham and

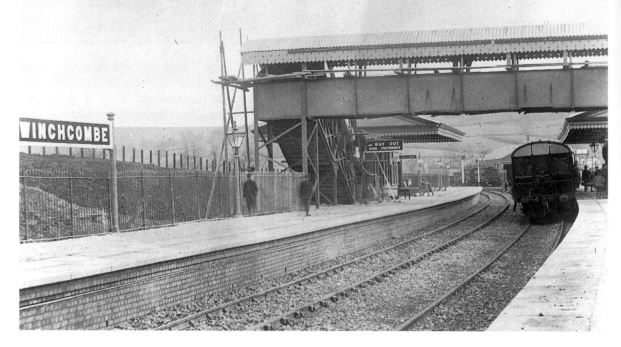

Honeybourne line was built as something of a protective measure by the Great Western, to prevent rival companies poaching a southern route into the heart of Birmingham[65]; one such venture was the planned Birmingham, North Warwickshire & Stratford-on-Avon Railway of 1894, which was intended to give the Manchester, Sheffield & Lincolnshire Railway (later the Great Central) a route into Birmingham. In 1900, however, the powers granted for this line lapsed, and were passed to the GWR which used it to add the finishing touch to its Honeybourne route.

The Cheltenham to Honeybourne line was authorized in August 1899, but was not fully open until 1 August 1906, when the last section between Bishops Cleeve and Cheltenham was finally opened. Running through the Cotswolds, the line was constructed to high standards and was well provided with stations, including one at Cheltenham for the racecourse; the cross-country traffic already mentioned was catered for, and the railway was 'engineered for the express working of through traffic from and to Birmingham and the North'[66].

The company called it a railway through the 'Garden of England', and in an article written in 1904 the General Manager, James Inglis, argued that the new line would aid the development of the fruit and vegetable farms already in evidence in the area. The Great Western enterprise, he wrote, would open up such areas of production to the large markets of numerous cities and towns. Furthermore, he added, 'the construction of this line…in the centre of England presents a more than usually interesting example of legitimate railway development, adding to the comfort and well being of all classes, from the labourer on the soil to the dwellers in the large cities'[67].

A railmotor service linked the stations on the new line when it was first opened, and until the final link between Bishops Cleeve and

A view taken at the southern end of the Great Western's new route from Birmingham to Bristol. A '517' Class 0-4-2 takes a train composed of both GWR and LNWR stock past Narroways Hill Junction in Bristol, heading north towards Ashley Hill.

Cheltenham was finished a road motor was used to complete the journey. In 1908, the Great Western began to run its north-south expresses over the line, but the Midland Railway not unnaturally made life difficult for its rival, and tried to prevent the Great Western from using the spur at Westerleigh already referred to, hoping that instead GWR trains would have to use the Midland's lines via Mangotsfield. After a legal battle, the Great Western won the right to use the spur, and from then on its cross-country services were established in earnest.

One further piece of enterprise worth noting before the end of this section was another north-south express instituted in 1910. In cooperation with another old rival, the London & South Western Railway, direct trains were run between Manchester, Birkenhead, Birmingham and the South Coast. Leaving Manchester at 10.10 am, the passenger could be in Bournemouth at 4.34 pm, a saving of over an hour on previous services. A handbill issued to advertise the new service argued that the new train gave 'a "straight through" journey from North to South in circumstances of comfort, and with all the attraction that a journey through country of great scenic and historic attraction can afford'[68].

As has been previously noted, Birkenhead was the northernmost point on the GWR network, and although the location had the

A piece of GWR paperwork from one of the company's most northerly outposts.

disadvantage that merchandise for Liverpool had to be ferried across the river Mersey by barge or Corporation boat, nevertheless the station was a busy one. It had a large goods shed and warehouse provided for grain and general merchandise, and a large amount of shipping business was done. Like Fishguard, substantial numbers of cattle were imported at Birkenhead, although most of the livestock brought in came from the United States, and was slaughtered when it arrived. Special trains of refrigerator vans were provided to deal with this home-killed meat, much of which went direct to the London markets.

One more precious cargo transported from Birkenhead to Paddington was bullion traffic; naturally, special care was taken with such trains, and special wagons were constructed for the purpose at Swindon Works. Robustly made, they were fitted with a door on one side only, which was sealed at the beginning of each journey to prevent any tampering. A contemporary Circular of the period records that bullion traffic was to be signalled as Express Passenger traffic, with class 'A' headlights; needless to say, signalmen were firmly instructed to keep a clear road for such trains.[69]

There is not sufficient space in this volume to fully document the GWR network north of Birmingham, and while the company did spread its tentacles further north than Birkenhead, it only had running powers to those locations. It had, for instance, a warehouse in Manchester, at Liverpool Road, but this was actually the property of the LNWR. W.S. Parnell felt that there was business for the company in that city, but did not know whether the expense entailed in increasing the GWR presence in the area could be justified. One rather telling example of the Great Western enterprise of the period provides a fitting conclusion to this book: one of the most unusual locations for a Great Western Booking Office must have been that at Crewe station, where GWR tickets and publications could be purchased right under the noses of one of its closest rivals, the London & North Western Railway, the headquarters of which was at Crewe!

CONCLUSION

THE year 1913 marked the 75th anniversary of the public opening of the Great Western, and the company used the occasion to review the extent of its network and in particular the achievements of the previous 10 to 15 years. There is some evidence to suggest that by this time the energy with which the Great Western had tackled many of the most pressing problems that had been facing it in the middle years of the 1890s was dwindling; this may well have been because most of the important projects carried out by the company in the 'Golden Age' were now complete.

But what progress had been made! As well as the magnificient lines and services chronicled in this book, which were of the highest standard, the Great Western had also increased its business; the improved facilities and high-profile publicity had made the 'Holiday Line' a popular one. In 1895 the GWR ran 721,090 passengers trains, an average of 2,319 per day; by 1910 trade had increased so much that the company ran 1,237,74 passenger trains that year, at an average of 3,843 per day.[1] This if anything really emphasizes the progress made during the 'Golden Age'.

Throughout this volume, much attention has been paid to the high quality of the work done in the 19 years before the First World War. The reader might also find a few more statistics useful in gauging the sheer extent of the company's 'enterprise'. The Great Western network took in 30 counties, and the company actually owned and operated more than 3,000 miles of track. There were over 1,100 stations, ranging from the biggest, like Paddington and Birmingham Snow Hill, to the smallest wayside stations and halts. The company also owned or leased vast amounts of land for other uses, including goods depots, marshalling yards and locomotive, carriage and wagon sheds.

A natural consequence of much of the new development carried out by the company in this period was that these lines and services required more staff. By 1913, the company was employing over 73,000 people; within this huge total were a wide variety of different occupations, from engine drivers to stationmasters, porters, motor car drivers, lock-keepers, ships' crews and so on.

Rolling-stock had also increased not only in sophistication, as we have seen, but also in sheer numbers; just before the Great War, the GWR owned over 3,000 locomotives, 8,162 passenger vehicles, and a staggering 78,387 goods and mineral vehicles. Added to this was an extensive fleet of horse-drawn and motorized road vehicles, and a substantial shipping fleet.

Contemplating these figures and the descriptions of much of the work done in the years before the First World War, the reader will understand why the author has on various occasions referred to the Great Western Railway as an 'Empire'; the comments of W.J. Scott, who by now the reader will have realized was both one of the company's strongest critics and one of its staunchest supporters, summed up this feeling in 1906, when he commented that 'a great railway is much more like a country or a state than it is like an ordinary business. I am sure that the most deadly mistake the General Manager and Chief Officers of the Great Western would make would be to fail to "think Imperially" '[2].

However, it is also probably true to say that not everyone was happy with the company's continued policy of enterprise. Speaking in 1912, W.S. Parnell argued that the remodelling of such a large railway system as the Great Western was not something which could be done in a hurry, or without a great deal of expense[3]; it also seems likely that by the end of the decade the shareholders in particular were beginning to take exception to the large amounts being spent by the GWR in improving its lines and facilities.

One can imagine the investor taking a dim view, for example, of a report from the *Great Western Railway Magazine* for February 1910

One of the company's ships, the SS Roebuck, *in some trouble off the coast of Jersey in 1911. The Channel Islands route needed careful navigation, and the treacherous coastline claimed several GWR ships over the years.* (GWR Museum, Swindon)

J.W.S.   S.S. Roebuck. on the Rocks. off Jersey. 19/7/11.

The GWR company flag, flown not only from company buildings but also on its shipping fleet. (National Railway Museum Collection)

which noted the work in hand at that date. The only major route to be finished was the Ashendon & Aynho Railway, although other work was being carried out on the Camerton branch, the Avonmouth & Filton Railway, the Cwncarn Branch, and the Swansea District lines. Widening works were going on at Newport, Hockley and Handsworth, and between Torquay and Paignton. New stations and rebuilding work were also reported as going on at the following locations; Paddington, Birmingham Snow Hill and Moor Street, Wrexham (Goods), Honeybourne, Newquay, Didcot, Devizes, Dulverton, Hallatrow, Bridport, Exeter, Aberystwyth, Abertillery, Skewen, Risca, Gilfach and Cradley. New goods facilities at South Lambeth, a new locomotive shed at Bristol St Philips Marsh, dock work at Swansea and a substantial amount of bridge rebuilding all over the system were also listed.

GREAT WESTERN RAILWAY.

ONE HUNDRED AND THIRTIETH
HALF-YEARLY GENERAL MEETING,
THURSDAY, 9th AUGUST, 1900.

REPORT
OF THE DIRECTORS, AND ACCOUNTS FOR
THE HALF-YEAR ENDING THE
30th JUNE, 1900.

Waterlow Bros. & Layton, Limited, 24, Birchin Lane, London, E.C.

The title page of one of the Great Western's half-yearly reports from 1900.

Despite spending so much money on modernizing its facilities, the Great Western was still, however, making a good profit; a glance at the balance sheet for the half year ending 30 June 1909, for example, reveals that the company's expenditure for that period was £4,283,118, balanced by an income of £6,487,507. In the same document it is noted that up to that date £1,444,500 had been spent on the Fishguard project alone, a large amount of money even by today's standards. So the shareholders were not doing that badly from their investment, and one dividend cheque which has survived illustrates this. A Mrs Lowndes, who had invested £2,000 in GWR stock, received a cheque for £46 6s 3d in the half year ended 31 December 1906, which included the subtraction of nearly £3 tax!

What is clear from contemporary sources is that the kind of high quality railway system which the Great Western built up during its 'Golden Age' did not come cheap. Records show, for instance, that Churchward's 'Star' Class 4-6-0 locomotives cost £3,340 each, allowing for not only wages and materials, but also depreciation and interest.[4] Similarly, the cost of carriage stock reflected the quality of material used, and the time and effort which went into its construction; in 1906 a brake tri-composite was recorded as costing £1,570, whilst a more lavish Dining Car cost £2,350.[5] The accounts of the substantial nature of the new lines constructed during the period will also have left the reader in no doubt that the Great Western 'built to last'.

Reports of the company half yearly meetings in the *Great Western Railway Magazine* seem to suggest that from 1905 onwards, searching questions were being asked by shareholders about the level of company expenditure. Clearly, although the Great Western continued to pay a dividend throughout the era, some investors felt that profits could be higher if some of the ambitious schemes embarked on were of a lesser scale. But the policy of the Great Western management was that the money spent was a future investment. In 1909, Viscount Churchill, recording a substantial increase in receipts, reflected that the investments of earlier years were now maturing, fully justifying past expenditure.

There is some evidence, indeed, that Great Western officials felt somewhat hurt by suggestions that they were squandering shareholders' money; W.J. Scott was moved to write that fierce criticisms of the Great Western Board's forward policy had come from people who 'whatever their knowledge of finance may be... had little understanding of modern passenger working'[6]. The *Great Western Railway Magazine* for March 1910 further reported that 'at recent Great Western meetings there has been a tendency to criticise the policy of consolidation and coordination which has so greatly improved the system'. There was, it added, a tendency 'to allow criticism to degenerate into mere comparison with other undertakings'.[7]

Despite the large amounts of money spent by the Great Western in this 'Golden Age', there can be no doubt that economy was never far from the minds of management. Numerous examples have already been quoted in this volume, but it is worth noting the minutes of a Superintendents' meeting held in October 1909. The question of 'expenses' was fully discussed, and numerous economies were suggested. The application of the Arbitrators' staff pay award was another factor adding to expenditure, as well as the opening of new stations and other works. Amongst the economies suggested at this particular meeting were the installation of automatic ticket machines, and the increased working of branch lines by railmotors, with fewer staff, since intermediate stations could be dealt with by conductors. Another idea was the employment of female clerks in Booking Offices, since presumably they could be paid less; it was noted, however, that 'in certain districts there has been a continual expansion of business, which has precluded the possibility of effecting substantial reductions'[8].

One aspect of company expenses which management was always keen to reduce was the mileage bill; in doing this, a consequent saving would be made in locomotive, rolling-stock and track maintenance, as well as staff costs. The mileage bill was bound to rise since the Great Western had built a substantial number of new lines, adding to the network by around 11 per cent, and had improved others; it had also put on new trains to serve these routes, and in

A view of Truro station which typifies the 'Golden Age'. Apart from the locomotive, No 3457 Tasmania, there is a wealth of detail to be seen, including the varied rolling-stock in the sidings, and the spire of Truro cathedral in the background. (Alan Parrett Collection)

Churchward 'Star', Knight of St Patrick, *seen at Plymouth in 1912. Many railway historians have argued that the 'Stars' were the solid foundation on which much subsequent GWR locomotive design was based.* (Alan Parrett Collection)

many cases had made great improvements to old services. For example, the new Ashendon and Aynho route added 1,622 miles per day to the mileage bill, and necessitated the use of seven more locomotives than previously. The new business stimulated by the route, however, added a revenue of £50,000 per year, an equivalent of £7,000 per engine.

The drastic reductions in train services forced on the Great Western during the coal strike of 1912 caused the Chief Accountants Office to look in some detail at the working of the whole network with a view to making economies, presumably mindful of the criticism levelled at the company in the previous few years. The report that was issued recorded the growth in passenger revenue due largely, it noted, to the improved facilities provided by the company in the previous decade. In the years 1908–10, its passenger revenue was greater than any other British railway company, and it was not until 1911 that its great rival, the LNWR, finally caught up, having experienced, the Chief Accountant remarked rather ironically, a 'Great Awakening' of its own[9].

It was further reported that the growth in the business of the GWR had aroused the envy of other companies like the LNWR, which was a warning to the Great Western to be on its guard, rather than an incitement to reduce services substantially from their present level. As already mentioned in the previous section, excursion traffic was a particularly useful asset to the company; in the years 1902–11 it had grown by a staggering 83.2 per cent, not a figure to be taken lightly. Passenger revenue, the report thus concluded, might well become dependent on this kind of traffic, since the trend appeared to be that the upper classes were tending to adopt the motor car, particularly after the industrial troubles of 1911 and 1912.

One particularly interesting point was that even at this time, branch line traffic was seen as uneconomic; in contrast to the Beeching era, however, the Company Accountant saw branch lines as an integral part of a railway *network*, feeding passengers and goods to other parts of the system; the attempts to make use of rail and road motors also suggest that the company was all too aware of the loss-making potential of many of its smaller lines.

One of the main conclusions made by the Accountant seems to to suggest that by 1912 the Great Western had reached some kind of impasse; all its major routes had been brought up to scratch, and the 'Great Way Round' tag had been banished for ever. All that seemed now to be done was the completion of a host of smaller modernization plans. What seems lacking is any vision of where the company was to go from there; the Chief Accountant ended his report by asking for a definite instruction on future policy, in order that economies could be made in proportion with the company's needs in the years ahead. It seems that at one stage it was suggested

Life in the more remote parts of the Great Western network changed very little in the 'Golden Age'. The leisurely timings of branch trains always allowed enough time for staff to catch up with the latest gossip! (Brian Arman Collection)

that train services be curtailed by 20 per cent, although this idea was dismissed out of hand since it would not only diminish receipts, but would also cut the equivalent of all the new mileage added since 1902! A more realistic figure was seen as around 3 per cent which, it was argued, would bring economies without drastically decreasing income.

To a large extent the problems facing the company with regard to its future plans became rather academic in 1914, with the outbreak of the Great War. International tension had been building for some years, particularly in the Balkans, and relations between Germany and Britain, ostensibly good in the early years of the century, had degenerated as the Kaiser's aggressive policy led to a rapid growth in the navies of both countries, far above what was necessary for defence. Indeed, it is worth remembering that one of Churchward's new carriage designs was nicknamed 'Dreadnought' after a new kind of powerful battleship introduced by the British Navy in 1906.

It is not the place here to chronicle the events surrounding the assassination of Archduke Ferdinand, heir to the Austrian throne, and the complex chain of events which eventually led to Britain entering into conflict with Germany on 4 August 1914. The archives show that in that first week of August, considerable 'midnight oil' was burnt at Paddington; one note was written by the General Manager at 11 pm on 3 August, recording that special embarkation platforms at Reading, Swindon and Hereford were to be constructed as soon as possible. Less than 24 hours later, at 4.55 pm on 4 August, a telephone message was received at Paddington from the War Office, authorizing Mobilization, and a few minutes after the call an official telegram arrived to confirm this. Special instructions were then telegraphed all over the system ensuring that the special plans for the mobilization of troops could be smoothly carried out.[10]

The work undertaken by the Great Western in the war years is

Since so many staff wished to enlist, the GWR was forced to make its staff apply for permission to leave the company's service; this enabled them to keep enough staff to prevent the system grinding to a halt. (GWR Museum, Swindon)

Great Western Railway.

(21.7.15)

5678.   Janʸ 16ᵗʰ 1916

To *Lovegrove N.*

You are hereby granted permission to report yourself for Military Service in accordance with Lord Kitchener's Proclamation of *Janʸ 8ᵗʰ* 1916.

Signature of Authorised Officer *C. C. Collett*

Address of   ,,   ,,

GWR 'Atbara' 4-4-0 No 3379 Kimberley with a train on Hemerdon Bank in the early years of the twentieth century. (GWR Museum, Swindon)

strictly speaking outside the remit of this volume; indeed, the day after war was declared, all railways in the United Kingdom passed under the control of the Government under the terms of the 1871 'Regulation of the Forces' Act. The purpose of this was to allow the railway system to be at the full disposal of the military, and throughout the war the lines of the Great Western resounded to the sounds of both troop trains, transporting men to the front, and ambulance trains, bringing home the injured from the carnage of the Western Front. As was the case in many walks of life, there was no shortage of volunteers from the ranks of the Great Western, keen to join the forces; indeed, this proved to be a problem for the company, since skilled workers were hard to replace. As early as 16 August 1914 clerks in some places, such as Newport, were having to work an extra two hours overtime each day in order to cover for colleagues who had joined up.[11]

By the end of the war 2,524 members of staff had been killed from a total of 25,479 who had enlisted. Even with the employment of female labour, the losses to the company in terms of expertise and training were enormous, the total number of men enlisting eventually reaching a third of the total workforce. It would take the

Great Western and the other railways some years to recover after the war.

At Swindon on the evening of 4 August 1914, the Works hooter mournfully blew ten times, and marked the beginning of a conflict which was to change irrevocably the face of the GWR, and the nation which it tried so hard to serve. It is, perhaps, a cliché to say that after the war nothing was ever the same again, but the phrase does sum up the feeling that the glorious years of expansion and development seen on the GWR in the 20 or so years before the conflict would never be repeated again on such a large scale, and that the events and achievements chronicled in this volume certainly were the 'Golden Age' of the Great Western Railway.

REFERENCES

INTRODUCTION

1. *GWR Magazine*, November 1904; Supplement to the *Statist*, 23 July 1904
2. *GWR Magazine*, October 1895, p160
3. *GWR Magazine*, May 1905, p88
4. GWR handbill: 'New Through Express Service between Manchester...and the South Coast', J.C. Inglis, July-September 1910
5. *GWR Magazine*, March 1895, p66
6. W.J. Scott, 'Some Turning Points in the History of the GWR', GWR (London) Lecture and Debating Society, 25 October 1906.
7. Quoted in Booker, F., *A New History of the GWR* (David & Charles, 1977) p102
8. Ibid, p107
9. *GWR Magazine*, April 1899, p59
10. *GWR Magazine*, February 1897, p41
11. *GWR Magazine*, June 1896, p96

PADDINGTON, GATEWAY TO THE EMPIRE

1. *GWR Magazine*, April 1913, frontispiece
2. Ibid
3. GWR 'Traffic Dealt with at Stations and Goods Depots', London (Traffic) Division 1903-1937
4. *GWR Magazine*, December 1896, p26
5. For further detail see A. Vaughan, *A Pictorial Record of Great Western Architecture* (OPC, 1985), pp16-21
6. *GWR Magazine*, August 1896
7. H. Holbrook, 'A Day and a Night at Paddington Station', GWR (London) Lecture and Debating Society, 19 March 1914
8. A. Vaughan, *A Pictorial Record of Great Western Architecture*, pp18-19
9. *GWR Magazine*, August 1910, p207
10. *GWR Magazine*, January 1913, p7
11. *GWR Magazine*, June 1906
12. *GWR Magazine*, October 1910, p167
13. Ibid
14. Lord Monkswell, *The Railways of Britain* (London, 1913)
15. PRO RAIL 253/667, p36

16. *GWR Magazine*, May 1907, p107
17. *GWR Magazine*, February 1913
18. H. Holbrook, GWR (London) Lecture and Debating Society, 19 March 1914
19. H.C. Law, 'A Day's work at Paddington Goods Station', GWR (London) Lecture and Debating Society, 26 March 1908
20. *GWR Magazine*, January 1913, pp10–11
21. W.S. Parnell, 'A Commercial Geography of the GWR' GWR (London) Lecture and Debating Society, 22 February 1912
22. H.C. Law, GWR (London) Lecture and Debating Society, 26 March 1908
23. Ibid
24. GWR Circular, 'Standard Provender Mixtures', General Stores Department, Swindon, 6 August 1900, PRO RAIL 253/422
25. H.C. Law, GWR (London) Lecture and Debating Society, 26 March 1908.
26. Ibid
27. *GWR Magazine*, June 1897, p92
28. Ibid
29. Ibid
30. Ibid
31. *GWR Magazine*, February 1901, p15
32. *The Times*, 2 February 1901
33. *GWR Magazine*, February 1901, p17
34. *GWR Magazine*, February 1901, p23
35. Ibid
36. *GWR Magazine*, November 1895, p2
37. Ibid
38. *GWR Magazine*, January 1901, p2
39. Ibid
40. For further detail see J. Russell, *Great Western Company Servants* (Wild Swan, 1983)
41. 'Regulations for the Guidance of Staff of the Chief Goods Managers Office', Paddington Station, November 1914
42. Ibid
43. Ibid
44. Ibid
45. W. Dawson, 'Selecting, Training and Disciplining Railway Men', GWR (London) Lecture and Debating Society, 31 March 1905
46. Ibid
47. 'Regulations for the Guidance of Staff of the Chief Goods Managers Office', Paddington Station, November 1914
48. Ibid
49. *GWR Magazine*, January 1913, p2
50. C. Gibbs, 'Railway Telegraphs and Telephones', GWR (London) Lecture and Debating Society, 28 January 1909
51. *GWR Magazine*, March 1913, p76
52. *GWR Magazine*, March 1913, p75
53. 'The Sights of London: Around the Metropolis by GWR Sightseeing Car', Paddington Station, 1 June 1909

SWINDON: HEART OF THE EMPIRE

1. Ausden, K., 'Up the Crossing' (BBC, 1981)
2. On display in the GWR Museum, Swindon
3. Quoted in Bonavia, M., *Four Great Railways* (David & Charles, 1980)
4. GWR Memoranda Book, GWR Museum, Swindon, Collection
5. *Swindon Works* (BREL, 1975)
6. Williams, A., *Life in a Railway Factory* (Duckworth, 1915), p100
7. GWR 'Rules & Regulations to be observed by Workmen employed in the Workshops of the Locomotive, Carriage and Wagon Departments', GWR Swindon
8. Griffiths, D., *Locomotive Engineers of the GWR*, (PSL, 1987)
9. Williams, Ibid p114
10. Millard, A.W., Swindon Engineering Society Ms, 1951
11. Evans, E.T.J., 'Locomotive Erecting', Swindon Engineering Society, 15 December 1910
12. Harris, M., *Great Western Coaches 1890-1954* (David & Charles, 1966)
13. Eversley, D.E.C., 'The Great Western Railway and the Swindon Works in the Great Depression', University of Birmingham Historical Journal, 1955-6
14. See PRO RAIL 258/262
15. Quoted in Peck, A., *The GWR at Swindon Works* (OPC, 1983), p166
16. Burrows, G.H., 'GWR Locomotives', GWR (London) Lecture & Debating Society, 16 December 1904
17. For further detail see Holcroft, H., *An Outline of Great Western Locomotive Practice 1837-1947*, (Ian Allan, 1971)
18. Swindon Engineering Society, Presidential Address, 8 November 1910
19. Ibid
20. For further detail on Swindon in this period see Peck, Ibid
21. *GWR Magazine*, March 1903, p32
22. *Locomotive Magazine*, 15 June 1950
23. Williams, A., Ibid p126
24. For further detail on the history of the Mechanics Institution, see Cockbill, T., *Finest Thing Out* (Quill Press, 1988)
25. *GWR Magazine*, August 1908, p165

THE CORNISH RIVIERA

1. Betjeman, J., *Betjeman's Cornwall* (John Murray, 1984), p31
2. *The Cornish Riviera* (GWR, Paddington, Jan 1904)
3. Quoted in *GWR Magazine*, April 1906, p59
4. *GWR Magazine*, August 1910, p195
5. *GWR Holiday Travel Books* (Paddington, July 1909), BR Collection
6. Envelope, 'GW Series of Travel Books', ND, BR Collection
7. *The Cornish Riviera*, p7
8. Ibid p9
9. Ibid p7
10. Ibid p13
11. Gibbs, J.A., *A Cotswold Village* (1898) p1
12. *GWR Magazine*, October 1913, p317
13. *GWR Magazine*, January 1909, p15
14. Proceedings of GWR (London) Lecture and Debating Society, 25 October 1906, p9

15. Quoted in *GWR Magazine*, April 1904, p49
16. Proceedings of GWR (London) Lecture and Debating Society, 25 October 1906, p9
17. *Holiday Haunts on the GWR* (Paddington, May 1906)
18. Ibid p5
19. Ibid p6
20. Ibid p61
21. GWR handbill: 'Weekends in the West', ND, BR Collection
22. *GWR Magazine*, April 1909, p109
23. *GWR Magazine*, May 1913
24. *GWR Magazine*, March 1912, p79
25. *GWR Magazine*, August 1909, p174
26. 'Timetables of the GWR', January–April 1902
27. Proceedings of GWR (London) Lecture and Debating Society, 17 January 1907, p2
28. GWR (London) Lecture and Debating Society, 1907, p9
29. *GWR Magazine*, October 1905, p175
30. Ibid p176
31. Ibid p175
32. *GWR Magazine*, November 1895, p2
33. *Handbook for Travellers from Overseas* (Paddington, July 1912)
34. GWR Circular No 40, March 1912, PRO RAIL 253/267
35. Quoted in *GWR Magazine*, June 1904, p87
36. *GWR Magazine*, June 1904, p87
37. Ibid
38. PRO RAIL 253/267
39. Ibid pp152–156
40. *GWR Magazine*, May 1910, p52
41. *GWR Magazine*, June 1904, p87
42. Ibid
43. *GWR Magazine*, July 1904, p74
44. Memorandum in PRO RAIL 253/267 dated 6/8/09
45. *The Railway Magazine*, July 1904, p92
46. *The Railway Magazine*, September 1904, p258
47. PRO RAIL 253/267, pp211–212
48. *GWR Magazine*, June 1905, pp107–108
49. GWR Restaurant Cars: Summary of Receipts and Expenditure 1912–1915' PRO RAIL 253/166
50. *GWR Magazine*, August 1905, p136
51. *GWR Magazine*, January 1909, p15
52. GWR Circular No 3136 in PRO RAIL 253/267
53. *GWR Magazine*, June 1913, p191
54. Proceedings of GWR (London) Lecture and Debating Society, 25 October 1906, p10

THE SOUTH WALES MAIN LINE

1. See Norris J., *The Bristol and South Wales Union Railway* (Railway & Canal Historical Society, 1985)
2. PRO RAIL 265/10, 'Statistics re Severn Tunnel 1906–1915'
3. Ibid
4. PRO RAIL 253/667, p29
5. *GWR Magazine*, October 1895, p4
6. Ibid

7. Great Western Railway (South Wales and Bristol Direct Railway) Act, 1896 (59 & 60 VICT)

8. *GWR Magazine*, March 1904, p33

9. 'Maximum Loads of Engines Working Freight Trains', GWR November 1908

10. Parnell, W.S, 'Commercial Geography of the GWR', GWR (London) Lecture and Debating Society, 22 February 1912

11. Roberts, C. 'The GWR in South Wales', GWR (London) Lecture and Debating Society, 13 March 1913

12. 'List of Collieries showing Proprietors & Invoicing Stations', GWR, June 1907, 31pp

13. Hadley, E.S., 'The Train Control System', GWR (London) Lecture and Debating Society, 23 February 1911

14. *GWR Magazine*, August 1896, p113

15. *GWR Magazine*, October 1905, p263

16. *GWR Magazine*, November 1912, p314

17. *GWR Magazine*, May 1907, p135

18. PRO RAIL 253/267, p32

19. *GWR Magazine*, October 1906, pp196–197

20. 'List of Collieries Showing Proprietors and Invoicing Stations', GWR, June 1907

21. GWR Circular 2325, 14 January 1913

22. *GWR Magazine*, November 1899, p153

23. Quoted in Cole, G.D.H & Arnot, R.P., *Trade Unionism on the Railways* (Fabian Society, 1917)

24. *GWR Magazine*, June 1906, p105

25. Anderson, H.D., 'Railway Accidents: Some Facts and Figures', GWR (London) Lecture and Debating Society, 19 December 1912

26. Cole, G.D.H & Arnot, R.P., *Trade Unionism on the Railways* (Fabian Society, 1917)

27. *GWR Magazine*, September 1907, p193

28. *GWR Magazine*, October 1907, p213

29. 'Rates of Pay & Conditions of Service of Railway Operating Staff 1907–1922' (GWR, Paddington, 1923)

30. PRO RAIL 253/267

31. PRO RAIL 253/280

32. Williams T.E., 'GWR Steamboat Services', GWR (London) Lecture and Debating Society, 10 February 1905

33. For detail see Morris, J.P., *The North Pembroke & Fishguard Railway* (Oakwood Press, 1969)

34. *GWR Magazine*, April 1899, p61

35. *The Times*, 10 September 1904, p4

36. PRO RAIL 253/293

37. Ibid

38. *Fishguard, 1797-1908* (GWR, Paddington, 1908), p2

39. *GWR Magazine*, October 1906, p193

40. *GWR Magazine*, January 1907, p3–6

41. *GWR Magazine*, August 1913, p247

42. *Southern Ireland: Its Lakes and Landscapes* (GWR, Paddington, 1906), p4

43. *GWR Magazine*, October 1910

44. *GWR Magazine*, April 1907, p84

45. *GWR Magazine*, May 1907, p97

46. *GWR Magazine*, March 1909, p51

47. *Southern Ireland: Its Lakes and Landscapes* (GWR, Paddington, 1906), p4
48. *GWR Magazine*, May 1908, p96
49. See Nock, O.S., *The Great Western Railway: An Appreciation* (Heffer, 1951), pp78–79
50. Quoted in GWR 'Leaflet: Cuttings from the Press', 30 August 1909, GWR Paddington
51. Ibid
52. *New York Tribune*, 20 April 1910
53. *Fishguard: Ocean Port of Call* (GWR, Paddington, 1910)
54. *Morning Post*, 3 January 1911
55. *New York Tribune* (Paris), 11 April 1911
56. *GWR Magazine*, September 1910, p232
57. *Morning Post*, 25 June 1912
58. *GWR Magazine*, May 1913, p126
59. *GWR Magazine*, March 1913, p67

SUBURBIA AND BEYOND: THE BIRMINGHAM ROUTE

1. Jenkins, S., *The Great Western & Great Central Joint Railway* (Oakwood Press, 1978), p7
2. *GWR Magazine*, September 1899
3. *GWR Magazine*, May 1904, p89
4. *GWR Magazine*, September 1899
5. Ibid
6. GWR/GCR Joint Meeting, 6 March 1901, PRO RAIL 253/16
7. Ibid
8. From Office of Assistant Superintendent of the Line, Paddington, PRO RAIL 253/16
9. PRO RAIL 253/667, p130
10. *GWR Magazine*, May 1906, p83
11. Ibid
12. See PRO RAIL 253/677
13. *GWR Magazine*, July 1910, p88
14. Ibid p90
15. Ibid p173
16. PRO RAIL 253/667, p135
17. *GWR Magazine*, August 1910, p241
18. *GWR Magazine*, July 1910, p171
19. *GWR Magazine*, May 1913, p140
20. GWR handbill: 'Shakespeare Festival, Stratford-On-Avon, April 21-May 14 1913'
21. GWR Half-Yearly Meeting, 11 August 1910, in *GWR Magazine*, September 1910, p225
22. *GWR Magazine*, September 1905, p156
23. McDermot, E.T., *History of the GWR*, Volume 2, p235
24. Simmons, J., *The Railway in Town and Country, 1830–1914* (David & Charles, 1986) p59
25. Ibid p60
26. Peacock, T.B., *Great Western London Suburban Services* (Oakwood Press, 1978), p7
27. Scott, W.J., 'Suburban Services: Particularly Great Western', GWR (London) Lecture & Debating Society, 7 December 1911

28. GWR handbill: 'Fares and Season Ticket Rates for the New Birmingham Line, May 1-July 11 1913'

29. *Rural London: The Chalfont Country & The Thames Valley* (GWR, Paddington, May 1909), p2

30. Ibid p9

31. *Homes For All: London's Western Borderlands*, No 1, January-March 1912

32. Scott, W.J., Suburban Services Particularly Great Western', GWR (London) Lecture & Debating Society, 7 December 1911

33. *GWR Magazine*, September 1903, p115

34. Ibid

35. Ibid

36. *GWR Magazine*, November 1903

37. *GWR Magazine*, March 1913, p77

38. GWR, 'Description of Rail Steam Motor Carriages', ND, GWR Museum Collection

39. Letter: 27 June 1905, Birmingham Reference Library Collection

40. GWR, 'General Instructions to be observed in Connection with Rail Motor Cars', J.Morris, Superintendent of the Line, 1905

41. Ibid

42. PRO RAIL 253/667, p102

43. GWR Circular No 907, December 1904

44. *GWR Magazine*, April 1912, p115

45. PRO RAIL 254/24

46. *GWR Magazine*, September 1903, p115

47. *GWR Magazine*, July 1904, p119

48. *GWR Magazine*, November 1905, p189

49. *GWR Magazine*, September 1910, p236

50. GWR, 'Instructions to Road Motor Drivers & Conductors', May 1904

51. PRO RAIL 253/667, p119

52. GWR handbill: 'Combined Rail and Road Observation Car Tours', ND

53. *GWR Magazine*, September 1910, p236

54. PRO RAIL 253/667, p119

55. GWR handbill: 'Cheap Fares for Workmen etc.', June 1903

56. Gleadow, F. & Shackle, C.E., 'The Reconstruction of GWR Snow Hill Station Birmingham', *The Engineer*, 12 September 1913

57. Quoted in Harrison, D.A.C., *Salute to Snow Hill* (Barbryn Press, 1978), p19

58. Quoted in Harrison, D.A.C., *Birmingham Snow Hill: A First Class Return* (Peter Watts Ltd, 1986)

59. Gleadow. F. & Shackle C.E., *The Engineer*, 12 September 1913

60. For further detail see *GWR Magazine*, August 1911 and March 1912

61. Gleadow, F. & Shackle C.E. *The Engineer*, 12 September 1913

62. *GWR Magazine*, April 1909, p81

63. PRO RAIL 253/667, p91

64. *GWR Magazine*, May 1906, p81

65. See Christiansen, R., *Regional History of the Railways of Great Britain: Volume 13 Thames-Severn* (David & Charles, 1981)

66. *GWR Magazine*, March 1905, p46

67. *GWR Magazine*, October 1904, pp167–170

68. GWR handbill: 'New Through Express Service etc', Paddington, July-September 1910
69. PRO RAIL 253/667, p88

CONCLUSION

1. PRO RAIL 253/667, 'Passenger Train Working 1890–1910'
2. Scott, W.J., 'Some Turning Points in the History of the GWR', GWR (London) Lecuture & Debating Society, 25 October 1906
3. Parnell, W.S., 'A Commercial Geography of the GWR', GWR (London) Lecture & Debating Society, 22 February 1912
4. PRO RAIL 254/19
5. PRO RAIL 253/667, p40, 15 February 1906
6. *GWR Magazine*, August 1909, p173
7. *GWR Magazine*, March 1910, p53
8. Minutes of GWR Superintendents' Meetings; Minute No 7221, 29 October 1909
9. PRO RAIL 253/667, p341: Memo to General Manager, April 1912
10. PRO RAIL 253/667, p237
11. PRO RAIL 253/653, 'General Instructions to Staff: Newport Goods Department'

SOURCES AND GENERAL BIBLIOGRAPHY

ALTHOUGH I noted in the Preface that this was not an exhaustive history of the Great Western before the Great War, I have nevertheless made much use of the rich store of archive material housed at the Public Record Office at Kew, London; individual file numbers are listed in the References to each section. Perhaps the richest source of information has been the *Great Western Railway Magazine*; as has been noted elsewhere, during this period, as later, the company was always keen to 'blow its own trumpet', both to the public at large and to its own staff. As others have remarked, in the inter-war period it may have been rather more candid about its shortcomings, but nevertheless the magazine provides a solid basis for much of this volume. Use has, of course, also been made of that other mine of information, *The Railway Magazine*, which gave the Great Western's exploits in this period much space.

Two other under-rated sources have also been consulted; the Proceedings of the GWR (London) Lecture and Debating Society, and the Proceedings of the Swindon Engineering Society. Both are excellent sources of information since they report both lectures and debates by the very people who were so instrumental in creating the new Great Western at that time, and often include first-hand information not available elsewhere.

Much attention has been paid to company handbills, memoranda, publications and timetables; specific items are again noted in the References section of the book. Many of these items are part of the collection housed in the Social Sciences Library at Birmingham Central Library, and I am grateful for access to this superb archive.

It was also noted in the Preface that, like many other authors, I owe an enormous debt to the many historians and writers who have tackled almost all aspects of the history of the Great Western. As in the case of anyone attempting to tell the story of 'God's Wonderful Railway', E.T. McDermot's two-volume History of the company, along with its later third volume by O.S. Nock, has been a valuable source of reference. Listed overleaf are some of the other informative publications I have consulted during my research; other specific items are listed in the References section.

Allen, C.J., *Railway Building* (J.F. Shaw, 1928)

Allen, C.J., *Titled Trains of the Western* (Ian Allan, 1974)

Bagwell, P.S., *The National Union of Railwaymen 1913–1963* (NUR, 1963)

Beale, G., *Edwardian Enterprise* (Wild Swan, 1987)

Body, G., *The Severn Tunnel* (Avon Anglia, 1986)

Bonavia, M., *The Four Great Railways* (David & Charles, 1980)

Booker, F., *A New History of the GWR* (David & Charles, 1977)

Burnett, J., *A History of the Cost of Living* (Pelican, 1969)

Cecil, R., *Life in Edwardian England* (Batsford, 1969)

Christiansen, R., *Regional History of Railways of Great Britain: Vol 13 Thames & Severn* (David & Charles, 1981)

Christiansen, R., *Regional History of the Railways of Great Britain: Vol 7 The West Midlands* (David & Charles, 1979)

Clinker, C.R., *Closed Halts and Stations* (Avon Anglia, 1978)

Cockbill, T., *Finest Thing Out: A Chronicle of Swindon's Torchlit Days* (Quill Press, 1988)

Griffiths, D., *Locomotive Engineers of the GWR* (PSL, 1987)

Edwards, D. & Pigram, R., *The Final Link* (Bloomsbury Books, 1982)

Hill, C.P., *British Economic & Social History* (Edward Arnold, 1971)

HMSO Census of England and Wales 1911, General Report and Appendices; cd 8491 (1917)

Holcroft, H., *An Outline of Great Western Locomotive Practice, 1837–1947* (Ian Allan, 1957)

Hutchings, D.F., *RMS Titanic: 75 Years of Legend* (Kingfisher, 1987)

Maggs, C., *Rail Centres: Bristol* (Ian Allan, 1981)

Maggs, C., *Rail Centres: Swindon* (Ian Allan, 1983)

Nock, O.S., *The Great Western Railway: an Appreciation* (Heffer, 1951)

Nock, O.S., *The Great Western Railway in the 19th Century* (Ian Allan, 1972)

Nock, O.S., *The Great Western Railway in the 20th Century* (Ian Allan, 1973)

Nown, G., *When the World was Young* (Ward Lock, 1986)

Pollins, H., *Britain's Railways: An Industrial History* (David & Charles, 1971)

RCTS, *The Locomotives of the Great Western Railway*, Parts 4,7,8,9 & 11

Russell, J., *Great Western Company Servants* (Wild Swan, 1985)

Russell, J., *A Pictorial Record of GWR Locomotives* (OPC, 1975)

Simmons, J., *The Railway in Town and Country, 1830–1914* (David & Charles, 1986)

Simmons, J., *The Railways of Britain* (Macmillan, 1985)

Slinn, J., *Great Western Way* (HMRS, 1985)

Thomas, D.J., *Regional History of the Railways of Great Britain: Vol 1 The West Country* (David & Charles, 1981)

Thomas, D.J., *The Great Way West* (David & Charles, 1975)

Trevelyan, G.M., *English Social History* (Pelican, 1977)

Vaughan, A., *Grime and Glory* (John Murray, 1986)

Vaughan, A., *A Pictorial Record of Great Western Architecture* (OPC, 1985)

Vinter, P.J., *Great Western Expresses* (Locomotive Publishing Co, 1901)

Weintrub, B. & Hibbert, C., *The London Encyclopedia* (Papermac, 1983)

INDEX